NORTH SEA

C000174174

Cragside

NORTHUMBERLAND

Wallington

TYNE & WEAR

COUNTY DURHAM

TEESIDE

Acorn Bank

CUMBRIA

NORTH YORKSHIRE

Sizergh Castle

Studley Royal

Beningbrough Hall

EAST RIDING
OF YORKSHIRE

LANCASHIRE

WEST YORKSHIRE

GREATER MANCHESTER

Dunham Massey

SOUTH YORKSHIRE

EYSIDE

Tatton Park

CHESHIRE

DERBYSHIRE

Clumber Park

Biddulph Grange

Hardwick Hall

Little Moreton Hall

NOTTINGHAM-
SHIRE

LINCOLNSHIRE

HAM

E N G L A N D

THE
WASH

Felbrigg

Blickling Hall

STAFFORDSHIRE

Calke Abbey

RUTLAND

NORFOLK

SHROPSHIRE

LEICESTERSHIRE

Peckover House

WEST
MIDLANDS

WORCESTERSHIRE

Packwood

NORTHAMPTONSHIRE

CAMBRIDGESHIRE

SUFFOLK

WARWICKSHIRE

Anglesey Abbey

Ickworth

HEREFORDSHIRE

Hidcote

Canons Ashby

Wimpole Hall

BEDFORD-
SHIRE

Snowshill Manor

Chastleton House

BUCKINGHAMSHIRE

Westbury Court

ESSEX

GLOUCESTERSHIRE

HERTFORDSHIRE

OXFORDSHIRE

West Wycombe Park

GREATER LONDON

Osterley Park

WEST
BERKSHIRE

Ham House

SHADES OF GREEN

SHADES OF GREEN

MY LIFE AS THE NATIONAL TRUST'S HEAD OF GARDENS

Negotiating change –
care, repair, renewal

John Sales

UNICORN

DEDICATION

For the professional gardeners of the National Trust

Published in 2018 by Unicorn,
an imprint of Unicorn Publishing Group LLP
101 Wardour Street
London
W1F 0UG
www.unicornpublishing.org

Text © John Sales 2018
Images copyright – see page 322

ISBN 978-1-910787-00-7

10 9 8 7 6 5 4 3 2 1

Designed by Nick Newton Design

Printed in China for Latitude Press Ltd

With Grateful Thanks to:
Stanley Smith (UK) Horticultural Trust
The Kew Guild
Royal Horticultural Society Bursaries

The Finnis Scott
Foundation

The Finnis Scott Foundation is a charity created
under the will of Valerie Finnis (Lady Scott), a
distinguished and well known Alpine gardener and
garden photographer. She died in 2006, 20 years after
her husband, Sir David Montagu Douglas Scott, an
ardent gardener and picture collector. It was her wish
that their important picture collection be sold and the
proceeds used for charitable purposes. The Charity
thus created makes grants to support Horticulture
and Plant Sciences together with Fine Art and Art
History, the two enduring preoccupations of Valerie
and Sir David.

FRONTISPIECE *Ilex x altaclerensis* 'Clumber Park' is
the only yellow-fruited Highclere holly, found as an old
specimen near the Parsonage. When I discovered its
significance we had it propagated and replanted in the
Pleasure Ground. It received an Award of Merit from the
Royal Horticultural Society in 2003.

CONTENTS

FOREWORD

John Sales's long reign as Head of Gardens at the National Trust gives his writing a particular and unusual resonance. Long memories are valuable and in *Shades of Green* we have a detailed account of his involvement in the acquisition and conservation of some of the most important of the National Trust's gardens. It is a wonderfully vivid and engaging story. The quality and range of these places (in all about 200) is remarkable, covering nearly 400 years of garden-making. In them is the world's largest and most diverse collection of cultivated plants.

John Sales arrived at the Trust in early 1971 and for the next twenty-seven years was at the centre of fashioning a whole new discipline: garden history. Discovering what lay under the brambles and crumbling terraces of the Trust's acquisitions was a long and exhilarating process that to those of us who love gardens is just as intriguing and important as the history of the houses or their contents.

It was John who fought for recognition of the Trust's gardens as important places in their own right, not just as adjuncts to the notable properties. He fought for proper appraisals of gardens, rather than just *ad hoc* planting. He fought for adequate funding, which proved to be a never-ending battle. He defended gardens against inappropriate and damaging use. He championed the gardeners of these places, understanding always that without their dedication the gardens would, all too soon, drift back into the undergrowth. His brilliantly vivid accounts here of Powis, Knightshayes, Clumber Park, Rowallane and Dunham Massey pay full and affectionate tribute to the likes of Jimmy Hancock, Michael Hickson, Neil Porteous, Mike Snowden and Peter Hall, all of whom gave to the gardens they looked after the kind of care and love that is way beyond mere duty.

By the time I met John in the late 1980s, he was rightly recognised as a key figure in the restoration and conservation of historic gardens. He had been deeply involved in the first full-scale restoration of a garden ever undertaken in Britain. This was at Westbury Court in Gloucestershire, an enchanting, small water garden of the seventeenth century, derelict when it came to the Trust in 1967. It was one of the first Trust gardens on which John worked, devising a richly diverse planting plan which included ancient varieties of fruit trees to be trained out against the original retaining walls. Now, perhaps, we are not surprised to be able to find a 'Catshead' apple tree of the seventeenth century, if that is what we want. Then, it required an extraordinary amount of dedicated research.

John has also, for nearly thirty years, been an important friend and mentor. I have learned a great deal from him because he was always so generous with his time and his knowledge. Over the years I have collected a kind of Little Red Book (it should be Green) of Sales *dicta*: 'Gardens are shaped by the quality of the gardening that goes on in them'; 'Present values should never compromise future possibilities'; 'A garden is a process, not a product'. This latter *dictum* should be engraved on the door of every garden shed in the land.

The fact that gardens never stand still was a difficulty within the hierarchical structure of the Trust. From the beginning, there were problematical but absorbing concepts to be thrashed out. What story should the Trust be telling about any particular garden in its care? In some gardens, like Westbury, which had been left quietly alone for hundreds of years, there seemed to be a clear picture to recreate, based on the detailed records of its planting by its seventeenth-century creator, Maynard Colchester.

Some would say the same was true of Stourhead, the most visited of all the Trust's gardens with over 400,000 visitors each year. Here, surely, was the perfect palimpsest of the eighteenth century: the lake with its circuit walk, the superb trees, carefully disposed, the grassy sward, the classical buildings. However, in the 1920s and '30s, Sir Henry Hoare, owner of Stourhead before it came to the Trust, had packed the woods with rhododendrons, for which he had a passion. Was this as valid a part of the garden's history as its eighteenth-century past?

John Sales was one of the key figures involved in preparing a hundred-year plan for Stourhead, finally published in 1978. It was the first long-term management plan that the Trust had ever commissioned for a garden; the forging of a policy to preserve the conception and design of the place, taking into account subsequent developments. That key final phase was John's. The rhododendrons stayed.

Many of the principles we now take for granted at a Trust property – that a car park should not get in the way of a view, that as visitors we should be introduced into a garden in the way intended by the original owners – were first worked out in this document, in the production of which John played such a seminal part.

However, so many other extraordinary things were achieved while John was Head of Gardens: the first massive recreation of a kitchen garden (at Tatton Park); the thrilling awakening of the Victorian garden at Biddulph Grange, which John considers the Trust's 'greatest achievement in garden restoration and renewal'; the establishment, together with Kew, of a Woody Plant Catalogue that finally recorded what trees the Trust had in its gardens and where they were.

The book John has written is an important one, and covers fifty gardens in which he has been intimately involved. Westbury appears in the first chapter, *Learning*, and Stourhead in the second, which deals with the process of 'inventing' the Conservation Plan. This might sound dry stuff, but in John's hands of course it is not. He is a man who laughs a great deal; who has often seemed to be able to overcome the occasional frustrations and difficulties of his job by finding the ridiculous within them.

John listens well, a rare talent, and an important skill on the occasions he had to deal with the often-formidable donors of properties. He gives us vivid and wonderfully entertaining portraits: the Countess of Rosse, self-styled 'Director' of the gardens at Nymans, whom an obituarist described as having 'raised the practice of insincerity to an art form'; of the indomitable Betty Hussey, clambering in her eighties over the chaotic mess to which the Great Storm of 1987 had reduced the garden at Scotney Castle.

John writes well, too, and nobody but he could have given us such a detailed and riveting account of the complex processes that have produced so many of the gardens we admire today. No-one who has sat in the sun on the terraces at Powis Castle, gazing out over the tumbling terraces to the borders below, or sniffed the smell of a thousand roses cascading from the arbour at Sissinghurst, can fail to give thanks for the vision of those who have brought these incomparable gardens safely through to the present day. It is both a delight and a privilege to contribute a Foreword to John Sales's superb book.

Anna Pavord

INTRODUCTION

Dating from
the early
18th-century,
John Aislabie's
tranquil Water
Garden, now
restored, is the
formal core of this
great landscape.

A FORTUNATE LIFE

I have enjoyed a fortunate life, professionally and personally. Things that grow have always fascinated me and I cannot remember being indifferent to the miracle of plant growth and development. This interest developed into a career in horticulture haphazardly, because of the times and circumstances of my upbringing which were characterised by constant change at every level, personal and national. My career spanned a huge arc of continuous change and development in the practice of horticulture and of its scope. The simple post-war certainties of commercial production on the one hand and local authority parks gardening on the other, developed and widened unpredictably to include amateur gardening (led by the Royal Horticultural Society), historic gardening (led by the National Trust), landscape gardening and garden design, garden centres and the nursery trade, organic gardening and the 'green movement', therapeutic gardening, as well as the extraordinary resurgence of the great country house as a place to visit for its garden as well as for its architecture and contents. My particular talent seems to have been to adapt to these changes, always following my personal interests as they evolved. I am no academic; I have always been motivated by clear goals, but at each stage in my career I have endeavoured to identify and assimilate something of the style and methods of those successful people with whom I have come into contact. This empirical, perhaps even erratic, approach to learning has usually inspired me to acquire new skills and follow new interests more deeply.

This book represents the sum of my accumulated experience and my own philosophy derived from it; also from the wise thoughts and great works of colleagues and others in the field, not least the head gardeners of the National Trust.

Germination

I was born in Hammersmith, as Hitler was coming to power in Germany. My early childhood was spent in Shepherd's Bush, where my parents struggled to make a living and bring up three children. They were ambitious and my mother, of gritty Yorkshire farming stock, had a great capacity for hard work and sound common sense decision-making. My father was from a family of rather unsuccessful shopkeepers; he set himself up as a shoe-repairer, also selling leather goods. Aged six at the outbreak of World War II, I was evacuated with my elder brother and, later, my much younger sister to our grandmother in a little village in the East Riding of Yorkshire, near Howden, where we went to school. It was not a happy time in my memory but, like most children, we soon adapted. It was a narrow world with few luxuries and little mental stimulation outside school – oil lamps and candles, one radio (with an 'accumulator' wet battery that had to be charged at a garage in Howden), coal-fired cooking range (to be black-leaded on Saturdays), outside earth closet, tin bath (Friday nights), water from a pump in pails, milk direct from the farm. There were no books but the *Beano* once a week was our one indulgence, ever under threat for bad behaviour. We knocked about with the village lads, soon learning the dialect, but were banned from the enticing muddiness of the river banks of the Ouse.

After the Blitz we returned to London, but not for long because of the buzz bombs and then the V2 rockets. I remember well a close shave while waiting for a Circle Line train at High Street Kensington on my way back to Yorkshire via King's Cross. A droning V1 suddenly cut out and we crouched, hearts in mouths, until it exploded alongside St Mary Abbots Church; broken glass tinkled around us, nothing worse. Back to London in 1943, I was genuinely astonished to be told that I had 'passed' my 11-plus and had a place at a grammar school.

Westminster City School is still situated in Palace Street between the now totally re-developed Victoria Street and Buckingham Palace Road. The school had been evacuated to Exmouth in Devon, another complete contrast. It occupied a big Victorian country house and grounds called The Grange, now demolished, which was my first (and formative) experience of a big private garden with fine trees, lawns and shrubs. My earliest experience of real gardening was through the retired teachers with whom I was 'billeted' for a term in a suburban Exmouth house with a well-loved and carefully cultivated garden, including cordon apple trees – 'Ellison's Orange', 'James Grieve' and 'Charles Ross'. I wondered who these people were; an indelible impression.

Back in London after the war, at first I used to cycle to school from West Kensington up the relatively empty Cromwell Road and through Belgravia, until the new Labour government gave us free travel passes for the bus and underground. There was a lack of any strong guidance from my nevertheless generally supportive parents whose lives were overwhelmingly taken up by the vicissitudes of small businesses – two shops, various unsuccessful ventures and three houses let as furnished accommodation – demanding, eventful, occasionally in crisis, never allowing much time for family life. Without any sense of purpose I drifted into an effortless world, delivering groceries for a local shop instead of homework, arriving late at school, taunting prefects and generally playing the fool; excelling only in art and woodwork. A serious threat of expulsion had a salutary effect on me and for a while on my parents. The turning point came from getting a weekend job in a small nursery in Twickenham that grew traditional pot plants under glass – begonias, Cape heaths, azaleas, cyclamens, etc. – for sale to florists. At last I knew what I wanted to do and there was just enough time, about a year and a half, to re-direct my school life to this end. Unilaterally I decided to concentrate on relevant subjects like science and those I enjoyed (English, history, woodwork and art), ignoring those in which I was too far behind (languages and mathematics). Suddenly I began to work comparatively hard; school certificate results were far better than expected by me and a great surprise to my teachers.

When I announced that horticulture was to be my career, at a school from which 90 per cent went into banking or insurance (the other 10 per cent to university), the firm recommendation was to leave immediately. My parents had recently bought a small bungalow in West Kingsdown, near Swanley, Kent, where there was a still-thriving market gardening tradition and many glasshouse nurseries, as well as a college on the site of the former Swanley Horticultural College for Ladies. I got a nursery job growing outdoor spray chrysanthemums and large-flowered, disbudded mop-heads under glass, another total change of environment and life-style – hard physical work and commercial pressure. After a year I moved on to work in the college greenhouses, growing tomatoes, cucumbers and again chrys-anthemums under glass, with the additional advantage of being able to attend day-release classes one day per week.

All too soon I was eighteen and called up for National Service in the RAF, where aptitude tests directed me into air traffic control: a wireless operator/clerk on the lowest rung. Service life, especially at first, was another abrupt contrast and not to my liking, but I learned to adapt. As a reluctant serviceman, my aim from the start was to become transparent, never to be noticed in any way through success or failure. Being inconspicuous was an effective strategy for avoiding extra duties and I had no ambition (or ability) to excel, preferring to spend my free time on reading, photography and listening to music with like-minded friends. Serving in Malta, a 'cushy' posting, our days and nights were spent either on shift in Luqa control tower or on the beach when warm enough. My main preoccupation was a correspondence course in general horticulture, which served me in good stead later.

Kew

Returning to civilian life in 1953, I thought no further than the one-year cer-tificate course in general horticulture at Swanley, although in fact I could have aspired higher. Lacking confidence, it suited me to be a comparatively successful fish in a small pool; I was offered a second year and returned, specialising in glasshouse crop production, which had been my experience to date. However, the general horticulture course had opened my eyes to other interests. I was drawn towards gardens and plants through my first real mentor, George Brown, who taught 'ornamental horticulture' at Swanley. Kew-trained, he inspired in me an interest in trees, plants and garden design. He eventually returned to Kew as an assistant curator and wrote an important book, *The Pruning of Trees, Shrubs and Conifers*, which stayed in print for many years and has been recently revised by Tony Kirkham. George Brown eventually suggested that I should apply to become a student gardener at the Royal Botanic Gardens, Kew as a means of further-ing my interest and obtaining the higher qualification to which I aspired, the National Diploma in Horticulture, always regarded as a degree equivalent – now succeeded by the M.Hort. (RHS).

I had met my future wife, Lyn, at Swanley and we planned to marry at the end of my two-year Kew Certificate course, for which I was eventually accepted in 1956. Meanwhile Lyn lived and worked in London. Formal education and training at Kew in those days consisted mostly of several series of after-work lectures of varying quality on separate subjects, in the 'Iron Room', an ancient corrugated-iron lecture room. This also served as a meeting room for the 'Mutual Improvement Society', traditionally run by the students according to sound Victorian values, to share knowledge and experience. Each student was expected to give at least one lecture; the whole thing was taken seriously and minutes were taken, with formal questions through the Chairman. As a hopelessly self-conscious and nervous public speaker, this was excellent experience for me as no doubt it was for others, and I became Secretary in due course. Throughout this period I pursued a correspondence course for the National Diploma, at the time a very wide-ranging examination, covering all aspects of horticultural theory and practice. Plantsmanship, especially plant nomenclature, never came easily to me and Kew was sometimes baffling, if always fascinating, in its extraordinary diversity. Nevertheless I did well at Kew, enjoyed my time there immensely and passed the NDH in 1957, thereby greatly widening the scope of my career.

Writtle College

Lyn and I got married in 1958 at the end of the Kew course, and after a few months working for Ealing Parks Department I was eventually appointed assistant lecturer at Writtle College near Chelmsford, despite little experience of lecturing. Nothing is more demanding than attempting to teach bright students of one's own age group. The learning curve for me was steep and the first year difficult, the college being run according to strict schedules designed, it seemed, to put constant pressure on staff and students alike – e.g. examinations every term to be set and marked. I soon established a rapport with the students and came to terms with my role once settled in. I discovered that much would be forgiven in someone with enthusiasm and a sense of humour. Lyn and I lived separately at first, then together in a borrowed caravan, but eventually we were able to buy a small bungalow locally.

I learned a lot at Writtle in a variety of ways, not least by having to keep one step ahead of the students. My colleagues were all specialists in their own subjects and I was required to assist with practical training in all departments – outdoor vegetables, glasshouse crops and fruit growing – as well as to organise practicals in my own section, garden and nursery practice. Above all I learned a lot by being responsible for managing the large garden, plant collection and nursery, which was, like much at Writtle, in an active stage of development. I was able to carry out a great deal of planning and planting (within a strict budget) with a young head gardener but all too few gardeners, making mistakes and learning by experience. Despite minimal resources and alternate interference and indifference from my superiors, this aspect of the job was immensely rewarding and the trees I planted still form the main structure of the much-changed campus. I learned a lot from my colleagues, especially my head of department/vice-principal Austin Healey. Although neither imaginative nor even highly intelligent, he was hugely effective and got his way in negotiation by being always meticulously well prepared and succeeding in his job by admirable thoroughness, perseverance and dogged determination: a universally respected but hardly a lovable character.

In the 1960s Writtle was a rigorous and effective learning factory, nevertheless incorporating many of the better characteristics of the public school system. Especially for younger staff there was a strong need for commitment to an intense regime, which could be wholly absorbing. Through meeting an external assessor, Raymond Evison,* Director of Brighton Parks, I was lucky to be appointed to examine at NDH level within a decade of passing the examination, and through Tom Wright to become an external assessor for the first course in nursery practice, at Pershore College. These were invaluable experiences of the

* John Raymond
Berridge Evison
(1910–81), not
to be confused
with Raymond
J. Evison, the
clematis nursery-
man, happily still
extant.

world outside Writtle, allowing me to absorb a wider range of educational and horticultural practice.

At this time my wife and I were buying our own house, a new bungalow on a comparatively large site in the village of Roxwell. This allowed me to try my hand at domestic garden-making and, when we moved into Chelmsford, to design and plant another small garden for a young family with all the constraints and opportunities of a modern housing estate.

While at Kew I had noted an immaculate hedge of × *Cuprocyparis leylandii* (as it is now known) in the arboretum nursery, planted as part of a trial of hedging plants. In the 1950s interest in evergreen, quick-growing hedges was stirring, *Cupressus macrocarpa* having been found unreliable. Seeing an opportunity, I took cuttings (with permission) before leaving Kew, rooted them in a window box in our temporary flat in West Kensington and eventually planted them as a hedge in our first garden in 1959, one of the first Leyland hedges in a small domestic garden. By the mid-1960s it was a thriving hedge almost 2m high, screening our neighbour and being clipped twice a year, as is necessary to create and retain a dense hedge. One of the Writtle students, from a fruit-growing family, was keen to diversify into nursery stock. He took my eulogy of Leyland cypress seriously and came to see our hedge. Soon we had a deal by which, instead of burning the hedge clippings, I would carefully prune the hedge to supply batches of cuttings (at a very reasonable price!) for him to build up a stock of the conifer. Mea culpa: am I really guilty of beginning that hideous rash of overgrown Leyland cypresses that have disfigured Britain the past forty years? Like Dukas's Sorcerer's Apprentice, I was unaware of the force I had released! Worse was to follow when the invariably hideous yellow form hit the garden centres.

Introduction to the National Trust

Although I enjoyed my time at Writtle, I had never aspired to a career in education and training. The mixture of garden management and direct contact with students suited me well but the educational world was becoming more bureaucratic and, having been promoted to senior lecturer, I could see the next step removing me into college management, which was not a happy prospect. At this point, in 1970, I spotted an advertisement in *The Times* by the National Trust for a 'Horticulturist, assistant to the gardens adviser' (whom I knew to be Graham Thomas) but with few details.

I was a member of the Trust, and familiar with some of its incomparable collection of gardens. It sounded like the perfect job (as it did to many others: I learned later that there were more than 400 applications). I wrote a letter explaining my situation – married with three sons, mortgage and salary much higher than that offered. The response, then typical of the Trust, was a telephone call from the Chief Agent suggesting that I should 'call in' at head office, Queen Anne's Gate, London, 'when passing'. It so happened that we were planning to go on holiday and could indeed 'call in' on the way. I had never encountered an office like it, created from two adjoining terrace houses, a rabbit warren of little overcrowded rooms, mostly populated by a mixture of distinguished-looking country house gents and charming Sloaney girls with cut-glass accents, occasionally banging away at typewriters. It was all very informal and after a chat with the Chief Agent, Ivan Hills, we called in to see the Secretary (Chief Executive), Jack Boles, and on the way to the communal teatime, met the Director-General, Freddie Bishop, and 'by accident' the Chairman of the Trust, Lord Antrim. This was the way the Trust seemed to operate in those days – interview by a series of happy (semi-planned) chance encounters.

I remember being asked how I might deal with 'difficult' former owners resident in some of the Trust's properties and replying that I had a 'difficult' Principal at Writtle. I then related an occasion when I had proposed growing Virginia creeper over the front of Writtle's main building, which had been built in the 'safe' neo-Georgian (George VI) County Council style of the late 1930s. Although thought an acceptable idea by many, it was turned down flat by the Principal (a farmer). My response was to plant it as 'ground cover' in front of walls, which went unnoticed. After a few years of establishment it was soon running up the walls as a self-clinging climber. No one objected and the building is now clad end to end, a lovely sight every October.

Afterwards I explained that I needed the prospect (obviously not the certainty) of succeeding Graham Thomas to warrant applying – apparently an unwritten assumption on their part; also that I could not move for a lower income – 'if it is only the salary please do not let that prevent you from applying'. These broad hints were followed later by a formal interview chaired by Sir George Taylor, who remembered me as a student gardener at Kew while he was Director. However, it was not an easy decision for us because the job entailed staying away from home on visits for at least one third of my working time, leaving Lyn alone with three young boys; furthermore my teacher's superannuation was not transferable and I had to buy into the Trust's pension scheme at considerable cost.

Strangely, Graham, who was to be my boss, was not involved in any way in my appointment as his assistant, which is just as well because I feel sure he would not have approved of me and my background. He worked for the Trust for only nine months per year, reserving December – February for writing. I went to meet him as soon as I was appointed, spending the day at Briar Cottage, West End, Woking. Apart from gardens our tastes were almost entirely dissimilar but he treated me with great courtesy, once he had decided that I 'would do'. The decision seemed to be based on a leisurely tour of his garden, during which he asked me 'tactfully' a series of questions, mostly plant names, all of which luckily I knew.

Astonishingly, Graham Thomas never worked full-time for the National Trust, always spending the three or four darkest months of winter writing his books. Nevertheless he found time to advise regularly in nearly eighty gardens! I began in January 1971 during Graham's annual 'hibernation' and I was left to tour the gardens alone, making my own arrangements with regional staff (sixteen regions) to meet head gardeners and glean what I could. If not universally welcomed, I was invariably treated with courtesy and respect. Without any brief I set about learning about the workings of the Trust and as much as possible about each garden, at the same time endeavouring to make myself useful by answering questions and solving problems. Clearly it would take many months and more visits to get to know even a proportion of the eighty or so gardens on which he then regularly advised and more where he did not. I soon realised how little money there was, even for essential equipment like lawnmowers, but also how much labour could be released by different approaches to mechanisation, plant health and weed control. Like Graham and most of the Trust's advisers at the time, I worked from home, with my wife, Lyn, working as my secretary, dealing with telephone calls and correspondence and typing my reports following each visit. In fact, she fulfilled this role for seventeen years, up to and including the establishment of the advisers' office in Cirencester.

Graham Thomas's emergence from hibernation marked the beginning of an intensive learning phase as we undertook a rigorous tour of properties. Graham had developed a direct and effective system of 'advice' based upon regular day-long visits in the growing season, during which priority was assessed and a programme of work devised in discussion with the head gardener. For important decisions involving cost, the managing agent was consulted. Graham was a model of efficiency and effectiveness in his role as adviser, always beginning with pleasantries (remembering the names of family members, etc.) but rapidly moving on and wasting no time at all. Discussion was kept short, every decision being recorded in his notebook as he pressed on with the gardener, examining every part of the garden; nothing was left to chance. At this rate he would manage two of the smaller places in a day. Finishing for tea, he would invariably settle down wherever he was staying and write full reports of several pages in longhand, complete with plant names. He wrote with carbon paper underneath so that he could present the report(s) the next day. These reports covered every garden decision made after 1955 (and indeed until I retired in 1998). After that the system, although demonstrably effective at Hidcote and elsewhere, and never adversely criticised, was unaccountably dropped during a series of management reorganisations by the National Trust.

During these tours I was actively involved with the head gardener in every decision, constantly being tested on a range of topics, many of which I had never before encountered. I progressively took over advice in properties where Graham felt it appropriate, and this gave me confidence and a sense of achievement. Working with the regional management staff and the head gardeners was mostly enjoyable as well as challenging, and required me to adapt to a wholly different culture. This involved a fascinatingly diverse range of people, including former owners and their families, as well as the many distinguished and experienced people involved in conserving the Trust's properties at that time.

The Trust had a Gardens Panel to which the Adviser reported: an unpaid advisory committee appointed to give an objective overview in all matters connected with gardens. Composed of a broad range of distinguished individuals, some expert professionals and others who may have known big gardens open to visitors all their lives, it is an invaluable source of wise counsel, able to react both philosophically and pragmatically to conservation problems and challenges.

It is difficult to realise, or even to recall, how immature the study of historic gardens and the practice of historic garden conservation were in the early 1970s. There was no body of knowledge, no coherent philosophy and no accepted procedures for conservation and renewal. The Garden History Society had been

Is this work? Break for picnic lunch on one of the islands at Stourhead with head gardener Fred Hunt in the foreground right.

founded only a few years earlier and it was more than a decade before English Heritage was formed, with its interest in historic gardens and parks. Since the mid-1950s the National Trust, through Graham Thomas, had been feeling its way, cautiously and parsimoniously discovering some of the realities of managing, opening and conserving gardens 'for ever'. I was fortunate to be employed at a time when interest in gardens, historic sites and our heritage generally was growing exponentially, fuelled by greater personal mobility and in the case of gardens by the excellence of places like Sissinghurst, Hidcote, Bodnant and Stourhead. My career has taken in the widest possible range of horticultural experience and I have been lucky enough to have been deeply involved with the remarkable growth and flowering of landscape, garden history and conservation as serious academic subjects and as effective professions.

I succeeded Graham Thomas as the Trust's Chief Gardens Adviser (later Head of Gardens) in 1973 and fulfilled this role for a further twenty-five years. Although an established and successful author, Graham needed the constant stimulus of the Trust, and I was glad that that it retained him as Gardens Consultant, with a diminishing portfolio of gardens, for another ten years. His knowledge and experience were invaluable, especially in ensuring the continuity upon which successful historic garden conservation depends. Becoming his 'boss' after having been his assistant was not an easy transition but between us we managed the situation successfully, despite a few skirmishes. Meanwhile he used the Trust to continue to build his career as an author, e.g. through shrub roses at Mottisfont, herbaceous perennials at Powis, garden restoration at Mount Stewart and garden conservation generally through *Gardens of the National Trust*, first published in 1979. It was a wholly beneficial partnership, especially after I was able to expand the work of the Gardens Advisers to cover a much wider range of advice and to cope with the flood of new properties acquired during the 1970s and '80s. As well as the purely horticultural and plant-related advice and design input provided by Graham, we progressively embraced conservation planning, visitor facilities, management challenges, help with staffing, cataloguing, plant sourcing and restoration guidance, especially in relation to contractors. The Trust had needed to become far more professional.

When I joined the Trust the only full-time advisers were Graham Thomas for gardens and John Workman for forestry and woodlands. They never really got on, especially while John Workman's influence in the Trust grew during the 1960s and

'70s. He became a dominant character in the Trust, looked upon as a guru by management staff and committees. Unsurprisingly, they fell out mainly over advice on designed landscape parks, especially where parks related closely to extensive eighteenth-century pleasure grounds like Stourhead, Attingham and Blickling. His understanding of designed landscape came from experience and the comparatively small amount of historical conservation guidance then readily available. He based his generally sound advice almost entirely, it seems, on the excellent first edition O.S. maps and whatever documentary evidence could be provided from the property. Luckily I had been recruited, along with John Workman and others, to provide the first-ever conservation/management plan (for Stourhead) in the mid-1970s through which I learned a great deal, by writing the whole thing jointly with the distinguished historian Kenneth Woodbridge. Rather than provoke a confrontation (which might have further entrenched the current division), my strategy for the Trust's historic landscape parks was to expand this exemplary approach for individual properties on the lines of Stourhead to show that a more professional attitude to their conservation would be more appropriate and effective. This began slowly with little or no central funding: using an unemployment relief scheme at Osterley, and employing John Phibbs and his Debois friends for a pittance at Wimpole. Nothing was said, but in this way the Gardens Advisers steadily took over advice on historic landscapes, and I added 'landscape parks' to my job title without anyone objecting, or perhaps even noticing!

LEARNING ABOUT GARDENS

Learning about gardens begins, I suppose, with experiencing them. I began visiting gardens as part of a school trip to the Loire Valley in 1947, aged fourteen. Not that I learned much French, but the chateaux and their gardens made an indelible impression despite the austerity of post-war France. It must have been the first time that I had seen grand gardens so obviously designed. I collected postcards of each of them and kept them for many years. My favourite chateau by far was, and still is, Chenonceaux, with its galleried bridge over the river Cher and a scale more human than elsewhere. Versailles is of course in a class of its own but Vaux-le-Vicomte seems to me to be the epitome of the genre. While admirable places to visit, they hardly seem places in which to live.

Around forty years after that school trip I was invited through *Country Life*, with Richard Dickinson of Painswick, to speak at a short conference, based at the Chateau de Blois, which I was delighted to accept. We were to speak before lunch on the first morning and travelled from Paris without breakfast – arriving, we thought, for coffee, but there was none. Having done our bit on water alone, we were ready for lunch, which turned out to be one of those two-and-a-half-hour events, including a reception for guests and 'bigwigs' from the Ministry of Culture. To my surprise I was placed next to a glamorous lady and introduced to her; but she was not introduced to me, everyone assuming, I suppose, that like the Queen, she would be familiar to me. I gathered that she was an actress or celebrity because everyone had their eyes on her and the press homed in for photographs. When the minister, whom I knew to be Jack Lang, arrived, he was placed opposite her and I swear never took his eyes off her during the whole meal. The lady was charming and we chatted happily through the meal. I was deeply embarrassed by being obviously the only person in the room who did not know who she was and why she was famous. I have to admit that we did not seem to have much in common and she obviously knew nothing about gardens. By the end of the meal my small talk was wearing thin but I gathered that she was a guest of the minister who was obviously an admirer, if not more. Afterwards I soon discovered that her name was Catherine Deneuve and that she was a very famous film star; not my interest, I am afraid, but an unforgettable couple of hours.

Learning about garden design

My career began with growing things for use and ornament. I never thought about gardens as a whole until I became a student at Kew and began to study garden design and construction. Frustratingly, the Kew course in the mid-1950s covered only some drawing board skills and methods of constructing garden features; nothing on garden design or on the history of gardens. Studying by correspondence for the National Diploma in Horticulture involved garden design, but it was taught largely by rote, referring always to recommended examples and concentrating on a satisfactory design and disposition of traditional garden features thought necessary for any respectable garden – lawns, paths, borders, buildings, rose garden, formal bedding, etc. For me it seemed difficult to identify and grasp any principles of design related to meaning, context, function, ownership, cost, etc.

The new wave of post-war landscape architects was generally scornful of gardeners and gardening in the traditional sense. Examples of their modern designs were invariably related more or less to pre-war Bauhaus (architectural) ideas of form and function dictating style, which had not yet been assimilated into mainstream garden design, at any rate in Britain: all very control-freaky and joyless. With no one to explain this dichotomy and the relationship of current styles to the history of garden design and planting, I found any sort of general philosophy elusive. I guess I was not alone in this but somehow always assumed that it was due to my inadequacy.

However, I had been inspired by the 1951 Festival of Britain and its celebration of modern design and innovation generally, including landscape as far as it went, none of which had yet become part of the world of gardens and gardening. On the same course as me at Kew was Preben Jakobsen, a Dane who went on to study garden and landscape design in Denmark. Although a dogmatic and inflexibly opinionated character, Ben became an extremely talented designer in the then forward-looking Scandinavian style. He certainly influenced me at Kew and became a successful and important garden and landscape designer. He was part of the emerging post-war international style which, with its emphasis on form, foliage, texture and function, became a feature of the communal areas of up-market housing such as the Span schemes of the 1960s. His contribution to *Landscape Design with Plants* (1977), edited by Brian Clouston, was outstanding, as was his espousal of landscape architecture as an art form.

When I went to Writtle College in 1958 I was charged with teaching 'Ornamental Horticulture' as part of a diploma course in general horticulture. With only passing reference to garden design, I was required to follow a syllabus covering the design and cultivation of garden feature, e.g. lawns, borders, etc., together with plantsmanship. Looking back, it seems obvious now that I should have begun with the general, i.e. the principles of design and the influence of history, before dealing with the detail, so that everything would be provided with a context.

Nevertheless, I became deeply interested in garden-making and landscape design, partly because of my role as garden manager at Writtle, which involved tree planting and the landscaping of the campus as well as the design and upkeep of horticultural features. There is nothing like attempting change and innovation under the watchful eyes of both senior staff and students to sharpen one's response to challenges of this kind. This role allowed me to learn from experience and make mistakes that were soon noticed, as well as to press for expansion of the meagre facilities assigned to my aspect of the college.

When I went to Writtle, the college was two-thirds agricultural and one-third horticultural, and within horticulture my contribution amounted to minor parts of the two-year Diploma and one-year Certificate courses. During my twelve years at Writtle the emphasis was reversed, following a national trend, with the introduction of new courses specialising in 'amenity horticulture': only the prelude to fundamental course changes that included garden design and construction, nursery practice and plantsmanship at higher levels. My early part in these changes was challenging and generally rewarding, and I took the trouble to learn more by attending, unofficially, a course in Landscape Architecture at Hammersmith Polytechnic (later Thames Polytechnic; now Greenwich University), haphazardly run by Timothy Cochrane, a Fellow of the Landscape Institute. With my other commitments and travelling to Hammersmith once a week, I was not able to participate fully but carried out some of the exercises, learning the 'language' of landscape design and the importance of first assessing all aspects of a site as a whole.

Through mixing with landscape architects my eyes were opened to a more flexible approach to landscape and gardens. There was understandably an emphasis on buildings, structures and hard elements – trees, shrubs and other plants being used mainly as monocultures, often crammed in for quick effect. Much of the work was urban and there was as yet little regard for creating, or recreating, ecosystems, whether semi-natural or exotic; nor much interest in conserving the historic environment. We were still part of the post-war 'brave new world' of reconstruction and urban expansion, the most successful from a landscape point of view being the 'new towns', worthy successors I believe to the 'garden cities' of the past.

My greatest inspiration while at Writtle was Sir Frederick Gibberd – architect, town planner and landscape architect – responsible, amongst much else, for the design of Harlow New Town during the 1950s and '60s. His garden at Marsh Lane, Harlow still exists as an icon of its time, though now under-resourced. In the early 1960s, having heard of his work in progress, I tentatively enquired whether I might bring a group of students and had an immediate and enthusiastic positive response. Despite his mighty achievements Freddie was a modest and charming man who had taken to practical gardening late and applied his visual skills and imaginative design abilities to creating perhaps the outstanding post-war modern garden. On successive visits (he invariably gave up a morning to us) we witnessed much of the garden's inception, construction and planting, always inspired by his enthusiasm and the features and sculptures that he created or placed. The best gardens are indeed those made and cared for by the person who designed them.

Show gardens and show judging

Having set up an 'Ordinary National Diploma' course in amenity horticulture at Writtle, I was fortunate, after leaving, to be able to accept an invitation to be educational assessor for the first four courses offered nationally – Lancashire, Yorkshire, Somerset and Essex – an excellent way of meeting staff and students and keeping abreast of horticultural and landscape training throughout the 1970s. I learned a lot from this and made many friends and useful contacts. However, this experience was eclipsed in every way when I was invited to join Lanning Roper and Arthur Hellyer as show garden 'assessors' at the RHS Chelsea Flower Show in 1985. Exhibitors had become understandably uneasy about show garden judging procedures, the brisk and apparently summary way awards were decided at the time. Judging then consisted of all members of RHS Council (encompassing a wide range of skills and experience but with garden design and construction barely represented) assembling after lunch on press day. Chaired by the President (then Lord Aberconway), this miscellany of distinguished amateur garden owners, professional horticulturists, nurserymen and various specialists would award a medal – gold, silver-gilt, silver or bronze – at each exhibit according to a briefing from the President and a short discussion, followed by a show of hands (actually umbrellas). Our little trio of 'assessors' was appointed in response to criticism of this approach, with the intention that we should assess the gardens at length on the previous day and present our recommendations to the assembled council members before judging. At first we seemed to make little impact, Lord Aberconway's views being famously difficult to influence but we hung on in there and gradually developed the judging process, especially after I became chairman of assessors after Lanning had died and Arthur Hellyer decided to withdraw.

Thanks to a series of mostly progressive Presidents, input from a variety of well-informed people, and our accumulating experience under Stephen Bennett as Shows Director, the Society has since developed a show garden judging system which has been much admired and copied elsewhere. Assessing and judging flower show gardens is demanding, contentious and inevitably disappointing to many, if not most, exhibitors and designers. It always generates complaints and misunderstanding from those who invest their time, expertise and often large sums of sponsors' money. Nevertheless, the whole procedure is fascinating, dramatic and televisual, resulting in the now huge and perhaps disproportionate popularity of the gardens at Chelsea and, to a lesser extent, Hampton Court. For me, thirty years of show garden judging has been intensely stimulating, enjoyable and educational through being exposed to the mostly wise (sometimes foolish) opinions of so many fascinating people reacting to exhibits of every-increasing diversity. It is not the real thing of course but a true reflection of current aspiration and expertise in garden design and plantsmanship; also in technical and organisational ability.

In a medium so obviously subjective and dependent on taste, any objective assessment of gardens in the context of a great flower show depends greatly on knowing the intentions of the design and construction team. In addition to a brief description in the catalogue, my suggestion that garden designers should be required to write their own brief, setting out their aims and assumptions, was taken up with increasing effect. This process was gradually refined and a marking schedule created, so that exhibitors would know in advance the weighting of the various criteria inherent in the design and construction of any show garden. In my view, however, the key factor in the success of the RHS system of assessment and judging was in taking the widest possible view of the meaning of the term 'garden' as a place made and arranged for production and/or effect, involving plants. There were many pleas for creating categories for this or that type of garden but, at least at Chelsea, I successfully argued that creating categories of style or function would in fact result in cramping the imagination of designers to fit the established categories. As a result of this freedom of expression Chelsea Show gardens have over the years become infinitely more creative, imaginative and diverse, as well as popular. They will always, I hope, remain a source of controversy and dispute, gardens being as unlikely to appeal to all tastes as pieces of music, sculpture or painting.

Over the past thirty years or so interest in garden design has burgeoned at all levels. The strength of the British gardening tradition has been for centuries an obsession with plantsmanship combined with the skills of horticultural production – fruit, vegetables, plants and flowers. Garden and landscape design has been the preserve of the servants of the rich, mostly landowning classes. Although through the inter-war years there developed a middle class tendency towards the employment of professional garden designers and contractors, the vast majority of practical gardeners clung to the belief that gardens were for growing plants for enjoyment or consumption. Of course the war years and their austere aftermath saw a concentration on gardening for utility, gardens as always accurately reflecting current mores.

The 1950s and '60s were the decades of the flowering shrub, as people looked for ways of making decorative 'labour-saving' gardens (a contradiction in terms), and we increasingly saw borders of miscellaneous flowering shrubs, combined with ground-covering perennial plants. At that time and through to the 1970s Chelsea Show, gardens were indeed dominated by great shows of colour from rhododendrons, azaleas and other flowering shrubs, together with traditional but diminishing numbers of rock garden exhibits, some of which were still using water-worn limestone plundered from the Cumbrian hills. We saw familiar rhododendrons used again and again, lifted for the Show and replanted in the nursery. As well as for publicity, Chelsea was still a place where nurserymen took orders for later delivery. The rise of the garden centre trade in the 1960s changed all that, plants and shrubs increasingly being grown for sale in containers at any time and at any size for immediate effect. There was a resulting increased interest in bush roses, shrubs and plants with coloured and distinctive foliage, including compact conifers, silver-leaved and variegated plants and heathers, which are all striking en masse in the garden centre and appealing all the year round.

Modernist garden design was slow to come to Chelsea, even following John Brookes's ground-breaking 1962 scheme with its firmly architectural layout and structure, which launched the 'room outside' concept in Britain. 'Architectural planting' (another contradiction in terms) had come to Britain. However, in the 1970s modern, family-oriented gardens with architectural structures were beginning to appear, aimed at prosperous urban and suburban dwellers who may or may not have an interest in gardening. Gradually the traditional Chelsea garden, reflecting the Edwardian pleasure ground of lawns, shrubs and roses, was giving way to more diversity, including a revival of Gertrude Jekyll floweriness.

From the 1970s the impact of television began an increasing focus on flower show gardens, as better filming and wall-to-wall exposure sparked a remarkable broadening of [the public?] understanding of the scope of garden design. Combined with the consequent rash of 'instant makeover' programmes on mainstream television, even non-gardeners soon got the message (only partially true) that gardens could be created and recreated almost immediately, given the funding. Suddenly Chelsea Show garden designers became, if not superstars, at least pundits preaching a creed based at last on John Brookes's Californian-inspired designs of the 1970s and his books.

Many distinguished garden designers began and developed their careers on this wave of enthusiasm for 'instant' gardens of modern design, which attracted increasingly lavish sponsorship from commercial organisations and charities as they recognised the publicity value of being associated with the benign qualities of gardens and gardening. The Society of Garden Designers is in many respects a child of the great RHS shows, especially Chelsea but also Hampton Court and to a lesser extent Tatton Park and Malvern. The SGD has promoted a renaissance of gardens as a widely available art form, an important and nationally underestimated cultural development which has greatly enriched the lives of the British of our generation.

Garden history

Even before I joined the staff of the National Trust, my taste in grand gardens had 'grown up' to embrace the subtleties of the English landscape style, including its pleasure grounds and their more exotic nineteenth-century versions. Becoming a Gardens Adviser allowed me to learn much more from visiting and considering their conservation. As a result of our Stourhead work I soon realised the need for a more inclusive approach based upon an in-depth study of the history, values and unique qualities of each place. For sheer delight there is nothing to beat enjoying a great historic landscape like Stourhead, Studley Royal or Petworth on the right day at the right time. Furthermore, the most rewarding days of my whole career have been when setting out trees on the ground in important designed landscapes, knowing that I was part of a continuing historic process of renewal and adjustment; a humbling, but joyful experience.

While at Kew I had already visited Sheffield Park, Wisley, Cambridge Botanic Garden and several London parks and gardens, but it was visits to Sissinghurst, Bodnant, Snowshill, Powis and, above all, Hidcote in the 1960s that inspired my interest in the National Trust. This was before the days of mass visiting while travelling and tourism were more difficult and comparatively expensive. Gardens generally lacked the amenities they now embrace, not wholly a disadvantage in many cases. My most satisfactory garden visits have been to places like Rousham which are presented as far as possible without distractions and where visitor facilities and interpretation do not impinge unduly on the experience. Running the gauntlet of car park, visitor centre, shop, restaurant, children's play area, etc., may or may not be necessary but every effort should be made to lessen their impact: also the intrusion of signs, advertising and the corporate stamp of the National Trust, or indeed of any ownership organisation. With the help of the owners I want to discover the garden and I do not want to see a preview of its highlights or be bombarded with information, whether visually or personally. Education is a wonderful thing but it should not be forced on people who want to engage with the place on their own terms. It is a pleasure to be welcomed but an irritation when so much intervenes between the visitor and what he has come to see. Conversely, I am happy to take advantage of facilities and I recognise the need to maximise income for the good of the place.

Unfortunately most of what is written about gardens, whether in the press or in the guide books or on television, is on the basis of a very few visits, or even a single visit. While it is interesting to know of anybody's immediate reaction to a great garden, so much depends on the knowledge, understanding, taste and

Snatching a photograph while advising at Castle Coole, County Fermanagh, Northern Ireland.

frame of mind of the visitor; also on the season, the weather, the number of other visitors and the circumstances of the visit. The very idea that gardens can be judged or properly appreciated from a brief encounter shows a fundamental misunderstanding of their nature. Every garden is composed of an integrated system of processes, more or less controlled by gardeners and subject to changes, weather patterns and to accidents, pests and diseases. Depending on its nature it is essential to experience any garden in a variety of conditions and seasons before beginning to understand its qualities and value.

After joining the Trust I soon recognised the recently-formed Garden History Society (GHS) as a potentially important ally in garden conservation as well as a source of information and wise counsel. I made it my business to become involved in their activities and understandably members of the Society were interested in our work. Before English Heritage was formed the Trust led the way in garden conservation and restoration, but was learning as it went along in the absence of any generally accepted philosophy and code of practice. For me the main value of belonging to the GHS was in mixing with erudite people from all walks of life with an extraordinary range of knowledge and expertise. I continually marvelled at their diversity and at the range of, often narrow, interests that seem to bring people into gardens. Being generally ill-educated, I was particularly glad to be able to listen to people with literary and art-historical backgrounds. Among these much the most helpful to me was Mavis Batey, first as Secretary, then as valued friend, who went on to become President. Not only was she a brilliant garden historian, researcher and author, she virtually ran the GHS from her kitchen table in the early 1970s and was its sheet anchor in those early years, always encouraging new members and establishing the beginnings of a learned society.

In 1975, along with my wife Lyn, Mavis and I represented the GHS at a conference on historic garden conservation at Schwetzingen, an important garden near Mannheim which was in the process of restoration. Mavis spoke about the challenges and opportunities affecting gardens in the UK and the developing role of the GHS, while I talked about the Trust's achievements with restoration and conservation, especially our work with conservation planning at Stourhead. At that time, because of the remarkable bond of secrecy surrounding Bletchley Park, no one was aware of Mavis's stellar role as a code-breaker, which did not come to light until near the end of the century. Mavis was clearly very bright and accomplished and told us that she had been an undergraduate reading German at University College, London in 1939. At the outbreak of war she was due to begin a spell, oddly enough, at Mannheim University from where she beat a hasty retreat! Nevertheless we had an inkling of her mental prowess on the way back from the conference, when we had to wait for two hours for a train at Mannheim station. Lyn had managed to get a newspaper and thought we should do *The Times* crossword together to while away the time. In fact it took less than ten minutes as Mavis produced the answers as Lyn read out the clues!

Mavis encouraged in me a more philosophical approach to gardens and opened my mind to some of the truths revealed in literature and poetry especially through Alexander Pope, but also Goethe, Horace Walpole and other writers of the eighteenth century. She was never in any way pompous about her extensive knowledge, and conveyed her enthusiasms in ways that avoided belittling those like me whose education in such matters was comparatively weak. After attempting to reconcile these profound thoughts with the practicalities of caring for historic gardens, I gradually developed my own 'home-spun' philosophy, tested by experience and judged by the work of others in the field of historic garden conservation.

In the absence of any kind of statutory protection for historic gardens in Britain in the 1970s, there had been talk in the Garden History Society of attempting an approach through ICOMOS (the International Council on Monuments and Sites, founded in 1963). In discussion with Mavis Batey and Peter Goodchild (who was starting a post-graduate course at York in the conservation of historic gardens and parks) we agreed to endeavour to make a list of sites of outstanding national and international importance. Putting our heads together, we assembled a simple schedule which was gradually added to and refined, covering at first England and Wales. By the time English Heritage was formed in 1983 the Society had a core list that formed the basis of the EH Register of Gardens of Outstanding Historic Importance. This allowed EH on its formation to 'hit the ground running' and begin the process of researching gardens for the Register without delay, in the nick of time. Four years later the great storm which swept through the politically sensitive south-east of England made influential people realise at last that gardens and parks, loved by so many, were fragile and in need of conservation and renewal. This in turn led to a programme of grant aid to historic sites for restoration and renewal based crucially on well-researched survey and research, the beginning of a new profession.

Restoration and conservation

Dramatic, televisual, self-indulgent and food for the ego, restoring historic gardens is in danger of becoming part of the makeover industry, combining instant gratification with emotional response. On the other hand, the burgeoning interest in historic houses and gardens certainly seems attributable in large degree to this swelling tide of publicity, which captures attention and stimulates interest in history and gardens. Over the forty years since I became involved with the National Trust's restoration of Westbury Court, the first in Britain to be based on the unique history of the site, interest in historic gardens has grown increasingly rapidly along with concern for other aspects of our heritage. As the body of knowledge and expertise has developed, so the magnitude of restoration projects has grown, together with the quality of the outcome. Since 1965, thanks largely to the Garden History Society, garden history has become a serious academic discipline. The Victoria and Albert Museum gardens exhibition 1979 was another turning point. Established only in 1983, English Heritage (now Historic England) has expanded into gardens with its Register of Gardens of Special Historic Interest. Following the great storm of 1987 in the south-east of England and the availability of funding from the Heritage Lottery Fund, a whole new garden conservation profession has been born.

Comprehensive and well-recorded restoration achievements like Ham House, Erddig, Biddulph Grange, Painshill and Hampton Court, ever larger and more complex, capture the imagination, give pleasure and may also be justified educationally. But full-blown restoration is not necessarily the best option. Restoration, in whole or part, should be looked upon as an option within the primary objective of sustaining, revealing and reinforcing significant heritage values. These values are not confined to objects and design or related entirely to history or horticulture, although these will be important considerations. Values significant to a garden may also be architectural, biological, environmental, social, educational, recreational, cultural, aesthetic or spiritual.

Simply to clear the site and restore an approximation of the original is usually the easier option. In reality we are incapable of precisely recreating any historical object or layout, however well researched. Inevitably there are so many unknowns that the best we can produce is our own version, our best shot at the original. Nor can we usually, if ever, afford to restore or care for everything, and our judgement is bound to be partly subjective even if guided by the most rigorous analysis of significance. An over-indulgent resort to restoration can well destroy elements of heritage value or damage historic evidence not yet identified.

This view does not render restoration valueless but should indicate the need to be realistic about its value. The fundamental question to ask is Why: what are the real reasons for any proposed act of restoration? Will the restoration be of greater heritage value than the original, before restoration? These questions need to be asked at all stages from clearance to reconstruction, and at every level from a total restoration to the reinstatement of a single feature or process.

Comprehensive restoration to a particular date can be justified under circumstances that are unlikely to occur often, especially in Britain where we are lucky to be able to enjoy houses and gardens that have been continuously occupied and cared for. At Ham House there had been no significant 'overlay' in the garden since its layout in the seventeenth century, and the house, at any rate on the garden front, was substantially unchanged, relating very strongly to the contemporary design of the garden. But even here we got it wrong in the east cherry garden (despite everyone liking the outcome!), and we found ourselves leaving mature trees on either side on the grass plats in the main south garden. The meticulous Hampton Court Privy Garden restoration can be justified similarly as a set-piece related directly to the west elevation of the house. Even here this was at the expense of destroying the archaeology and removing the original overgrown yew topiary. But these circumstances are rare and research is liable to raise as many questions as answers, especially about details of planting, upkeep and renewal: e.g. what did the grass look like and how often was it cut? At Kenilworth Castle English Heritage went to great trouble and expense to re-create an elaborate garden made for a specific occasion – a single visit of Queen Elizabeth I, all based on a written account: no plans and no archaeology because the Castle was subsequently 'slighted' (i.e. largely demolished) by Cromwell. How does this smart new garden relate visually, historically and logically to the deliberately ruined castle? How do you sustain all year the beauty and excitement of a garden made for a single occasion? The answers to these questions must be balanced against the undoubted added value and interest of an accurate re-creation. There are no easy solutions and every case needs a separate philosophy, driven by its unique history and circumstances rather than by short-term commercial considerations.

Bogged down as it has been by architectural and archaeological philosophy and terminology, Historic England still uses totally inappropriate terms in relation to garden restoration and conservation. The architectural and archaeological approaches of 'preserve as found' and 'minimum intervention' – 'as little as possible and as much as necessary' – are impossible to apply in gardens, except in relation to the artefacts within them. Gardens can only be sustained by constant 'intervention', i.e. gardening, and no garden process can be halted. Similarly, it is arrant nonsense to refer only to 'repair' and 'maintenance' in relation to sustaining, renewing and caring for gardens and their features. These terms are relevant to structures and artefacts but not to living organisms, which are constantly developing and decaying. Gardens are about processes, not simply products.

Gardens are about process

All landscapes and all gardens are fundamentally about process. They are constantly and inevitably developing and decaying; indeed this is why we value and appreciate them, not simply as a series of immutable experiences occasionally enjoyed. Gardens are shaped by their environment and those who use and manage them; above all they are determined by the values of those who care for them. Dereliction is a process that can be guided or tempered but cannot be stopped. Nor is it possible to recreate dereliction artificially in gardens, or even to retain a bogus sense of 'romantic' decay by inadequate care and cultivation. Any attempt is doomed to failure because decay is a transitory process. With plants you eventually have to start again. All plant life needs to be cultivated – weeded, pruned, trained, manured, protected, renewed – on historic sites according to a pre-determined but flexible ideal. Every repeated garden task has a cumulative effect as well as an immediate impact, and accidental change is unavoidable.

The glamour and excitement of the initial restoration is merely the start of a process of development. Putting the clock back in a garden does not stop it; it will go on ticking and the garden will need to be sustained, modified and renewed if it is to survive and retain the qualities for which it was restored. Few significant gardens, or even landscape parks, in Britain have been made to a definitive plan, i.e. designed overall and laid out according to a single vision composed on paper and executed completely. In most cases they were developed over a period, either by trial and error in a lifetime or created over several generations by a dynasty of owners and their servants. Gardens like Hidcote, Sissinghurst, Mount Stewart, Rowallane, Snowshill, Stourhead and Studley Royal and, more recently, Knightshayes and the Gibberd Garden, were created through a series of inspirational innovations and embellishments, guided in each case by a developing ideal in the minds of the creators; never stable and never complete. Stourhead and Studley Royal were developed by subsequent generations who clearly respected their inheritance, in the English tradition. Other gardens of great beauty, historic importance and horticultural merit like Powis Castle, Blickling Hall, Wimpole Hall, Killerton, Cliveden, Lanhydrock, Hatfield House and Chatsworth, have gained significance thanks to an evolving series of changes and contributions, each generation adding to the richness and diversity of the place. Continuity has arisen from respect for previous generations' achievements and dynamism from their successors having the courage and ambition to add something of their own, to do their own thing, according to their taste and the values of the time.

Any attempt at re-creating 'historic' gardens at a stroke is contrary to all this accumulated experience. Too often the result, although admirable in many ways, seems to lack the spontaneous humanity that goes with a garden made with the freedom of a personal vision to temper a rigid academic blueprint. The fundamental point

Harry Burrows, head gardener at Hidcote throughout the 1960s and '70s, in the White Garden.

Head gardeners on their annual conference tour visiting Rowallane with the host, Mike Snowden, offering the oldest gardener Jimmy Hancock a wheelchair tour of the garden.

about gardens, however formal, is that they are about change – hour to hour, day to day, month to month and year to year. The accidental and the ephemeral often enhance the well planned; we can relax a little because in gardens most change is reversible. Provided that the concept remains clear and easy to appreciate, deviation in detail should be welcomed; change from year to year is necessary to retain freshness and vitality. Even in a garden strictly tied to date, adherence entirely to plants documented to have been in the garden (as distinct from those available at the time) is unnecessarily restrictive. It misses the point that gardens are primarily for production and enjoyment, giving pleasure by change and development. They should never be regarded as museum pieces or even as tableaux, like Chelsea Flower Show gardens, assembled only for a few days.

Britain's unmatched quantity and diversity of gardens exists because garden-making has been a national obsession for centuries and because many of them have been consistently cared for. This has been possible because of our social stability and institutional continuity. However, the real reason for their survival is that they have been consistently loved and cherished for their individual values, an almost infinite range of qualities from design to wildlife and from recreation to fashion. They have also provided owners with a way of identifying with the values and achievements of past generations as well as a means of self-expression, an accessible way of making their own mark. They have survived because they have been enjoyed, constantly being adapted or modified to meet different needs and demands. Our greatest historic gardens are of this kind, bearing the imprint of successive owners, their value residing largely in the extent to which they demonstrate their age. This is shown most obviously by the deliberate accumulation of features, but also by maturity and by change, development arising from site, climate and style of upkeep.

Gardens are inherently dynamic and cannot remain static, needing to be constantly renewed and adapted to changing circumstances. Historic garden conservation should aim at retaining the garden's significant qualities, characteristics and values, and any innovation should be consistent with, or complementary to, this inherited character. It is emphatically not the role of the conserving organisation to impose whimsical new features, plantings or styles on a garden of great historic importance, however distinguished the designer or plantsman. Nor is it right to justify new development entirely on the perceived need to pursue management goals, especially financial.

Procedures for conservation

However 'complete' the restoration, it still has to be managed into maturity, a process more demanding and more exacting than the initial works. On the other hand, the standard of the preparatory horticulture – drainage, soil improvement, perennial weed control, planting, staking, as well as plant quality and trueness to type – is soon discovered. There is a lot to be said for those who will have to care for the garden being closely involved in the landscape works. Similarly, contractors can do a great deal of damage that may not be apparent at first – soil compaction, dumping of toxic materials, fires near trees, contamination of tree roots from cement mortar, etc. Competent and responsible contractors are a key to success but even they need careful supervision to avoid inadvertent damage. In my experience this is best achieved by appointing the eventual head gardener or garden manager at the earliest possible stage and giving him or her authority over the garden contractors and equal status with the clerk of works of any parallel building restoration.

Needless to say, without good gardeners it is impossible to sustain good gardens. The garden's staff are by far the most important factor in its conservation. In addition to their initial training, gardeners at all levels need to be consistently guided in the ways of the place and encouraged to develop relevant expertise and judgement based on acute observation. They need to be confident about promoting necessary change and development, and be able to grasp opportunities and anticipate threats. Gardeners also need to be involved in decision-making at their level and to understand the general strategy. Only in this way can the garden hope to retain and sharpen its unique qualities and special character over time.

Not everything can or should be preserved. A set of significant values, in order of precedence, should help to formulate a philosophy for conservation specific to the site, relevant to changing circumstances and new opportunities. Conservation principles arising out of this philosophy need to take account of foreseeable change but must also seek to preserve significant values and characteristics whatever they may be – plants, objects, skills, local relevance, etc. – while pursuing other management objectives such as income generation, education and public participation, which may indeed be the means of the garden's survival. Success with garden conservation is measured by the extent to which the place retains its individuality: the degree to which its traditional processes can be retained despite changing circumstances and resources.

It is comparatively easy to assemble a list of significant values and characteristics for any garden, historic or otherwise, the larger and more complex gardens producing the longest lists. Historic significance is revealed by research and survey, including plant cataloguing and analysis and archaeological investigation. Other elements of significance need to be arrived at by the joint efforts of those who know the garden, perhaps those who have managed it in the past, together with someone who is able to make expert and informed comparisons with other gardens so as to define the garden's special characteristics. But a raw list is not helpful for

John Sales in his office at Cirencester in 1980 – no computer!

decision-making, which is the purpose of any conservation plan. To be useful to future managers, on whose decisions the future of the garden rests, elements of significance must be set out in comparative terms, compared on local and national levels and with one another within the garden. This vital order of precedence needs to be negotiated with all involved, not an easy process, and established unequivocally if the conservation plan is going to have any real meaning. The inevitable conflicts need to be resolved without fudging the issue. National and regional designations, having statutory backing, will be useful in guiding the ranking but cannot be allowed to dominate. The presence of significant archaeology, scientific interest, badgers, bats or newts does not necessarily constitute the dominant values of a site, especially one of great historic or cultural complexity, although these things may contribute to the full meaning of the place.

John Sales discussing proposals for a border at Tatton Park with head gardener Sam Youd. Beyond is James Rothwell, now the National Trust silver specialist.

For example, in the absence of statutory protection for the key elements of a garden, the presence of an SSSI (Site of Special Scientific Interest) should not be allowed to distort the evaluation. To some degree there is an inevitable conflict between nature conservation on the one hand and landscape and garden restoration on the other. Semi-dereliction often creates rich habitat for wildlife which restoration threatens. On the other hand, enlightened management of parks and gardens creates and sustains a wide range of habitat and food sources for wildlife. Furthermore, the very fact that landscape parks have been managed (or even mismanaged) for centuries according to a consistent regime, whether for use or beauty, has ensured the conservation of much valuable, even unique habitat. Narrow perceptions of conservation on all sides arise from over-specialisation that creates inflexible attitudes based on a fundamentalist, almost religious 'conservation' creed. Even now this myopic approach to nature conservation is all too prevalent, presumably the result of narrow teaching and lack of a multi-disciplinary approach in universities.

With historic garden conservation and management, nothing is more important than an unequivocal statement of significance set out in relative terms, arising out of rigorous enquiry and research, negotiated with all concerned. However, for clarity in management terms, significance needs to take account of constraints and opportunities – financial, planning, current legislation, change of use, etc. Combining these changing realities with the comparatively immutable statement of significance should give rise to realistic management principles reflecting both. These principles must state clearly, in order of precedence, the fundamental bases and assumptions that should govern all decision-making – management priority, planting style and renewal, buildings restoration policy, repair of the fabric, standards of upkeep – as well as related issues such as access, education, interpretation, trading, staffing, training, etc. The management principles should be sufficiently comprehensive to guide the general style of management and to contribute to any decisions, large or small, that may arise. They should form the basis of any long-term conservation management plan devised for the garden and the property as a whole.

The National Trust has changed in many ways in recent years, sometimes but not always for the better. With the dissolution of the independent Gardens Panel and the demotion of the Gardens Advisers and curators to consultants, there is an obvious danger of gardens being propelled entirely according to the values and priorities of the largely autonomous managers, perhaps only influenced by the head gardener. Neither will necessarily have had the opportunity of considering an authoritative alternative view. Gardens are constantly formed and reformed over time, and even in the presence of a conservation management plan the cumulative effect of alterations, even minor changes, can have a profound impact over a period. Conservation management plans, however well written, are only as effective as their interpretation over time.

My loyalty was always primarily to the properties, and I saw the Trust as a worthy agent ensuring the continuing care of the place and upholder of its essential values. However, we have seen the promotion of over-visiting in sensitive flower gardens, disruptive developments (such as children's adventure playgrounds inappropriately sited), and the over-frequent staging of damaging commercial events. There seems to have been a relentless and indiscriminate drive to augment visitor numbers whether or not the property can continue to support the increase. It would never have occurred to me that the Trust would compromise the obligations of preservation in the interest of unnecessary commercialisation, nor of proselytising popular causes and pursuing campaigns, however worthy. Let us hope that as it pursues its many worthy campaigns the National Trust does not overlook its responsibilities in preserving the individual, inherited values of each place.

Chapter 1

LEARNING

Crane lifting a new lantern on to the restored pavilion at Westbury Court.

WESTBURY COURT
GLOUCESTERSHIRE

It was no coincidence that the National Trust's restoration of the late seventeenth-century Westbury Court garden coincided more or less with the formation of the Garden History Society in 1965. The garden had miraculously survived until after the Second World War, if a little shabbily, and was well remembered in Gloucestershire, as well as having been photographed for a *Country Life* article in its Edwardian phase. Including the house, the third to have been built on the site, the whole property had been bought by a developer in 1960, and would undoubtedly have become a housing estate had it not been for the early eighteenth-century pavilion that had been listed by the Department of the Environment. This had been incorporated as a wing of the Edwardian house, and it came to light during demolition works in 1963, sparking a halt at the eleventh hour. At that time historic gardens had no protection unless the structures formed the essential curtilage of a listed building. Even the seventeenth-century garden walls at Westbury, still in reasonable condition, had no protection. Disastrously, the developer had already demolished the west wall that once separated the house and its flower garden from the formal water garden with its canals, hedges, topiary, fruit and vegetables.

Despite the resulting chaos, the local authority, to their great credit, denied planning consent. Under great pressure, Gloucestershire County Council acquired the whole site and decided to build a care home and sheltered housing on the then derelict area west of the demolished wall. Recognising its historic importance, the Council gave the remainder of the site to the National Trust on the understanding that it would endeavour to restore the garden, assisted by a grant from the HBC for the repair of the pavilion. By then a head of steam had been built up through regional interest and local public opinion, together with the efforts of founder members of the Garden History Society. Miles Hadfield, one of these founders, had published his influential book *Gardening in Britain* in 1960, and he took a great interest in Westbury in every respect. Thanks to pressure from the region and the enthusiasm of Anthony Mitchell (Historic Buildings Representative), and also through the benign influence at a higher level of the Earl of Rosse, the Trust, to their eternal credit, rather reluctantly took on the restoration without any endowment. They did this despite knowing that the garden would never be able to balance its budget through visitor income or any other sort of property initiative. I cannot imagine that the equivalent of such a far-reaching and imaginative act of faith in an historic garden would ever recur with the present governance of the National Trust, despite it now having more than ten times as many members as it did in the late 1960s. Through a public appeal the Trust raised funds, helped by an anonymous gift, and acquired the place in 1967.

By that time the pavilion, minus the adjoining house, had deteriorated much further, having been stripped of its roof lead by thieves. The garden too had gone back seriously as a result of flooding after the cold and snowy winter of 1963–4, made worse by blocked culverts and sluices, which are integral to the control of water levels in this low-lying riverside plain below the Forest of Dean. Most of the

ABOVE The south-facing wall border showing the urn-topped piers of one of the clairvoyées and the roadside 18th-century gazebo. (1967)

RIGHT The replanted roadside wall border with the restored 18th-century gazebo originally intended for sitting and watching the passing road traffic as well as enjoying the garden. (1985)

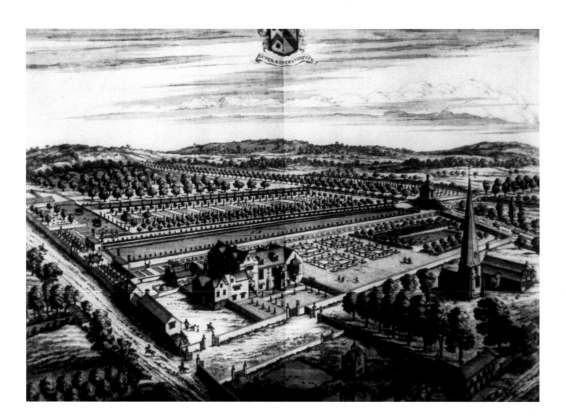

yew hedges were dead but I doubt from their girth that they were of the seventeenth century; they were much more likely to have been a Victorian replanting following a similar flood, or even simply replacements for overgrown originals. Replanting was along the lines of the dead hedges, although some argued that they were not true to the Kip engraving.

Apart from its incredible survival, the joy of Westbury is the wealth of evidence available about its past layout and plant content, mostly carried out by the owner Maynard Colchester between 1696 and 1705. It was little changed thereafter, except for the addition eastwards, before the middle of the eighteenth century, of a gazebo and small walled garden. This was all enclosed by a further diversion of Westbury Brook, which effectively forms the boundary on its eastern and northern sides. The Kip engraving of 1705, published in Atkyns's *The Ancient and Present State of Gloucestershire* (1712), seems to be based on an accurate survey, but characteristically makes the layout appear much grander than it is. It formed a 'blueprint' for the restoration and was ideal in giving people a vision of what was intended. However, the real breakthrough and incentive was the discovery of Maynard Colchester's meticulous accounts in the Gloucestershire County Record Office, covering the whole period of the garden's making. These had formed the basis of a thesis on Westbury Court by a student at the Gloucestershire College of Art in Cheltenham. Her work was in turn used to guide the reconstruction and the main structural planting. Crucially, it included descriptions and costs of ornaments and other artefacts as well as hedging plants, evergreens and fruit trees.

Despite the seemingly comprehensive records, we quickly learned how much of any 'restoration' is dependent on conjecture and practicability. We could never

Kip's engraving of Westbury Court from a survey of 1705 published in Atkyns's *The Ancient and Present State of Gloucestershire* (1712). This shows the existing church and shingle tiled spire and the original house and flower garden in the foreground, with the now-restored garden beyond.

have afforded an archaeological investigation (nobody suggested it), but I doubt whether it would have revealed anything crucial. It is, however, the mass of essential detail that really determines the character of any garden. Plants (including grass), and their arrangement, pruning, training, support, cultivation, etc., were inevitably largely conjectural, and in the early 1970s there was almost no body of knowledge apart from what we could glean from contemporary illustrations. Furthermore, we were acutely aware that the most the Trust could possibly afford was going to be one gardener, rather than Maynard Colchester's seemingly elastic workforce, which included various 'weederwomen' (this was before the days of volunteers in gardens – the modern weederwomen?). In the last resort, gardens are about gardening and what is possible in the prevailing circumstances and with the resources available. There was another consideration at the time – that of making what was in fact only a little more than half of the original garden (i.e. minus the flower garden) interesting enough to satisfy the average visitor making a special trip to see it. Purists and academics care little about such matters, but at the time enjoyment was important and is after all the main purpose of gardens, along with production. Compromise is inevitable in garden restoration.

Most of the initial work between 1967 and 1971 was structural. The Trust's consultant, Christopher Bishop of Eric Cole Architects of Cirencester, brilliantly designed the tall pavilion, including elements recovered from the demolition, and cleverly contrived a house for the gardener, Ken Vaughan. Funding was so tight that the west wall, demolished by the developer, had to be rebuilt three courses of brick lower than the original. But in an effort to mollify residents of the adjacent care home, two wrought-iron clairvoyées, reflecting those in the north wall, were made so that residents could peep through. When I first went to Westbury

The small early 18th-century walled garden after repairing the gazebo and setting out a simple conjectural layout of flower borders. (1971)

in 1971 this wall was being rebuilt, the pavilion was complete, the canals had been dredged of silt with their retaining walls rebuilt and most of the yew hedges had been planted. Without prior chemical or physical analysis, the dredgings had been spread across the eastern part of the site, thereby creating problems when it came to planting the area. In quality and makeup the dredgings were predictably variable, resulting in uneven settlement, impeded drainage and contrasts in fertility from place to place.

My predecessor in the Trust, Graham Stuart Thomas, was of course involved from the start and was a founder member of the Garden History Society. He claimed to have first visited Westbury Court in 1960 and he was certainly consulted when it was first mooted as a possible acquisition in 1963.

Following my appointment, as a new boy who had not yet time to prove my usefulness, I was surprised to be delegated to deal with Westbury. It transpired that Graham had assumed that transplanting would use what he would have termed 'suitably appropriate plants' – i.e. traditional old country house species and cultivars chosen for an extended display throughout the opening season and arranged in the style he knew best. This important matter should have been part of an agreed overall philosophy of restoration, but at this stage the Trust was making things like this up as the restoration went along. Graham's first design for the south-facing wall border (which he thought faced east) was apparently overruled by the Historic Buildings department, no doubt influenced from outside the

The walled gazebo garden after planting with a collection of plants, all known to have been grown in England in the 17th century. (1980)

Trust, in favour of a policy of using only plants introduced and firmly in cultivation before *c.*1700. The Trust was feeling its way with what was after all the first intentionally historicist, comprehensive garden restoration in England. Having been rebuffed, it seemed that Graham could not back out quickly enough. The situation was never explained to me; that was not the way of the Trust at the time; decision-making at the higher levels was often a mystery to me. In this tortuous way the Trust arrived, with hindsight, at the right decision.

Nevertheless, Graham continued to encourage me and always commented very helpfully and constructively on proposals I had formulated with the regional staff. It was unrealistic to attempt a precise representation of the layout shown by Kip, except in respect of the area of the first canal stretching north from the tall pavilion to a clairvoyée on the A48. Elsewhere either too much had changed or the area had been developed post-Kip. Strictly speaking, we should have kept to fruit trees, vegetables and hedging, except perhaps in the little walled garden beside the roadside gazebo, where it was entirely legitimate to recreate an appropriate formal flower garden. East of the T-shaped canal was the large area of dredgings, now being sown down to grass, and we decided for the sake of additional interest to recreate two sections of the flower garden parterre shown by Kip behind the seventeenth-century house. To give this a firm setting I devised a quincunx of

The blocked
west canal and
ruined pavilion
in 1967 after
floods, vandalism
and death of
the flanking yew
hedges.

small ornamental trees and clipped evergreens entirely without precedent but of the period.

At the time it was a challenge to locate a wide range of plants known to have been grown in gardens before the eighteenth century. Many species were represented in cultivation by cultivars and hybrids that had supplanted the earlier forms. We gradually accumulated a fascinatingly wide range but, as Graham pointed out, they tend to be predominantly for spring and early summer display, most of our summer-flowering herbaceous plants and annuals having been introduced later from the Americas, South Africa and Australasia. Even most summer-flowering roses derive from cultivars produced in Europe in the eighteenth century or later. In the seventeenth century summer was primarily for fruits and berries. We were aware from the records and the Kip engraving that the garden contained a wide variety of fruits, which were grown as much for their aesthetic and sensual pleasure as for merely satisfying hunger. At a time of privation for the masses and very restricted diets, abundance was prized for its own sake and as a mark of status. Like most gardens of the time, Westbury Court was perhaps more about use than beauty; production than ornament. We had to leave what seemed to be the former vegetable garden as grass because there was no one to do the highly labour-intensive gardening on this scale, but more recently the Trust has been able to remedy this deficiency.

Wall-trained fruit was an essential element – apples, pears, 'plumbs' and peaches were all part of Colchester's grand plan. Here again almost nobody was planting old fruit cultivars at the time, particularly those current before 1700. Only

The west canal with restored pavilion, fountain pond, and flanking hedges as indicated in the Kip engraving. On the right is the rebuilt west wall with wall-trained apples, pears and 'plumb' cultivars, all of the 17th century. (1992)

a few nurserymen were able to supply any, and others had to be ordered and grafted specially for Westbury Court. More diverse than those at Erddig or Ham House, the Westbury collection of seventeenth-century wall-trained fruit was by far the largest of its kind, with fascinating old names like 'Bellissime d'Hiver', 'Catshead', 'Black Worcester' and to our delight 'Col. Vaughn' in honour of the gardener-in-charge Ken Vaughan!

Clearly we were guilty of planting an unrealistically comprehensive range of plants available in the late seventeenth century. Rightly or wrongly, we justified this on the grounds, first of giving the garden maximum interest and second of forming a reference collection for education and conservation purposes.

Although modest in extent and done on a shoestring, Westbury Court has, for its size and scope, been consistently enjoyed by visitors and much praised, even by academics, historians and aesthetes. But no one would go about it the same way today with so much more accumulated experience and expertise. After forty years this is hardly surprising but I believe Westbury Court to be highly significant among historic places, partly for being a recognisable recreation of Maynard Colchester's garden, but also for being the first garden restoration of its kind in England. It should be conserved as such.

However thorough and objective we may think we are, with a garden restoration we cannot escape the assumed values and unconscious attitudes of our time. We do not work in a vacuum and the next generation would inevitably do it differently, even with the same constraints – financial, social, functional, etc. – as today, which is also unlikely. Garden restorations say almost as much about the time they are carried out as of the history of the garden and its makers.

FELBRIGG
NORFOLK

My first solo visit as assistant adviser in January 1971 was to Felbrigg, which the Trust had acquired with 686.8 ha (1697 acres) in 1969; but it had only just assumed management. With a stone-mullioned south front of the early seventeenth century and a red-brick west front of slightly later date, the house sits unadorned on the edge of ancient woodland, overlooking the eighteenth-century park. There is little hint of serious gardening until you walk across the donkey paddock, with its hugely handsome sweet chestnuts, to the walled garden. Apart from the orangery, gardening seems to have receded during the twentieth century to leave the house splendidly stark in all its glory.

Felbrigg's donor, Robert Wyndham Ketton-Cremer, was evidently a great scholar, whose books included several important biographies and a variety of works about Norfolk history. He wrote a brilliant essay on Humphry Repton, who lived at Sustead, not far south of the park, and who certainly had a hand in the eighteenth-century 'improvements' by William Windham III. The Windhams were always strong on trees, gradually enclosing the park from the North Sea; near the house are majestic sycamores, beeches and sweet chestnuts. There never seems to have been much garden apart from a walled garden for fruit, flowers and vegetables, which since 1842 has been a sheltered haven from the bracing climate. However, there is a short pleasure ground walk, with shrubs, leading westwards from the house to the eighteenth-century orangery, full of camellias. Ketton-Cremer does not seem to have been much interested in gardening and cultivation of the walled garden gently declined as the regime, including his head gardener, got older, while funds available for employing gardeners became less.

The managing agent, David Musson, took me to the beautifully walled early Victorian kitchen garden, which had survived more or less intact with its lovely old dovecote and modest greenhouses. We were met by Mr Knight who had worked for Mr Ketton-Cremer for many years, loyally fighting a losing battle as the staff dwindled and the garden contracted. He was by then working virtually alone but the walled garden remained his pride and pleasure, although beyond him physically. His greatest joys were the double borders across the whole width of the garden which he planted annually with dahlias. This spectacular late-summer display predictably absorbed most of his time and energy, the plants being grown from tubers lifted and overwintered in the frost-free cellars of the house. The effect was uniquely enhanced in September by thick bands of *Colchicum tenorei*, thousands of them, inside the box hedges. In the strong East Anglian light and low rainfall, colchicums obviously thrived, and we later decided to use this distinctive touch in making a national collection of *Colchicum* at Felbrigg – now sadly discontinued, presumably because of lack of interest.

Despite the walled garden being in some ways charming with pockets of interest here and there, the process of steady dereliction plainly needed to be reversed. However, I was firmly informed as a new boy that the Trust would be able to afford no more than the one gardener currently employed. So here was my first challenge, upon which I would no doubt be judged if I were to aspire to succeed Graham Thomas as (Chief) Gardens Adviser. Graham did not emerge from his annual hibernation (for book writing) until April so, apart from a brief discussion, it was left to me. I am not sure he ever went to Felbrigg. The only practical solution, I concluded, would be to cut down on labour-intensive and strictly unnecessary work to make way for regenerating the walled garden as a whole. The aim would be to retain and strengthen the traditional layout while substituting semi-permanent planting of greater diversity and interest for some of the labour-intensive features like dahlias and vegetables.

In those days, under the chairmanship of the Duke of Grafton, members of the regional committee were deputed to watch over gardeners and Gardens Advisers. The critical amateur eye of a committee member was thought to be an essential counterbalance to the mere professional. At Felbrigg I was lucky to have Lady Harrod, wife of the distinguished economist Sir Roy Harrod, as my constant companion. She was charming and always tactfully helpful to someone who could not be expected to appreciate the finer points of country house living and gardening. In fact I learned a lot from her, but mainly about the benevolently feudal assumptions of the Trust's East Anglian committees and management at the time. I very much enjoyed her company and she invariably made me feel at ease, often entertaining us to lunch in her lovely old vicarage in Holt. Perhaps the most telling remark I remember is: 'the trouble is that so many people do not know the difference between what's nice and what's nasty'. 'Good taste' was the order of the day in the 1970s. To be fair, Lady Harrod knew Ketton-Cremer well socially and did have a grasp of what he may not have liked, even though what he may have liked

LEFT Main axis through the Felbrigg walled garden in 1971 soon after acquisition by the National Trust.

RIGHT View through to the repaired greenhouses and dovecote with box hedges renewed and borders replanted. (1991)

was rather more difficult to define. Her best piece of advice to me was 'not to try quite so hard'.

The interregnum between Ketton-Cremer dying and the Trust taking over management at Felbrigg, a matter of nearly two years, created our first dilemma. For a memorial to the well-loved former owner, the tenants and estate staff had contributed a fund and Ketton-Cremer's former agent had agreed to plant a rose garden with the proceeds, choosing a very conspicuous position adjacent to the south front of the house outside the estate office. Enclosed only by park rail fencing, it was planted throughout with slabs of modern bush roses, mostly upright floribundas, each cultivar brighter and brasher than the next, orange-scarlet being the main theme. A dazzling eye-catcher in summer and a dreary forest of thorns at other times, the style was that of the average 1960s housing estate front garden: not at all to the taste of the East Anglian Regional Committee. We all agreed that it was a total mistake but we had to take local sensibilities into account. Clearly it had to stay for the present, and my advice was to do something constructive before contemplating its replacement. It is all too easy to destroy and much more difficult to agree and implement something new. After a few years we did decide the time was ripe for removal and I designed an inoffensive new rose garden in pink and white, using rugosa shrub roses. However, in retrospect I believe it was a mistake. If a similar situation arose again I would argue for retaining the memorial roses much longer because they had more meaning than my replacement, being in effect part of the history of the place. I would have felt more strongly about them if they had actually been chosen specifically by people associated with the estate but I feel sure the choice was left to Mr Knight. Nevertheless, I now believe it should have been retained long enough for the roses to see out their time. Historic garden conservation is not about good taste.

Sadly, within a few months Mr Knight suddenly died. While obviously a matter of great regret at the time, the hiatus made it possible to engage a gardener-in-charge who would perhaps find it easier to make changes. Ted Bullock was the ideal solution, a 'refugee' from the garden centre world, trained at Wisley and desperately keen to escape commerce and get back to 'real gardening'. He was a lovely man, highly principled, loyal and conscientious as well as professionally skilled. He took to the task of renovating and converting the walled garden with great enthusiasm and contributed much to strategy as well as practice, the only problem being to get him to state his always intelligent opinions boldly enough.

To reduce upkeep and increase interest, our first step was to replace the long dahlia borders with a new design, incorporating mostly shrubs, together with bulbs and permanent ground-covering perennials aimed at providing a successive display without staking and with a minimum of dead-heading. The two southern quarters formerly devoted to vegetables, comprising almost half the walled garden, were grassed over and planted with a collection of *Crataegus* and *Mespilus* species and cultivars, intended as a way of furnishing the space with interest and variety from flowers and fruits. This was fairly successful but the effect tended towards the miscellaneous, lacking in clear meaning and firm pattern. Although perhaps an obvious solution, fruit trees might have been better. We made a pair of short, traditional herbaceous borders along the north-south axis and filled the

Twin borders
through the
walled garden in
1991, replanted
with perennials
with the box
hedges reduced
and reshaped.

perimeter borders with traditional blocks of herbaceous perennials – peonies, asters, irises, etc., as it were for cut flowers; also the displaced dahlias.

Half of the upper northern part of the walled garden was reserved for vegetables and soft fruits, together with space for nursery rows of young plants. This became in effect Ted Bullock's private kitchen garden, cultivated and harvested voluntarily by Ted and his family in their 'spare' time. The overgrown figs having been pruned and re-trained, the two big south-facing borders either side of the pretty dovecote were planted with a pattern of herbs, with climbers trained on smart wigwams. Gradually the walls were clothed again, partly with traditional fruits – apples, pears, plums, cherries, etc. – according to orientation, and partly with ornamentals, including climbing hydrangea on the north-facing wall. We also began a phased programme of cutting back the box hedges hard to regenerate them, combined with gapping up the spaces. Perhaps more than anything else, this gave the whole walled garden a sense of purposeful neatness and an air of trim continuity.

Ted accomplished this with virtually no help and with great enthusiasm. To our surprise there was little adverse reaction to the upheavals from visitors who had known the place before, not even to the resiting of the dahlias. Visitors soon took an interest in what was going on and I learned an important lesson – that visitors who come back time and again like to see change, reworking and development in historic gardens. This is hardly surprising because gardens are after all about change; it is what we enjoy about them.

In historic gardens the challenge is to promote change within the style and traditions of the place. This is a difficult judgement. Above all it is necessary to suppress the ego, to avoid change whose purpose is simply to please one's own whims and preferences, or simply to promote commerce, visitor attraction, etc.: cultural vulgarity in its fullest sense. It would be useful to carry out objective analyses of the content and layout of gardens like Felbrigg today as an audit of individuality and traditional values.

SNOWSHILL MANOR

GLOUCESTERSHIRE

Snowshill, or as they say 'Snozzle', must have been the first National Trust garden my wife, Lyn, and I visited together, while on holiday in the mid-1950s in the Cotswolds. I thought then that it was the best comparatively small garden I had ever seen and since then I have not changed my mind, despite all the pressures and modifications it has suffered. The Manor is part of the village and used to be entered from it via a 'Wade blue' front garden gate. Inside was a cool, shady place darkly enclosed in evergreens with just a glimpse of the house. Emerging along the gravel path into the light, the full south front of the house was revealed and then further on a tempting view across the garden to the valley beyond. This is the proper way to experience the garden.

Above all, Charles Wade's gardening eye was for structure, creating a succession of spaces, each with a separate character, linked by the sound of water dripping and tinkling on its way. He studied architecture and was sufficiently interested in garden design to enter a national competition, winning second prize. But when after the First World War he acquired Snowshill with its derelict garden, he employed a distinguished architect, M.H. Baillie Scott, to design a master plan. However, he seems to have used this in the honourable English tradition merely as a guide, imposing his own ideas and his personality as he went along; quite right too.

As the antiquarian in him gained ascendancy over his architectural leanings, the garden became, like the house, a place to display some of his incomparable

View from the Well Court towards the house.

collection. Unlike the ubiquitous 'sculpture trails' seen in almost every open garden these days, Wade integrated this fascinating range of objects into his design, giving the garden its special significance. The air of whimsical eccentricity he created at Snowshill as a private garden is not easy, perhaps impossible, to sustain with many thousands of visitors. The Trust has never made any real effort to lessen their impact; quite the reverse, in fact, as every member and every child must now see and engage with everything. Certainly much of the magic of Snowshill has gone, especially now that it is approached via the back gate from a visitor centre: all inescapably institutional.

However lovingly cared for (as it has been since the Trust's acquisition), a garden the size of Snowshill, under such intense pressure, inevitably loses its special character as eccentricity gives way to logic, surprise is lost to practicality, and excitement is tamed by health and safety legislation. This is a universal problem as 'honeypots' are in danger of being eroded by their popularity. With gardens the challenge is particularly acute because they depend for effect on the sum of their important details, qualities only too readily discounted by managers intent on maximising income. There is a fine line between, on the one hand, opening gardens (or houses) for conservation, education and enjoyment of their special qualities, and on the other hand opening to exploit them for other reasons, however honourable these may seem to be.

Although the garden had already lost some of its more fragile contents, I suppose I was guilty of the first well-meaning 'improvement' in the early 1970s. The elder grove had collapsed under heavy snow as far back as 1963. The elders grew in a sunken enclosure next to a barn at the end of the well court, providing a dense canopy. Although they were probably self-sown, Wade clearly realised that they helped provide a classic succession of contrasts from the orderly brightness of the flowery well court, through the pitch blackness of the barn and into the disorderly strangeness of the elder grove, carpeted in autumn by purple-staining elderberries. No one wanted the elders replanted because of their messiness and I suggested the guelder rose (also a native) instead: equally vigorous and arguably

The Well Court from the terrace: Cotswold stone with 'Wade blue' paintwork.

The double borders between the walled gardens and the orchard showing Wade's preference for unsophisticated cottage-garden perennials in soft colours with roses, a fig and other climbers on the stone walls.

more decorative in flower and fruit. Planted now on a square grid instead of randomly arranged, the result achieved its main purpose of providing a green roof for the little open-air room and everyone liked it. But was I trying too hard by inserting a more obviously designed space for something that at least looked as though it had just happened?

Because they are not far apart and have some similarities, Snowshill and Hidcote are often compared, both influenced strongly by the Cotswold Arts and Crafts tradition and created mainly between the great wars. On the other hand, there is no evidence that Charles Wade ever met Lawrence Johnston or even visited Hidcote. They certainly moved in different social circles, if indeed Charles Wade was part of any such identifiable group. Although, like Hidcote, Snowshill consists of an asymmetrical composition of room-like spaces, connecting corridors and contrived views, Wade never aspired to horticultural excellence, sophisticated plantsmanship or stimulating colour schemes. He liked simple cottage garden plants and old roses artlessly arranged in colours, mostly on the cool side of the spectrum. He specifically avoided employing a well-trained and perhaps opinionated head gardener in favour of a countryman who would more readily do his bidding. The gardening style at Snowshill should remain 'cottage garden' in its original sense and not in the self-conscious interpretation adopted now by its modern practitioners.

A welcome recent development has been renovation and renewal in the kitchen garden, which barely ticked over in the 1970s. But since the Trust has managed to recruit volunteers, more can be done to add interest. Vegetable gardening has been revived to good effect in many gardens, including Snowshill. As in the flower garden, any sophisticated design, elaborate system and over-indulgence in detail would not have suited Charles Wade. He would have left it to the gardener to grow fruit and vegetables in the conventional, country garden way: perhaps old dustbins for forcing rhubarb and a ramshackle old greenhouse for tomatoes; certainly not trendy, raised beds or step-over cordon apples?

RIGHT View to the back door of the house from the yew walk.

BELOW The garden incorporates a fascinating range of features and surprises created by changes of level, stone walls and buildings.

HAM HOUSE
LONDON

Although the Trust was given the property by the Tollemache family in 1948, it did not control Ham House until 1991, taking it over from the Victoria and Albert Museum which had been managing it. The garden had been run quite separately by the Royal Parks authority on behalf of what became the Department of the Environment, with advice from the Trust. There were the sad remains of a gardenesque feature east of the house, but gardening was confined largely to a border below the terrace, lavishly and gorgeously bedded out. The remainder was maintained at a basic level and the situation seemed immutable.

By 1975, when I got to know the place, Graham Thomas had engendered some enthusiasm for change. This was augmented in 1979 by the ground-breaking and influential *The Garden* exhibition at the Victoria and Albert Museum, which included a superb model of Ham. This interpreted a 1672 plan very precisely and must have had an influence. The breakthrough arose out of anonymous (at the time) offers of funding for the garden's restoration. Understandably the donors wanted to see a result in their lifetime and stipulated a very short timescale. Nevertheless, we could hardly miss the opportunity. Despite tight funding the Royal Parks were entirely cooperative, so together with other generous gifts the project became a practical proposition.

Research to date had been mainly confined to drawings and paintings in the house, the most important being a convincing plan of 1672 by John Slezor, showing eight grass plats with wide gravel paths south of the house and the formally hedged 'wilderness' beyond. This was largely corroborated by a later engraving of house and garden from the south, and crucially by a series of aerial photographs of the 1950s showing unmistakable parch marks of gravel paths with the overgrown wilderness beyond. Along with a splendid painting by Henry Danckerts, which hangs in the house, showing the Earl and Duchess of Lauderdale in their garden in 1675, these enabled us to build up a sufficient picture of the south garden at a key moment in its history, contemporary with the remodelling of the house.

In view of the unusual absence of any significant later 'overlay' to destroy, we felt entirely confident that a re-creation of the seventeenth-century scheme would be entirely beneficial in experiencing the place. There would not have been time for archaeology but neither did anyone suggest it, such was the unprecedented nature of the restoration. Later investigation revealed some discrepancies but not enough to make a difference; certainly not visually. Furthermore, there needed to be a great deal of pragmatism in the planting because (not surprisingly) none of it was recorded. For example, in the paintings trees in the wilderness looked like elms, ideal for quick effect but hopeless long term, so we eventually used field maple, smaller but still robust and native. Similarly, we picked on hornbeam as a practical as well as historically appropriate hedge plant.

With a notional two-year deadline, we needed to move fast. Luckily Paul Miles had joined the staff as Assistant Gardens Adviser, bringing with him his experience in

View from the Wilderness before restoration. (1975)

View from the Wilderness in 1979 after clearing and replanting trees and hedges. On the right are Graham Thomas and Jim Marshall.

garden construction and planting. He took on the project with great enthusiasm and resilience. He needed these qualities in the wet winter of 1975–6 while contractors were felling what remained of the wilderness – predictably bogged down in mud and inevitably criticised by locals for removing healthy trees. In fact the reaction both locally and nationally was surprisingly muted. This first dramatic stage of transformation was somewhat delayed by the weather but within two years the wide gravel paths and eight grass plats were laid, and the main structure of the Wilderness hedges and trees completed.

The construction and planting phase of restoration is always exciting and good for the ego, but subsequent care and development are the crucial parts of the process. It was easy enough to correct nutrient deficiencies in the grass plats but it soon became clear that there were soil problems in the wilderness. In our haste soil analysis had been neglected; locally extreme acidity and severe nutrient imbalances were later revealed. In places there was also serious soil compaction from the use of heavy machinery on wet ground, despite efforts at alleviating this before planting. The resulting uneven growth took a few years to correct. Furthermore, although the field maples chosen for the outer framework did well, my choice for the other trees of the historically correct 'Azarole' (*Crataegus azarolus*), a large-fruited thorn from north Africa and west Asia, was a mistake. They did not thrive and became diseased, eventually having to be replaced by more field maples, which with hindsight would have been the right choice originally. It took several years of persistent endeavour by Jim Marshall, who had by then replaced Paul Miles when he moved on, to put things right and develop the wilderness further in cooperation with the regional staff, especially Christopher Rowell, the Historic Buildings Representative.

By the time I retired in 1998 the essential elements of the south garden were in place, complete with the four summer houses and the statues and furniture shown in the Danckerts painting (the chairs being copied from one we saw at Helmingham Hall, the home of Lord and Lady Tollemache, whose seventeenth-century ancestors owned Ham House). Since the turn of the twenty-first century much has been done to revive the productive function of the western walled garden, with fruits, flowers and vegetables being grown in profusion. One day perhaps the orangery, maybe the oldest in Britain, will also be fully restored to its proper purpose and appearance?

The so-called 'cherry garden' east of the house was something of a mystery to us in 1975, there being nothing to see on the ground that seemed to refer to the seventeenth century. John Slezor's plan clearly shows a parterre based on diagonals, which seemed appropriate. Although there was no other reference to a parterre east of the house, to be consistent we decided to implement a version of this plan as a more intimate and sheltered flower garden, in contrast to the plain grass and gravel of the south garden. Graham Thomas suggested a pattern of box hedges and cones planted with cotton lavender and English lavender set in gravel

The Cherry Garden after setting out John Slezor's parterre and structural planting, still immature.

paths for maximum impact and minimum cost of upkeep. This was agreed but I strongly felt it needed a firm framework to enclose the pattern, act as background and bring down the scale. Hence my scheme of tunnel arbours and double yew hedges giving views out over the parterre was implemented at the same time as the south garden.

Although the garden restoration was approved of generally, most visitors understandably found the plain grass plats and immature wilderness lacking in interest in the 1970s and '80s. But the cherry garden was an instant success, greatly enjoyed and much photographed, appearing time and again in publicity literature. Quite apart from needing to be correct historically, gardens like Ham should also be enjoyed by visitors while keeping to what is appropriate to the place. Research had revealed that Ham was known in the seventeenth century for the many tender plants overwintered in pots and stood out each year for display. With too few gardeners and the Orangery in use as a tea room, this important horticultural dimension was absent.

The Cherry Garden has been much photographed from its perimeter hornbeam tunnel arbour; all conjectural.

Large scale garden restoration in the 1970s was rare, each case breaking new ground, and Ham was in the vanguard. There was little body of knowledge to draw upon and a paucity of experience of the techniques. The Garden History Society was less than a decade old and English Heritage did not exist. Further research revealed more and more of the history of the garden, and eventually in the late 1980s the Trust was able to afford a post-restoration archaeological

investigation. This revealed that, apart from visually undetectable variations, the main south garden restoration was as accurate as could be ascertained. On the other hand, it revealed no evidence that the east ('cherry') garden parterre had been implemented before the twentieth century. It seems that the area was used for standing out in summer the many potted plants, including cherries, overwintered in the orangery: hence the absence of ground evidence.

This seemed to come as a great shock to garden historians and to academics generally, and there were tentative suggestions that the parterre should be removed or much altered. But in its favour it had been a genuine proposal in the seventeenth century (if not implemented), and the outcome was undeniably successful, giving pleasure and interest to thousands of visitors. The Trust's Gardens Panel wisely took the view that as long as visitors were not misled into believing it was an authentic restoration, the whole feature should remain intact to be enjoyed as an example of garden re-creation of its time. If and when it is replaced, it should be exactly according to historic precedent, with sufficient resources and skills available for sustaining a full restoration.

There is no such thing as authentic restoration, especially in gardens. Nothing is forever and we should always be mindful of enjoying what exists before contemplating its replacement.

A model of proposals for the garden at Ham House made for the 1979 historic gardens exhibition at the Victoria and Albert Museum, showing the formal Wilderness and the grass plats.

Seen across the river Nene in Wisbech, the handsome Georgian front of Peckover House, part of an elegant terrace of town houses, gives no hint of the character of the garden beyond. Presumably there was an eighteenth-century layout but the walled gardens are now wholeheartedly Victorian in style and content, although the maidenhair tree is said to have been planted much earlier. The property came to the National Trust more than a decade before Graham Thomas began advising in 1955, and seems to have continued undisturbed apart from the vegetable garden being mainly grassed over for economy, there being only one gardener for the 1 ha (2.5-acre) garden.

Graham recognised the garden's significance as an intact survival of the nineteenth-century gardenesque style – a term coined by John Loudon in the 1830s for a style that displayed the character of each plant and the art of the gardener. The aim was to grow and display the many exotic plants becoming available and to enjoy the dazzling colours of new tender hybrids being produced. Nothing was left to nature; artifice was the name of the game. The result was a deliberate conglomeration of formal and semi-formal features and a plethora of flower beds for roses and herbaceous plants with trees and shrubs dotted within and between them. There was also a lugubrious shrubbery in which evergreens and ferns predominated, and several borders for flowers and foliage plants.

Perhaps because it was not much valued by anyone else in the Trust, the garden seems to have escaped attention and 'improvement', but to his great credit the Regional Director, Nicolas de Bazille Corbin, found scarce funds to repair the two greenhouses, one a remarkable fernery and the other a conservatory ('the orangery'), and to keep the little Victorian summer house and the garden walls in good order. Somehow in the 1950s a circular fountain pond got moved from the main lawn to a position in front of the summer house. Graham Thomas was complicit in this alteration – understandable from a 1950s design perspective but a change that would be thought inexcusable from an historic conservation point of view nowadays.

Graham designed a series of matching mixed borders along the walk between the greenhouses and the summer house, which are a good example of his design and plantsmanship in an historic setting, aiming at economy of upkeep. When I took over advising in 1971 there was still a good deal of overdue renovation and renewal needing to be worked through steadily with the one gardener, George Peeling, on his own. He was a doughty Fen man, not easily convinced but doggedly determined to improve 'his' garden according to the high horticultural standards locally.

My main single contribution at Peckover, before handing on the advisory role to Jim Marshall, was to redesign a long south-facing border. Luckily the Regional Committee took little interest in the garden and while I was still Graham's assistant

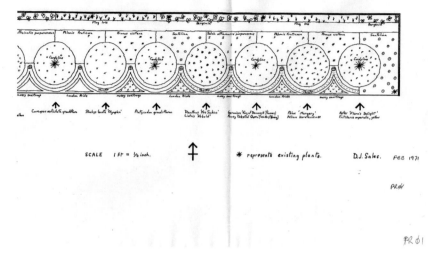

My plan for a Victorian-style ribbon border, adapted using semi-permanent planting rather than twice-annual bedding plants.

he encouraged me to create something in Victorian style as far as possible within the limited resources available. George Peeling was cautiously supportive but needed to be reassured as to how much extra work I would be making for him.

Instead of a mixed herbaceous border in the Jekyll tradition, I decided to copy what in high Victorian times would be called a ribbon border, as remorselessly repetitive as anything William Andrews Nesfield might have designed (on a larger scale of course) but without the need for so much annual or twice-annual bedding out. This was an interesting challenge and I concocted a design based on repeated circles set among permanent dwarf plants, including dwarf shrubs for foliage effect that could be cut back annually. After some early modification this innovation was generally well received and did at least preserve something of the garden's distinctiveness. The first of its kind, my attempt at period gardening was

The pattern of the ribbon border emerging but as yet lacking its background, 1973; perhaps the first since the Queen died?

ABOVE The ribbon border faithfully replanted in 1988 with various amendments in the light of experience; now at last appreciated.

RIGHT The pond was moved to this site near the summerhouse by Graham Thomas in the late 1960s and the rose arches have been added more recently to good effect.

not universally appreciated in the execution, especially by people who understandably misunderstood or simply disliked what they saw. Nevertheless, as I had hoped, the border has been faithfully conserved and developed to incorporate some annual bedding as more help became available. Even at this scale one should be looking forward to the possibility of modification and improvement.

LITTLE MORETON HALL

CHESHIRE

Soon after joining the National Trust and becoming Graham Thomas's assistant, I went with him to Little Moreton Hall. I was bowled over by the intricate asymmetry of the house on its starkly moated site. Apart from a scattering of appropriately ancient-looking fruit trees, one or two yews near the house and a plant of the locally ubiquitous *Rhododendron* 'Cunningham's White', the garden consisted of some soft-fruit bushes and a border round the house designed by Graham, 'unhistoric' but low-key and effective.

According to Christopher Wall, the Regional Historic Buildings Representative, who was very supportive, there was no record of a garden anywhere nearby contemporary with the house. However, the romantic beauty of its sixteenth-century timber-framed construction, embellished with carved gables and Elizabethan plasterwork, seemed to demand a rather more sophisticated response from the garden.

As with Moseley Old Hall before, it seemed obvious in the 1970s that a garden recreated from evidence of the style of the time was called for. Nowadays perhaps more consideration would be given to archaeology, motive and context, but I believe that our self-justification at the time still holds good. The garden adds to the enjoyment of a superb historic building by giving it a pleasurable and sympathetic setting. Provided that the Trust remains honest about its origins, the garden also functions as a means of learning for visitors, especially for the many school groups that see the place. We were anxious that it should not be too

Little Moreton Hall in the 1970s surrounded romantically by its moat enclosing an orchard and a small garden behind the house.

grand but with hindsight it may be a little over-smart; too southern and sophisticated? Rather than twenty-first-century 'interpretation', the place needs a bit of seventeenth-century mess – chickens in the orchard and ducks on the moat to eat the duckweed.

Graham suggested looking at Leonard Meager's *English Gardener* of 1688 for inspiration, especially for the knot garden proposed for the small square site behind the house. From the variety of patterns illustrated, I proposed a fairly simple quatrefoil, one that seemed to reflect the strapwork patterns of the house, bearing in mind the need for ease of upkeep (there was only a part-time gardener for the 0.4 ha (1 acre) site). This geometric design would be set out in gravel (laid on a geotextile base to obviate weeding) and edged with semi-dwarf box. The pattern of gravel was to be set in grass and the whole layout enclosed in yew hedges. To separate it from the rest of the garden, a tunnel arbour of yew

The knot garden after planting 1975 before gravelling, with box hedges and a perimeter hedge of common yew.

The knot garden circa 1986 reflecting the strap-work boarding patterns on the house.

Plan for the knot garden at Little Moreton Hall by Leonard Meager from *The English Gardener* (1688).

with 'windows' to see out would be established. Apart from a narrow border of contemporary plants on the arbour side, the only other incident would be four specimen yews to be clipped into obelisks.

Apart from some tidying-up near the house and a few new standard fruit trees of old cultivars, the orchard covering half the site was to be left unchanged so that the place would retain its acquired character. There was already a muddy perimeter path, later to be re-laid in gravel and provided with an adjacent mixed hedge in seventeenth-century style to separate it and the moat from the orchard. In one corner of the site was a steep, grassy mound which we liked to think may have been an Elizabethan mount for looking out across the flat farmland, but there is no record and it is more likely to have been a result of dredging the moat!

The cost was met largely by a grant from the Leverhulme Trust, and it was fortunate that the project coincided with the appointment of Paul Miles as Assistant Gardens Adviser soon after I succeeded Graham Thomas as (Chief) Gardens Adviser (although the latter continued as a part-time Consultant for more than a decade). Paul's experience had been with garden design and construction for Notcutts of Woodbridge, so he was the ideal person to pick up the scheme and see it through.

In retrospect I rather regret our having to remove the many gooseberry bushes, the fruit of which the Custodian's wife used to make into jam to sell to visitors – a nice, individual touch. In fact, gooseberries are traditional to the area and along the road at Rode Hall they are grown for competitive exhibition. We did include a few standard gooseberries in the formal scheme but should have found room for a proper patch.

When the National Trust accepted Ickworth back in the 1950s, it would certainly have been on account of the impressive eighteenth-century house with its huge elliptical rotunda and curved wings; also for its priceless collection of furniture, pictures and silver. That Lancelot ('Capability') Brown was involved in laying out the park in 1782 would perhaps have been a minor consideration. Certainly the formal garden which wraps around the south front would not have been valued; in those days almost anything of the nineteenth century later than Repton was deeply out of fashion and a candidate for 'simplification' (i.e. removal of anything remotely interesting as at Ickworth) or adaptation (i.e. providing the structure and framework for a new flower garden, as at Knightshayes and The Courts).

My first visit to Ickworth was a dreary affair, the only spark of colour being a mixed border north of the house designed by Graham Thomas on a generous scale but overwhelmed almost into insignificance by the faded magnificence of its surroundings. The south formal garden contained some fine trees but the surviving layout was meaningless to me, saved only by the elevated terrace walk around it that provided glorious views across Brown's park, although at that time mainly under arable cultivation. Some of the structure of hedges and all the gravel paths had survived but the place was dominated by lugubrious evergreens; dignified but dull. Furthermore, the Trust had accepted the place on condition that Lord Bristol and his successors would be granted tenancy of the east wing in perpetuity, resulting in a row of little 'no entry' signs arranged across the east lawn to ensure his privacy: nothing welcoming here!

In East Anglia the Regional Committee, headed by the Duke of Grafton, took a very hands-on approach to its responsibilities, especially in gardens, insisting on a member of the committee being present at every gardens advisory visit. The Duke would also sometimes ignore even the Regional Committee and staff as well as head office advisers. He would visit properties alone and inadvertently confuse property staff, including gardeners, by giving them direct instructions, sometimes countermanding an agreed proposal. In the 1960s, as Lord Euston, the Duke had acted in an honorary capacity as an historic buildings representative for the Trust, and seemed to have acquired this rather cavalier habit of taking decisions with a minimum of consultation, if any. At Ickworth he also persuaded the Regional Committee to move a small porticoed open temple from the north-west corner of the garden to create a focal point at the end of the long, hedged vista that cuts east–west through the formal garden. Will it ever be put back? It could be argued that this sort of thing was entirely in the tradition of the Bristols, ever since the eccentric 4th Earl, Bishop of Derry, built the house and laid out the garden! For my part I thought the result a success and a few years later we put a small rose garden in front of the little temple, more or less according to nineteenth-century precedent.

Evidence that there had been a geometric Italianate layout existed both on the ground and in the archive, such as it was then. But from the house the effect appeared almost entirely informal, the hedges mostly gone and the lawns running into the trees. In the vanguard of 1820s fashion, the garden had been one of the first in a decisive swing away from the naturalistic pleasure grounds of Brown and Repton to formal Italianate flower gardens, inspired by the rise of the Italianate villa; perhaps also by the work of James Wyatt and Richard Westmacott at Wilton in the 1820s; stimulated certainly by John Claudius Loudon's *Encyclopaedia of Gardening* of 1822. Some of the trappings of this scheme had survived with a few fastigiate Lawson's cypresses (although the original Italian cypresses, *Cupressus sempervirens*, had evidently perished in one of the many cold winters of the past hundred years). There were some large and elegant phillyrea (to resemble olives) near the house and a range of other evergreens such as laurustinus, box and holly cultivars and a number of yews and holm oaks, which had grown large although probably intended as 'bosco' (in Italy a formal arrangement of pruned trees). There was also a huge copper beech but the nineteenth-century parterre near the orangery had gone, inadequately replaced by a sad pair of oblong beds planted 'tastefully' with 'Iceberg' roses.

It would never have been possible, or even desirable, to attempt to turn the clock back completely, even if we had known exactly how the garden looked at any one time. Our agreed aim at Ickworth, in summary, was to re-establish the structure and character of the original, highly significant, layout as far as possible through a good deal of replanting of hedges and Italianate trees and plants, while also reducing and pruning the overgrown evergreens to reinstate the pattern as seen from the upper floors of the rotunda. With only three gardeners at the time for the whole of the pleasure ground and garden, flower beds would come later if possible.

Unfortunately the Duke much preferred the existing informal, overgrown and mildly 'Georgian' look, and carried his committee with him in rejecting our recommendations outright. Like many of his era he saw nothing of merit in nineteenth-century gardens, a widely held sentiment in the Trust, which accepted Ascott House near Leighton Buzzard in the 1950s, on condition that only the

Ickworth after planting the mainly conjectural Italianate scheme for the south formal garden. (1989)

The replanted Italianate scheme framing the Rotunda with clipped balls of Phillyrea and fastigiate Incense Cedars on either side. (2006)

contents were to be declared inalienable. Not a single Victorian garden was valued highly until the 1980s, Brent Elliott's *Victorian Gardens* of 1986 being the real turning point. Italianate gardens of the first half of the nineteenth century were not understood, even in gardening circles, and were firmly labelled 'bad taste' by the aesthetes. Chief of these in the National Trust was Robin Fedden, Deputy Director General and head of the Historic Buildings Department, which had an Historic Buildings Representative (now termed Curator) in each region, usually someone with a fine arts or architectural history background, to whom questions of 'taste' were invariably referred, even in gardens. Historic Buildings Representatives rarely began with any knowledge or interest in gardens and a few never acquired any! However, through necessity, most took gardens seriously and would attend many visits of Gardens Advisers, the best of them in time fulfilling a valuable role as experts on the history of the property as a whole, setting the standard against which proposals would be judged. In this way, together with the day-to-day experience of the head gardener, a constructive dialogue was created where every proposal was examined.

In contrast, in the early 1970s the Duke of Grafton (no doubt inspired by Robin Fedden) saw himself, the Trust's Historic Buildings Representatives and the Regional Committee as guardians of taste. This was an indefinable quality, acquired perhaps by going to the right school or by reading the right subject at the right university but also by having been brought up in the right house surrounded by the right objects: culture absorbed through the skin rather than acquired by diligence. As Lady Harrod of the Regional Committee once said, 'knowing the difference between what is nice and what is nasty'! This, now unfashionable, attitude led the Trust to be strongly influenced by some dilettante staff and committee members at all levels, who were not only pre-eminent in their field of expertise but also brilliantly imaginative and far-sighted. Often they were also charming and extremely entertaining. As well as envying their style, I learned a great deal from them. By definition, gardeners, including Gardens Advisers, did not have taste and were never likely to acquire it.

Gardens of the Trust are too important to be left to the whims of a single person in charge. At Ickworth the seemingly immutable attitude of the Duke and his committee could only be tempered, it seemed, by the intervention of someone whose position in the Trust was unassailable, whose knowledge and judgement were universally respected and whose charm was legendary. In every way except title, the Earl of Rosse was a match for the Duke of Grafton, and by good fortune at the time was Chairman of the powerful Properties Committee as well as the putative Gardens Panel. To my surprise at the time, Lord Rosse came away with an agreement that the conservation policy should follow precedent and that the formal scheme should be gradually restored as opportunity allowed, i.e. a general green light with cautionary overtones. As resources were very limited and visitors relatively few, there was in any case no likelihood of precipitate action.

Starting with the least controversial elements like removing the hopelessly inappropriate 'Iceberg' roses, we were after 150 years able gradually to reinstate the essence of the Earl Bishop's layout, including phased pollarding of the big yews and holm oaks and planting of hedges, once the broken drainage had been repaired. We planted many evergreens and fastigiate conifers to renew the Italianate effect, including greater diversity so that the result would be more resilient

The restored symmetry of the formal south garden leading from the Rotunda to the raised perimeter walk. (2001)

to the extreme weather in this cold part of Suffolk, as well as to pandemic diseases and pests. I chose phillyreas for the internal avenues because they were nearly always used to give the effect of olives, which could not be relied upon, even with global warming. These are now being neatly clipped against my original intention that they should be pruned to shape, similar to olives in Italy.

Flower gardening was gradually revived, but nothing approaching the kind of colourful Victorian bedding once in the former parterre on the west lawn. The head gardener in the 1980s, Jan Michalak, keenly entered into the spirit of the restoration and created small secret gardens in two of the quarters on the themes of gold and silver, with a fern-clad stumpery and a range of uncommon shrubs to contribute to the nineteenth-century effect. He also assembled a collection of box (*Buxus spp.*) which became a national collection.

There were recurrent problems throughout the 1980s arising from the erratic activities and presence of the Marquess, his unconventional friends, his big unruly dogs, his fast cars (scattering visitors!), his helicopter and his complaints; but a great deal was achieved. Thanks to the later (unforeseen and superbly designed) conversion of the granary in the west wing for visitor services, linked to the restored orangery, the garden now attracts many more visitors to enjoy the maturing garden. Furthermore, after the departure of Lord Bristol, the redevelopment of the east wing has at last freed the garden from the constraints imposed by his presence, while losing forever the thread of family influence.

The north front overlooked a large lawn and extensive pleasure grounds, well endowed with trees, including many evergreens and cedars – Atlas, deodar and Lebanon. The high water table never allowed deep rooting, and by the 1980s

Snowdrops and winter aconites in the pleasure grounds.

many of them had become unstable; then came the serious storm of 1987 that severely affected East Anglia as well as south-east England. After clearance, comprehensive replanting was necessary, and for this I suggested reviving the nineteenth-century technique of mound planting. This was widely and success-fully used in transplanting large, semi-mature trees with big root balls which were securely anchored on a shallow depression and covered with topsoil into which they would root readily, avoiding any danger of waterlogging. It also proved to be a valuable technique at Ickworth where the water table sometimes rises for weeks at a time almost to surface level. While older trees, even conifers, seem to be able to tolerate this when well established, recently transplanted trees are doomed to die. With mound planting the trees, given firm staking at first, root readily into both the mounded soil and the undisturbed topsoil below, and at Ickworth they all prospered, except where they were attacked by rabbits or deer. No special watering is needed but, as with all newly-planted trees, they should be kept scru-pulously clear of grass and weeds, which would compete directly for water.

Many of the National Trust's houses and gardens came to it with inadequate endowments, together with a lack of any obvious source of income for upkeep and repair. In 1958, when Beningbrough House, garden and park were transferred to the Trust through the National Land Fund, few people would have foreseen the explosive increase in the visiting of historic houses and gardens of the second half of the twentieth century. Wider car ownership revolutionised the ability of people to travel locally and nationally, and the National Trust, along with other owners of historic property, supplied the need for places to visit. In the 1940s and '50s, with limited demand for opening, the Trust's usual solution was to find a tenant able (especially financially) and willing to live in at least part of the house, act as custodian and open the place on a limited basis to visitors.

Finding the right tenant for any property is never a predictable exercise and for an important historic house the uncertainties are unavoidably compounded. In the 1960s Beningbrough Hall was one of the relative failures. The 1960s tenant seemed to command neither the resources nor the will to manage a house and garden on this scale and open it to visitors according to an agreed schedule. There were many problems and the garden suffered. When the tenant eventually left, it seemed highly unlikely that a place so large could ever be managed again through a tenancy agreement.

Beningbrough Hall south front with enclosed formal gardens on either side.

John Garrett became Regional Director for Yorkshire in the early 1970s and clearly decided to take this superb house and potentially glorious garden and park in hand. With great energy he took every opportunity to drive forward a major restoration of house and garden, crucially negotiating a novel and imaginative

partnership with the National Portrait Gallery for a special exhibition of portraits on permanent loan in the principal rooms. The whole property was revived and quickly became an inspiring flagship for the Trust in Yorkshire and beyond after reopening in 1977.

Although always paid by the Trust, no gardener had lasted for long under the previous regime, but determined advice from Graham Thomas in the 1960s made the best of the situation. His efforts gave rise to a characteristic mixed border between the house and the walled garden, which was later revived in his honour. Elsewhere, the garden of 2.8 ha (7 acres) was barely respectable and the 0.4 ha (1 acre) walled garden had yet to be cleared of accumulated dereliction arising from a disastrous horticultural tenancy. However, with an eye for the irreplaceable, Graham did ensure the survival of a characterful espalier walk including arches of pears, probably dating from the heyday of the walled garden under its outstanding mid-nineteenth century head gardener, Thomas Foster.

Much of the initial garden work was connected with a new car park and visitor centre, using the former coach house and derelict nursery area. The walled garden was dedicated to events and was cleared and grassed over, only later to be revived for gardening.

At this time in the early 1970s Paul Miles was appointed Assistant Gardens Adviser and Beningbrough was one of the gardens I assigned to him, along with others in Yorkshire, East Anglia, Devon, Wessex and Northern Ireland. Beningbrough was an exciting restoration, urgently needing more colour and interest, especially near the house. As well as replanning the double borders west of the kitchen garden, he realised a scheme for a pair of formal gardens flanking the south front of the house. The west garden was laid out with a pattern of box hedges and low plants in strong colours, and the east garden in contrast was given a cool scheme with lavenders around a formal fountain pool. Hedged off from the main lawn, which stretches away into the park, these two little gardens provide sheltered sitting space and small-scale borders for enjoying a wide range of plants and flowers.

The redesigned west formal garden. (1988)

The head gardener in the 1970s was David Masters, who was recruited after training at Sheffield Park, but had little experience. Quick to learn and immensely keen, he was a great success as he guided the garden's rapid transition from horticultural backwater to regional flagship with skill and dedication, moving on in the 1980s to an even more important role at Nymans, the famous garden in Sussex. He led a small team with energy and intelligence, always planning ahead and foreseeing the many challenges that inevitably occur in a comprehensive scheme of this kind. Under David's charge the whole garden was renovated, including the formal north front, the little wilderness walk and the 'American garden', an early nineteenth-century feature that occurs in many country house gardens and is often misunderstood. The term arose from the many North American trees and plants being introduced, most of which thrive only in lime-free soil, including some rhododendrons and azaleas. As plant hunting and introduction spread in the nineteenth century to China and the Himalaya, these also mostly lime-hating plants were added to 'American gardens', the term coming to be understood as an informal arrangement of trees, shrubs, herbaceous plants and bulbs requiring acid soil. Many of them were further developed late in the century as 'wild gardens' in the William Robinson sense, using a wide range of exotic plants among the American trees already established. With such a potentially wide range of plants to choose from for the American garden, the aim at a property like Beningbrough should be to investigate clues as to who inspired the original planting and the sources of the plants, so as to define the present and future character of the collection. Simply replanting with a whimsical selection of what is easily available will not do.

The redesigned east formal garden. (1988)

John Garrett had always resisted our recommendations for any planting in the walled garden, despite its prominent position in the middle of the property, the first feature seen on entry. Aware of the need to avoid creating extra work, we

ABOVE The pear arches and cordons are the only surviving feature from the old Kitchen Garden, now underplanted with borders including catmint and campanulas.

LEFT The walled Kitchen Garden replanted with box hedging, pyramid fruit trees and with cut flowers and vegetables in the borders. Upkeep relies largely on volunteers.

confined our suggestions to a modest restoration of the path system and a pattern of fruit trees to furnish the structure. All sorts of ideas, including pick-your-own lavender, fell upon deaf ears in favour of retaining the space for unspecified events and 'kick-around' games for visiting families. However, in the mid-1980s a surprise legacy specifically for the garden provided an opportunity. Rather than spending it on capital projects, the Region agreed after much discussion to use the money to endow, at least in part, an additional gardener dedicated to the walled garden. My calculation was that, once started, it would be perfectly possible to raise capital sums for separate restoration projects within the walled garden. Dedicated skilled labour was the limiting factor and the key both to getting the project started and to attracting volunteers for its development and upkeep. We soon learned how much could be achieved with one professional gardener providing effective leadership and training to a group of increasingly dedicated volunteers. The restoration went from strength to strength in adding a different dimension of ever-changing interest and development to the garden, and in providing a model for the Trust's many kitchen garden restorations of the twenty-first century.

With the substantial red sandstone house leased to Sue Ryder Homes, only the garden was open to visitors, along with walks along Crowdundle Beck, when I first went to Acorn Bank in 1971. The nursing home never having been able to provide for the garden, Graham Thomas had, two years earlier, cooked up a scheme with the then Regional Director, his great friend Cuthbert (Cubby) Acland, for the Trust to take the garden in hand and restore it for opening. All the better valued for being in an area of widely-scattered gardens, the garden and grounds were much enjoyed from early days by visitors and residents alike, despite being quite tiny by National Trust standards.

There was one gardener to cope alone with the opening, the gardening and the upkeep of the woodland walks, including the watermill. Of little more than 0.4 ha (an acre or so) in extent, the garden consists of a small formal piece with a pond near the house, linked to an old walled orchard. Alongside is an oblong cultivated enclosure facing south, with a then ramshackle lean-to greenhouse. In full sun and probably intended for vegetables, it was already sheltered from the park by damsons which do well locally. To give the place more interest and some individuality, Graham had set out a plan for rows of medicinal herbs to be grown in continuous borders, each labelled with its botanical and common name.

Chris Braithwaite was the gardener, a cheerful and willing young man in need of guidance, especially with the care and cultivation of unusual plants. Malcolm Hutcheson used to drive over from Sizergh regularly to lend his horticultural expertise and plantsmanship. The place was never going to be perfect, nor was it appropriate to aim for over-smart or horticulturally sophisticated gardening

Acorn Bank house from the wildflower meadow and orchard.

in such an isolated and countrified spot. Nevertheless, it needed to appear cared for and loved. The arrangement worked well enough, and through Malcolm we gradually acquired a fascinating assembly of over 180 herbs and medicinal plants, capable, according to the literature, of curing everything from dyspepsia and dropsy to 'The King's Evil' and all those unmentionable 'female complaints'. There were purgatives, aphrodisiacs, narcotics and enough poisons to wipe out the whole population of Temple Sowerby. No locked gates, fences or prominent signs were there to dissuade people foolish enough to try eating something clearly labelled POISON. To my knowledge there has never been a fatality or even a serious disorder attributable to any garden plant owned by the National Trust, despite millions of visitors over many years. The use of herbs and medicinal plants has a long history and their use in the kitchen and the pharmacy is now as widespread as ever. Homeopathy has gathered many devotees. Curiously, for many people there is something less threatening about poisons, however virulent, derived from plants (i.e. 'organic') than those developed synthetically (i.e. 'chemical'). I enjoyed part of a winter in the early 1970s writing a short guide to herbs and medicinal plants in the Trust covering principally Acorn Bank, but also Hardwick Hall, Sissinghurst, Scotney Castle, Batemans and other smaller collections.

The decrepit little lean-to greenhouse was used to house a complementary range of aromatic plants, which were much more successfully overwintered when eventually it was rebuilt. In this wet and windswept climate shelter is often needed and always welcome for plants and people.

Acorn Bank's former owners were famously keen on wildlife as well as gardening, and their legacy to the Trust included a garden well stocked with wild and naturalised plants, as well as along the steep banks of Crowdundle Beck. In the old walled orchard the grass is richly populated with all sorts of plants and bulbs,

Part of the herb garden facing south.

including wild tulip, Lent lily and the late-flowering pheasant eye daffodil, all left to be cut in early autumn to encourage diversity. Only the paths are regularly cut to separate the orchard meadow from the wall borders, in which thrive a surprisingly wide range of herbaceous plants and shrubs which enjoy the cool climate and high rainfall. A hedged axial path through the orchard of old northern apples runs to the garden gate. In an effort to give the garden a firmer structure, I suggested the avenue of the double form of the sour cherry *Prunus cerasus* 'Rhexii', a highly floriferous tree of ancient origin with white flowers. Flowering in May, it follows the apple blossom. Old orchards are invariably homes to honey fungus, a soil-borne disease that spreads by 'bootlaces' through the ground from infected stumps left behind by careless gardeners. Gappy orchards are picturesque, but apples rarely last more than three quarters of a century and need to be replenished by planting 20 per cent within each decade to ensure continuity, even though some may need to be removed before they mature.

Every so often the National Trust, in common perhaps with other organisations, either becomes anxious about its future finances or decides to spend a significant part of its income on some sort of project or campaign. In the Trust this precipitated a period of hair-shirt austerity imposed from the top. During the 1980s Acorn Bank was caught up in one of these economy programmes. The Trust was determined on some blood-letting, and gardens were thought to be expensive luxuries unless deemed nationally important. In spite of its relatively modest cost to the region (minute by any national standard), Acorn Bank was picked on as the sacrificial lamb, and I remember the then Chairman of the National Trust Lord Gibson's incredulity that anyone should defend its status as a garden and grounds open independently of the house. The only too-logical plan was to cease direct management and include the garden in the lease of the house. That this would have marked the end of the garden as we knew it was neither understood nor of any concern. While the staff and residents of the nursing home and their visitors clearly enjoyed seeing the garden and the Trust's visitors, their natural concern was with the care of the patients. The garden would have been well down the list of priorities.

All seemed lost until the very strong local membership heard of the Trust's plans. There was a spontaneous and horrified reaction which quickly revealed how much locals had come to love the little garden and its countrified charm, combining simplicity and interest, historic continuity and artless plantsmanship. (I promise that neither the regional staff nor the advisers had any part in this!) The Trust was no match for the formidable Cumbrian membership who knew what they wanted. After a comparatively short skirmish the hawks in the Trust backed off, convinced that the supposed saving would not be worth the likely damage. How many legacies would have been lost?

One of the lessons I learned from this disquieting episode was that, for gardens at any rate, values are comparative not absolute, and that the significance of a place can transcend the accepted considerations of, for example, history, design, contents and associations. Less tangible and more spiritual qualities of character, ethos and meaning can be equally important. Gardens are loved.

Chapter 2

CONSERVATION PLANNING

The Pantheon at Stourhead seen across the lake from The Shades 'look down at water and up to woods'.

STOURHEAD
WILTSHIRE

I had never been to Stourhead before joining the National Trust, a serious gap in my education. After hundreds of visits in all weathers and seasons since then, I can never recall a time when the experience has not raised my spirits; my definition of a great work of art. Change – deliberate and accidental – and maturity have served to enrich Henry Hoare II's eighteenth-century concept, as realised in his lifetime. It takes a masterpiece of supreme strength and resilience to absorb two and a half centuries of development and go on to give ever more pleasure and spiritual refreshment to so many.

This incomparable work of art has accumulated many qualities and characteristics, ever widening its appeal so that hardly anyone can visit without being engaged in some way, eventually to be captivated by the magic of the place. There are great eighteenth-century buildings, an important arboretum, a rich diversity of wildlife, colour from bulbs and shrubs, poetry and mythology; above all there is visible evidence of the history of the place and the tastes of those who have contributed. Being able to 'read' a landscape in this way is one of the acquired pleasures of garden visiting.

My first few visits to Stourhead were with Graham Thomas, who had been advising there for about fifteen years. Without the benefit of any sort of fundamental policy appraisal, his had been a sensibly conservative approach, aimed at raising standards generally, looking forward pragmatically, improving neglected areas and reopening views to enrich visitors' experience. Advisory visits consisted of a walk round the lake from the village entrance (the traditional way for ordinary visitors; only the family and their guests enjoying the full experience from the house). Attention was concentrated on what could be seen from the path. Much

View from the village entrance and the stone bridge to the Pantheon; Watch Cottage can be only glimpsed among the trees on the right.

was done to renovate silted ponds and overgrown rhododendrons, replant wood-lands and plant more specimen trees and flowering shrubs, while steadily remov-ing some of the nineteenth-century conifers that had by then survived beyond their most attractive phase of life. Not much clearance and planting had been done up to the mid-1950s and there was a backlog.

The head gardener at that time was Albert Marshall, a real countryman and loyal servant of the National Trust. He irritated Graham (it was easy to do!) by always having to stand still, legs apart, ponderously to proclaim the rejoinder to any suggestion or query. However, he got things done with the support of his eventual successor Fred Hunt, who took everything in his stride and gleaned the names of every one of the extensive and important collection of mostly nineteenth-century rhododendron cultivars. Albert was most famous for his, now unthinkable, secret method of controlling moles. He used to carry a loaded shotgun on his wheel-barrow, ready to blast any molehill in which his eagle eye could detect the slight-est movement. Effective maybe, but not the sort of thing that Health and Safety would approve, and eventually the inevitable accident (relatively minor) exposed Albert's transgressions.

The garden's popularity had never waned and visitor numbers increased rapidly to around 100,000 in the 1960s, almost two-thirds of them coming in a six-week period for the rhododendrons, a spectacular annual display created mainly by the late Sir Henry Hoare, by reputation a wonderfully Edwardian character, during the first half of the twentieth century. With only a tiny car park at the Spread Eagle pub, visitors' cars were ranked densely across the park in front of the house, hideous at best and a quagmire in a wet year. Totally at odds with historic prece-dent, a now forgotten 'cattle rush' path had been made directly down the east bank to the lake, ignoring Henry Hoare's zig-zag route which gives successive glimpses of the principal buildings and contrived views across the lake, always obeying the eighteenth-century precept of walking indirectly to the object in view.

That Stourhead absorbs nearly three times as many people, now spread through-out the year, is not only proof of effective management aimed at minimalising the visual impact of visitors, but also of their progressively wider and deeper enjoyment of the special qualities of this icon of eighteenth-century gardening and culture.

The late Sir Henry's mountains of hardy hybrid rhododendrons certainly had impact, especially in late May with huge bushes of 'Cynthia' next to the Pantheon, bringing to mind a well-endowed barmaid leaning across a grand hotel bar at a rugby club booze up! Elsewhere 'Britannia' gorgeously disrupted every subtle eighteenth-century vista; the rhododendrons were relentless. *Rh. ponticum*, an eighteenth-century introduction, had seeded everywhere, infuriating the aes-thetes who should never have gone near the place in May.

Stourhead consistently created controversy, especially among historians of eighteenth-century culture and aesthetes taking an increasing interest in historic gardens around the time of the formation of the Garden History Society in 1965. Chief among these critics was Kenneth Woodbridge, an ex-teacher and fine arts author who made a special study of the history of the Stourhead landscape. He wrote a series of learned publications from 1965, including *Landscape and Antiquity: Aspects of English Culture at Stourhead 1718–1838*, the definitive history, and *The Stourhead Landscape* (1982), a more accessible, illustrated account.

Woodbridge was highly critical of the Trust's management and gave the Regional Committee and the Regional Agent, John Cripwell (one of the most polite people I have ever met), a difficult time. Lord Head (Anthony Head, formerly a Minister in the Macmillan government), Chairman of the Regional Committee in the mid-1970s, became tired of the constant wrangling, including sniping from the media. In 1973 he declared the need for a 'hundred-year plan' for *The Conservation of the Garden at Stourhead*, a long-term policy based on the historical background, for the preservation of the original conception and design of the gardens, taking into account subsequent developments. (The last phrase was my humble, but crucial, contribution!) This was to be guided by a committee of six, chaired by Lord Head, including Robin Fedden (Deputy Director General), Kenneth Woodbridge, John Workman (Forestry Adviser), John Cripwell (Regional Agent), and myself (recently appointed Gardens Adviser).

In the event it fell to Kenneth Woodbridge and me alone to produce the report, with John Cripwell acting as the patient referee. Stourhead became a fascinating obsession and we agreed a series of meetings at the garden between which we would each do our homework, Kenneth to prepare the historical precedent and me to suggest long-term proposals for the place as a whole and for each part of it, having first divided it into management areas.

Woodbridge was a prickly little man with a formidable intellect for whom only the most rigorous analysis and precise language would do. He invariably arrived in the morning with a series of aggressive complaints about the Trust, but I soon learned that after half an hour's patient listening and a cup of coffee he would calm down and we could get on to examine our brief objectively. Received wisdom among historians, initially including Woodbridge, was that the 'recent' additions, especially the rhododendrons, should be removed. We began by looking at the implications of this kind of approach, i.e. attempting to return the landscape to its eighteenth-century appearance. But it quickly became clear that there is more to historic garden conservation than destroying accumulated evidence of the past in favour of a supposed version of the original.

Woodbridge was expert at writing precise descriptions of the known precedents for each area and the relationships of one area to another and the place as a whole, a challenging example for me. My approach was to explore which, if any, of a series of precedents should be followed, and why; while also attempting to relate the proposals to visitor circulation, management imperatives, likely visual impact and other practical considerations. Before long it became clear that a policy of 'peeling back' the layers of history would be indefensible. Where does one stop, and why? Are not the nineteenth and twentieth centuries integral to the history of the place? What are we to take out first? What would we be left with?

Examining an outstandingly important landscape based precisely on its known history and present value was a steep learning curve for me, and I believe also for Woodbridge. We soon began to formulate a series of principles, accepting that Stourhead does not represent a purely eighteenth-century concept and that the aim should be to reconcile the successive changes in a way that reveals and emphasises the original intention, while retaining and gradually adjusting many of the subsequent developments. Hence the offending rhododendron collection, much admired by some, would be preserved but gradually redeployed in a way that does not detract from Henry Hoare's ideas and historic views. Like the conifers and other nineteenth-century trees, they would be used to enrich the sequence of contrasting experiences, which had been a fundamental element of the place.

After three years of erratic progress, the report was completed to the exacting standards of Woodbridge and published in 1978, by far the earliest, well-researched conservation plan for any significant historic garden approaching the complexity of Stourhead. It was an important landmark for the National Trust, followed by Osterley Park and then John Phibbs's first efforts at Wimpole in the late 1970s, both important steps towards the conservation/management plans of today. After more than thirty years it is still in use, with modifications.

Some revolutionary and far-reaching general proposals arose out of considering the landscape as a whole in relation to its history and ever-increasing mass visitation. These included creating a new car park and visitor centre well away from the historic landscape, and re-opening a route from the house so that discerning visitors can now see the landscape in its proper sequence. Most controversial and potentially difficult was Woodbridge's entirely logical idea for re-routing much of the main circuit path below the east bank and on the west bank leading to the grotto. Although at first mostly resisted by habitual local walkers, the new paths improved the visitor experience by moving back the inevitable line of people along the hard path into the shade and concealment of trees and shrubs, while still allowing access across the grass.

Another important principle was in reaction to evidence that in several places the canopy of trees near the lake had moved back as trees had died and were not

Autumn view from the dam with Diana's Temple now properly framed by trees and shrubs which also screen the path (and visitors on the path) from the village entrance. But 19th-century conifers still interrupt the skyllne. (2003)

19th- and 20th-century flowering shrubs are now mainly situated out of the principal historic views across the lake.

replaced. This had the effect of making visitors more prominent in the views and revealing the rhododendrons, easily if slowly corrected by replanting trees near the lake. By coincidence, within a couple of years of the report's completion, a freak snowstorm of heavy wet snow caused the tall rhododendrons alongside the Pantheon to collapse forwards, the answer to our prayers, so that we were able to blame a different authority for the demise of big 'Cynthia'!

Perhaps the most exciting revelation was the rediscovery of the 'fir walk', a straight ride between house and garden leading to the obelisk, which before the trees grew up gave glimpses across the lakes and the landscape beyond. It had been in existence since 1734, before the garden. Carefully described by Sweden's most important eighteenth-century landscaper, Frederick Magnus Piper, after a visit in 1779, it consisted of a level terrace bordered by 'Scotch fir' trees, later removed by Richard Colt Hoare. The late Sir Henry Hoare had presumably let it grow over after the turn of the twentieth century. Through the undergrowth we measured the width of 9.75 m (32 ft) as described, once 'clad in the finest turf'. Removing the mass of self-sown trees, 12–18 m (40–60 ft) high, was a thrilling act of faith, entirely justified by the grandeur of the result. We were mightily relieved when the obelisk materialised centrally at the end of the vista, as Piper predicted!

Does being almost on the end of Heathrow's runway make Osterley, in a way, the nearest English country house and park to the rest of the world? More to the point, by a miracle it is the only nearly-intact country estate to have survived a century of being engulfed by London's sprawl. Even now, apart from the noise of roads, rail and aircraft, there is a real sense of escape from the stresses of town life when entering the gates. All things are relative, but the comparative calm of the park is much valued and enjoyed locally.

Given to the Trust by the 9th Earl of Jersey with an arbitrary 57.5 ha (142 acres) of grounds after the war, the house is a pre-eminent eighteenth-century remodelling by Robert Adam of its Elizabethan predecessor. Adam seems also to have been responsible for laying out the park in the English landscape style, together with the pleasure ground and a larger walled garden. The latter was sadly sold off separately in the 1940s. In Brownian style Adam created a string of lakes, planted woodland belts and clumps and made an informal pleasure ground called the American garden. (The term, as explained above in the section on Beningbrough, refers to the many new plants being introduced from North America, most notably rhododendrons, azaleas, and the like, which were mostly lime-haters and needed an area of special growing conditions.) He also set out a linear pleasure ground walk around a grazed inner paddock west of the house.

An idealised view of Osterley Park by Anthony Devis (displayed in the house) after Robert Adam's alterations and landscaping in the 'natural' English landscape style.

Thanks to Lord Jersey's gift and our much-maligned planning legislation, a huge area of green space has survived, albeit partly as playing fields and golf course,

spoilt only by the M4 motorway which was brutally driven through to cut off the northern part of Adam's park, including one of the lakes, his exquisite bridge and the Menagerie, now a private house. The odd-shaped parcel given to the Trust is merely the central core of Adam's park.

Although undoubtedly valuable as urban green space for recreation, as an historic park Osterley had become seriously degraded by the 1970s. The National Trust had accepted the house and park without endowment but with an agreement from the Victoria and Albert Museum to manage and maintain the great house and the lovely Elizabethan stable block; the park and grounds were to be separately managed and funded by the Royal Parks authority. The Trust's role as owner was in practice entirely advisory, and it showed.

My visits in the 1970s were deeply frustrating, despite everyone I met from Royal Parks being pleasant and cooperative. There was no funding for change and the place was managed at a basic level as though it had no significance other than its assumed role as a public park for dog walking, children's play and feeding the ducks. Recent planting was confined to a couple of lorry loads of miscellaneous ornamental trees – rowans, crab apples, cherries, etc. – deliberately scattered throughout the grounds. The grass was gang-mown at the same level throughout and the place was kept more or less tidy, with black tarmac paths and drives, urban street lights and car parking on the old tennis courts, only thinly screened from the house across the upper lake. Tree work was confined to health and safety measures and there had been no positive woodland management since acquisition. The second lake was invisible from the house because of a dense line of self-sown alders and it was impossible to discern anything of Robert Adam's intentions.

At the time none of the Royal Parks were managed according to any sort of long-term plan aimed at conserving its significant qualities, including historic value, in a sustainable way. Safe public access, control of vandalism, dog management, grass mowing and floral display were the main considerations but there was also a quite high-powered quango, the 'Committee for Trees in Royal Parks', which had to be obeyed.

Encouraged by my work at Stourhead with Kenneth Woodbridge, which had resulted in the first long-term conservation plan for an important historic landscape, I was anxious at least to begin the daunting task of doing the same for every major National Trust property. Until then the Trust had relied entirely on archive sources for its historic research, and always this was carried out piecemeal when time and opportunity was available. The approach was all very gentlemanly and dilettante, although far from ineffective. It is axiomatic that documentary evidence, especially historic plans, needs to be carefully evaluated to assess its accuracy. In many cases plans record intention rather than outcome, and the same applies to written accounts, drawings and paintings, which often (very usefully) indicate aspirations rather than reality. In order to produce a valid historic account it seemed obvious that a field survey was needed alongside archival research to reveal the full historical development of the place – intentional, accidental, social, biological and environmental. A measured survey of the whole site, including levels, fixed objects and their remnants, trees and shrubs, roads and paths, was the obvious first step.

There was no money for this potentially expensive exercise and the Trust's central priorities emphatically did not stretch to its unparalleled collection of historic parks and gardens. Apart from special cases like Hidcote and Sissinghurst, gardens and parks were invariably thought subsidiary to the great houses and useful mainly for attracting and absorbing visitors. Subsequently nature conservation came to the fore, and now the pendulum has swung further towards 'engaging' and entertaining visitors and volunteers. Even now gardens and parks continue to be thought of by the highest levels of the Trust more for their peripheral qualities – recreation, wildlife, events, etc. – than for their core values.

As Gardens Advisers, our role was to reveal all the many qualities and values inherent in each of the Trust's gardens and parks. However, perhaps for personal and organisational reasons, the blatant anomaly was that historic parks traditionally came under the wing of the Forestry Adviser for advice, along with woodlands and forestry production. John Workman had been the Forestry Adviser since the mid-1950s, and by the 1970s was approaching the apex of his considerable influence in the Trust. He was a remarkably far-sighted person with great charm and presence. He had a good eye for landscape and his experience was unmatched; but he was primarily a forester. Even he would have admitted that his historical research, although practical and sound, was rudimentary, relying mostly on consulting first edition OS maps, which are indeed the single best source of what was actually done and planted in most eighteenth-century and nineteenth-century parks. Unfortunately he and Graham Thomas, my predecessor, could never see eye-to-eye and tacitly agreed to differ, each having his own sphere of influence. As a new boy on the block, I was in no position to challenge John Workman's supremacy on any matter. The best tactic seemed to be to demonstrate the necessity for properly integrated, in-depth survey and research. Osterley was the opportunity and Jim Marshall, who had recently succeeded Paul Miles as Assistant Gardens Adviser, was the means.

In response to rising unemployment the government had introduced a nationwide unemployment relief scheme called TOPS (Training Opportunities Scheme), which was useful to the Trust at all levels and did indeed introduce many young people to the workplace. Winkled out by Jim Marshall, part of this scheme allowed suitable employers to put together teams of graduates for a two-year period, at government expense, to undertake approved projects requiring expertise that unemployed graduates could offer. We agreed a brief (based on the Stourhead plan) with the regional staff and Royal Parks, and Jim Marshall patiently waded through the bureaucracy towards eventual approval, plus the interviews and practical arrangements. Thanks to his careful supervision and the key appointment of an enterprising and capable leader, the scheme exceeded all our expectations.

The Osterley historic survey and plan, while not perfect, was an important step towards a more professional approach to park and garden conservation. Osterley also set the ball rolling for historic survey and research in the Royal Parks and the creation of a new profession, soon taken up and perfected by Land Use Consultants and others. All this was of course before the creation of English Heritage in 1983.

We were particularly anxious to obtain a full survey and catalogue of the trees, their accurate locations, identification, condition and ages. The surveyors adopted a system of dating by stem girth according to species, and comparing this with any records. In this way we could trace any original trees and track the increase in tree numbers and diversity of species over 200 years; this was especially revealing when expressed by giving each age band a different colour on the plan. It became clear, for example, that tree planting usually coincided with the advent of a new generation in charge.

Particularly useful at Osterley was the extraordinary wealth and diversity of aerial photographs from the 1920s onwards, which graphically illustrated the site's increasing complication and muddled development. An extensive and obviously labour-intensive formal layout on the east front had survived in outline until after the war and had never been conclusively dismantled. This was particularly damaging to Adam's concept. Equally damaging were the dense ranks of alders screening the middle lake, cutting off the principal vista from the house. Aerial photographs showed how this arose: until the war the park had been grazed and when the cattle were removed the alders were allowed to develop unchecked.

View from the west front before restoration of the park rail fencing which separated the pleasure ground walk from the grazed paddock

The fencing restored to define the pleasure ground

The Regency flower garden, a recent conjectural scheme appropriately incorporated in front of Adam's garden house.

From this research we were able to formulate a restoration and long-term conservation plan. This aimed at a sustainable layout based primarily on Robert Adam's intentions because his work was most significant, especially in relation to the house. But there was no intention of extinguishing the more recent past where this could be successfully integrated. This was particularly important for the range of exceptionally fine specimen trees planted over the past century. Although largely pragmatic, this deliberately value-based approach was novel at the time.

One lesson that was emphatically learned at Osterley was the cumulative impact that management style and upkeep have both on day-to-day appearance and on long-term development. One of our seemingly unachievable objectives was to reinstate the fenced area and reintroduce cattle grazing. This was eventually achieved west of the house, and had a profound effect in transforming the scene from urban park to private estate. Another lesson learned was always to state the ideal, however remote its realisation may seem to be at the time. At Osterley the Trust owned only a fragment of the whole and we resolved to include in the conservation plan a clear ambition for the Trust to acquire the whole of the historic parkland south of the M4, though we never expected to see it happen. We should have had more faith; miraculously the historic landscape is now united under the ownership of the National Trust. It now has a precious opportunity to acknowledge its full historic significance in restoring and sustaining its unique qualities while adapting it for everyone's use and enjoyment.

WIMPOLE HALL

CAMBRIDGESHIRE

It must have been in spring 1976 that I received a telephone call from my friend Peter Thoday, who was a student at Cambridge Botanic Garden at the time I was at Kew. He was at the time running a highly-regarded 'sandwich' degree course in horticulture at the new University of Bath. It catered mostly for the normal run of school-leavers but occasionally attracted older people looking for a second degree. Straight to the point, he said a very gifted Oxford graduate on the course, who did not quite fit the mould, was interested in historic gardens and needed a live project on which to base his thesis. I immediately invited them both to Cirencester and was impressed not only by John Phibbs's intellect but also by his commitment and single-minded drive.

Luckily the Trust was in the process of acquiring Wimpole Hall and park, left to it in the will of Mrs. Elsie Bambridge, the daughter of Rudyard Kipling. My first visit had been in January or February 1976 with the Regional Director, Nicolas de Bazille Corbin, a brusque and business-like land agent of the old school, whose energy and discipline were legendary. We approached the house through the rather rundown park from the gates on the A10, much the best way but unfortunately never safe for mass visiting. My first impression of the great house was how isolated, bleak and unloved it seemed, and my first concern was for its security, made more acute when I was told that only three, less than robust, people were living there at the time.

We were met at the front door by Mrs. Bambridge's companion, a charming but frail old lady, who was bravely holding the fort during this vulnerable interregnum. I was given a cup of coffee and asked to wait in the entrance hall while Nicolas attended to important matters not affecting the garden. To keep me occupied while waiting, I was invited to look through the garden scrapbook (album), which lay casually on the hall table. As I turned the pages I was more and more astonished by its contents – letters and drawings from the likes of Lancelot (Capability) Brown, Humphry Repton, Robert Greening, Sanderson Miller and William Emes, all of whom had a hand in the development of the park in the eighteenth century in succession to a seventeenth-century formal layout by London and Wise, and a grand formal scheme by Charles Bridgeman of the 1720s. If I did nothing else that day, I resolved immediately that this priceless archive must be locked up securely in a safe before one of the many succeeding visitors, official or unofficial, walked off with it!

Without needing to know any more about the history and content of the park and garden (who did at the time?), I was already convinced of the need for an in-depth research and field survey to establish its full significance. The garden had been progressively simplified under Mrs Bambridge to the point where it was almost totally devoid of horticultural interest – bland, windswept and 'maintained' at a basic level. On the other hand, the place contained many fine mature trees despite Charles Bridgeman's great double avenue of elms having recently succumbed to Dutch elm disease, which had swept westwards from Essex. As well as oaks, beeches, walnuts (black and common) and ash in the park and Indian bean, manna ash, and copper beech in the pleasure ground, most impressive were the limes of various kinds, both in quality and abundance. These later turned out to be mainly clones of the hybrid, so-called common lime, *Tilia × europaea*, from which we were able to choose one of suitable form to propagate as replacements for the elms.

It was Professor Donald Pigott of the University of Lancaster and the University of Cambridge who untangled so much of the mystery of the many historic clones of lime that exist in parks and gardens throughout Britain. From the seventeenth century the Netherlands was the principal source of lime trees (and other species) for English parks and gardens, each nursery apparently propagating its own clone of common lime (*Tilia × europaea*), a hybrid between the small-leafed lime (*T. cordata*) and the broad-leafed lime (*T. platyphyllos*), both natives of England. Common lime grows vigorously upright, ideal for avenues and tall enough to rival the English elm (*Ulmus minor* var. *vulgaris*), now sadly lost to its native landscape. Only in maturity is it possible to distinguish between the 'worst' lime clones, which tend to produce a mass of adventitious growth on the main stem, and the best like 'Hatfield Tall' which are tall and elegant. Between these extremes there are several distinct forms, often characteristic to a place, thereby contributing greatly to its individuality. Choosing a suitable clone, even if unnamed, from the park at Wimpole seemed an obvious way of ensuring the integrity of the great avenue when it came to replanting, rather than bringing in a readily available clone like 'Pallida'. From this initiative, the Trust began to collect characteristic clones of common lime and we later established a nursery at Dunham Massey to provide stock for propagation (since transferred to Knightshayes).

Having seen Wimpole and its potential, I needed to persuade the regional staff to include a significant sum of money in their budget for a measured survey. The young Historic Buildings Representative, Julian Gibbs, who soon became an enthusiastic garden historian, was sympathetic but funding was tight. I suppose £3,000 seemed reasonable to them at the time, but there needed to be ten times

The principal south front overlooking the park. (1980)

that to employ anyone (who?) to do the job adequately. Julian wanted to engage a landscape architect, until I pointed out that at their rates of remuneration none of them would be able to scratch the surface. Very reluctantly he agreed to see John Phibbs from Bath University, and was immediately converted to the unlikely proposal that John would survey and research the park on an expenses-only basis (with a little bit of help from his friends) as his degree thesis. This marked the birth of a new profession of which John Phibbs was the first full-time practitioner; he later became a partner in the Debois Landscape Survey Group, having since then been responsible for surveying and researching an enviable number and variety of historic landscapes throughout Britain.

It was not long before we were receiving interim reports of tantalising quality and diversity, and I was receiving telephone calls from Julian Gibbs, who guided the whole process, beginning 'do you know what John Phibbs has found out?'! I never enquired too deeply about their living arrangements or means of support (for fear of it all being illegal) but I know that he soon persuaded some of his friends to join him in this huge enterprise and that they camped out through the summer months. The resulting tome, once it eventually arrived, was fascinatingly dense and rivetingly interesting but impenetrable to most laymen and unusable to anyone attempting to manage the place. John had an entirely correct but time-consuming tendency, like any good academic, of following every lead on every subject to its ultimate conclusion. So we had, for example, a long essay referring to the many walnuts in the park, linking them to the possibility that they were planted and grown for the manufacture of rifle butts. As a result of this we eventually established the national collection of *Juglans* (walnuts) at Wimpole.

In due course this ground-breaking survey report was re-drafted and revised to make it more readily usable for decision-making. We began to learn the basic requirements of garden/park survey and research reports. Essentially they need to be easy for managers to refer to and to provide the basic data for the production

A view from the north front of Wimpole Hall showing the formal flower garden during restoration. (1994)

Aerial photograph with low light indicating, amongst other things, the 19th-century formal layout in the garden north of the house. University of Cambridge copyright.

of long-term conservation plans, e.g. all historic plans converted to the same scale and orientation; a clear and concise chronology of major changes; illustrations well keyed to the text.

As John was further employed by the Trust at Ickworth, Felbrigg, Blickling, etc., his always excellent reports became more professional but they never lost that spark of originality in reaction to the character of the place. Now that English

A recent view of the mature parterre with box hedging.

Heritage calls the tune, both surveys and management plans are required to fit into a bureaucratic mould which seems to ignore the size, scope and character of the place in an effort never to leave any stone unturned.

By 1980 the Trust had begun to restore some of the garden's horticultural interest to match the renaissance of the house, but gardens are about upkeep and strictly limited staffing meant that new features had to be relatively easy to sustain. Jim Marshall was the Adviser and he guided much replanting in the pleasure ground walk to the walled garden; also formal flower gardens near the house.

One aerial photograph, which emerged as part of John Phibbs's research, was remarkable in having been taken following a light fall of blown snow across the big lawn north of the house. This showed the unmistakeable impression of a huge nineteenth century parterre, forming a Union-Jack-like pattern which turned out to be traceable on the ground. The energetic and charismatic head gardener, Philip Whaites, had already begun to recruit and deploy volunteers in the walled garden, and believed he could do more. Between them, with Jim Marshall's guidance and support, they drew up a scheme for reinstating the whole parterre, a case of 'all or nothing', modified only to incorporate showy permanent plants in part to reduce the number of annual bedding plants. The result was a triumph and put Wimpole back on the horticultural map, reinforced by an equally ambitious walled garden restoration, all on a shoestring and thanks to the initiative and endeavour of a capable head gardener and his loyal band of volunteers; a sign of things to come.

Every garden is strongly influenced by its site but some, like Prior Park, are determined by it. Looking across a little coombe to an incomparable view of the Georgian city of Bath, the position Ralph Allen chose for his impressive mansion could hardly have been bettered. This single vista has become a defining image of the eighteenth-century English landscape style, almost overused in literature and publicity. Like Stourhead, it is in danger of being diminished by its chocolate-box associations. In a way, however, this is apt because the house was first intended as an advertisement – for the usefulness of Bath stone that Ralph Allen was quarrying beyond the house. This principal view with its cunningly sited Palladian bridge and contrived water is deceptively simple but, like much great art, the landscape has many less obvious qualities that only become apparent on closer inspection. There is more to it than seems likely at first sight and even this commanding panorama develops as one crosses on the National Trust's valley-head path.

Gardens are not simply objects to be admired passively from a series of viewpoints – windows, gateways, gazebos or even television sets. They are there to be experienced by all the senses on moving through them: a succession of incidents, contrasts of light and dark, contact with plants, glimpses of wildlife, different scents and smells, the feel of wind and rain. This is particularly the case

The iconic view from Prior Park across Brown's landscape and the city of Bath autumn. (1993)

with informal pleasure-ground landscapes like Prior Park, which manages a huge variety of experience in 11.5 ha (28 acres) of pasture, lake and woodland. Such landscapes tend to be judged by pundits from an occasional visit, together with a few well-worn images. Places are understood differently, and much better, by owners, gardeners and regular visitors who develop a continuing relationship with the garden, day-to-day and season-to-season. Prior Park's historic interest underlies its purely sensual pleasure for those willing to enquire. However, neither are gardens simply academic exercises in preserving historic significance; they should speak for themselves as satisfying experiences, even works of art. Primarily they are there to be enjoyed, not to be preached about. As with a symphony concert, you do not need to know everything about its composer, history, structure and technical challenges to enjoy it, but knowing more can enrich the experience.

The genius of Lancelot Brown in the early 1760s provided the final flourish that transformed Prior Park's series of separate improvements into the inspiring landscape we now enjoy. Beginning with Alexander Pope's small-scale 1730s 'wilderness' of rock and water, which has now (apart from its grotto) been restored by the National Trust, Ralph Allen made a serpentine walk on the west side leading to a pond. On the east side there was an elaborate vegetable garden enclosed by a straight hedge, leaving a more or less V-shaped lawn stretching halfway down the slope. In the 1750s, after Pope's death, the layout was extended to the bottom of the valley where the old fish ponds were enlarged and the Palladian Bridge built. On the steepest part Allen constructed a cascade and the whole landscape was given a softer outline by informal fringes of trees. Brown's masterstroke was to sweep away the cascade and its attendant planting and to unify the whole, much in its present form, using the eye-catching Palladian Bridge and reconfigured ponds as a carefully composed foreground to the city view.

Although the great house had been a school since 1867, the main components of the landscape had survived more or less intact for over a century. However,

The Palladian bridge after repair. (1998)

school priorities do not necessarily include historic landscape conservation, and gradually the garden's features were lost through neglect, beginning with Pope's garden which eventually became a rubbish tip, causing a landslide in the 1970s. Until that time there had been no new planting for one hundred years and then Dutch elm disease destroyed many trees, especially on the western side where the ground is always wet.

For years I had been intrigued by pictures of the landscape, but my first real look at it came as a result of unofficially joining a group assessing elm disease losses with a view to providing the school with replacement trees and help with clearance and replanting. My misgivings about a successful outcome arose from the obvious lack of preparation and a predictable lack of aftercare, but some trees survived – better than none. This was several years before the Trust began any moves towards acquisition but it was abundantly clear that this important historic landscape, soon to be registered Grade I by English Heritage and integral to what would become a World Heritage Site, before long would disintegrate unless managed soon with long-term conservation in mind.

Although the need was obvious, the challenge of separating management of the school from that of historic landscape was problematic to say the least, and was discounted as impracticable by many people. Nevertheless, it seemed the only hope, and there would be advantages for the school in having its landscape well cared for without cost by the National Trust. To the school it was a liability, but there remained serious concerns over security, access, circulation (especially across the principal north front of the mansion), and, worst of all, there was no hope of providing a car park. It is to the huge credit of the Trust at that time that it persisted, patiently negotiating with a reluctant local authority, against intense local opposition, for permission to open to visitors, the only basis upon which it could be restored. Eventually, in 1993, the property became a gift from the Christian Brothers to the National Trust and opened for a two-year trial period in 1996, full permission being granted in 1998 after all local fears had been proven groundless, with over 40 per cent of visitors arriving by bus.

The conspicuous concrete revetment of the lower lake dam in the process of being screened by planting. (1995)

The interregnum was nevertheless a valuable respite because the Trust needed to arrange its finances and set up a new property administration. Organisation of the site had to start from scratch with no base and almost no infrastructure; even the path system needed renewal. There were no service buildings but there was a house (Fishponds Cottage) and luckily we were able to recruit, first Richard Higgs, and then Matthew Ward from Stourhead, as successive head gardeners. Matthew has very competently continued to guide the restoration despite little in the way of skilled help in the early days. The labour force from the beginning was largely composed of staff on short-term agreements, usually willing but always inexperienced.

Like most neglected gardens from the eighteenth century Prior Park was full of overgrown and self-sown evergreens, some being original old yews but mostly common cherry laurel enjoying the alkaline soil and sheltered woodland on either side of the valley. I had seen a similar effect before at Claremont where it was Pontic rhododendron that cast a blanket over the land form. You could not see what was there at Prior Park either, the laurels having spread to create impenetrable masses of late nineteenth-century gloom.

To some alarm I firmly recommended cutting the whole lot to the ground to reveal lost features, like the ice house, and to assess the lie of the land. This was a big job but also an ideal opening gambit, entirely suitable for enthusiastic, unskilled help so long as the bonfires were carefully sited and the (poisonous) smoke carefully monitored. Archaeologists are invariably horrified at first by this robustly horticultural approach, always preferring the site to be left untouched until they have crawled all over it. But ubiquitous exotics like laurel are rapidly renewable and cutting them down first allows easy access and quick visual assessment as to whether they may or may not be retained.

Another essential early strategy was to secure the boundaries as far as possible from intruders, especially along Ralph Allen Drive, down which his Bath stone was transported on rail wagons to the canal – now a city thoroughfare. Against predictable opposition we first had to arrange the removal of the many self-sown sycamores growing too close to the boundary wall, to create space for planting, for which we chose a mixture of common thorn and holly – unexciting but hostile and eventually effective. At the same time we needed to remake a circuit path for visitors and a tractor route for access to and from a new storage yard and buildings near Fishponds Cottage. This area urgently needed screen planting with trees and evergreens. Much of the first few years was spent dealing with structural changes and replanting of this kind, to reconcile this profound change of use with the Trust's conservation imperatives.

The vitally necessary repair of the lower dam, which threatened properties below, left the unfortunate legacy of a very conspicuous concrete ledge half a metre or more above the water line. To incorporate brutal twentieth-century engineering on this scale seemed like an insoluble challenge, especially as the lip was wide and the dam behind was composed of hardcore. Nor did we want to see visitors congregating on the dam to emphasise the horizontal structure. The large lower pond needed to merge imperceptibly with its background. Oh dear! After much hand-wringing by the aesthetes and further discussion with the perpetrators, it

Archaeology in Alexander Pope's garden, revealing the edge of his lake as well as some more recent drains.

was conceded that shrub planting (certainly not trees) would be acceptable along the top of the dam to screen the path (apart from a single viewpoint over the outflow), exchanging topsoil for hardcore between path and dam edge. However, it would have been a long time before the concrete lip was covered, if ever, so we devised a cunning scheme. This involved inserting a band of biodegradable ground cover fabric into the topsoil behind the concrete lip and draping it over the edge of the dam into the water. This quickly took up water and greened over, eventually to be covered over by our careful selection of shrubs, including some dwarf, spreading willows at the edge, arranged more or less according to the repetitive pattern now obligatory for eighteenth-century borders. Thanks to good preparation and aftercare the screen of shrubs developed quickly and soon grew out over the edge, which disappeared from view. In cases of this kind it is important to focus on the ideal and never to take no for an answer from architects, builders and engineers, who are invariably allergic to having plant life anywhere near their structures.

Apart from a few specimen trees and several old yews, by the 1980s most surviving trees were either nineteenth-century additions or seedlings, mostly of common ash (now seriously threatened by disease), the many elms having gone. In the absence of much evidence it seemed reasonable to assume that the garden woodlands were mixed and a new generation of trees was urgently required. Overcrowded areas of self-sown ash needed to be thinned, unsafe trees removed and the spaces planted as soon as possible. Bearing in mind the increasing threats from pandemic tree diseases, as well as grey squirrels and the area's ever-present deer population, we agreed on a mixed plantation using native trees with others readily available in the eighteenth century. These were chosen according to site and function to control views and provide shade and cover. Whatever the exact precedent (if known), the imperative is to provide a resilient population of trees of suitable character that can be expected to survive to maturity in sufficient numbers in spite of all threats. Precise placement is necessary in some gardens but always tempts providence, since a single accidental loss can set back a scheme by several years, usually at great cost. In most cases in gardens a more broad-brush treatment is a better strategy, allowing for unpredictable losses by the generous planting of (cheap) small trees in carefully composed mixed populations. This allows thinning to favour the most desirable and successful trees for the place. It is important to leave your successors with as many options as possible.

Chapter 3

ENCOUNTERS WITH DONORS

Glendurgan, the
Bamboo Bridge
created through
a grove of tree
ferns using
home-grown
bamboo, rope-
rigged according
to local fishing
boat tradition.

FLORENCE COURT

It was love at first sight for me with Florence Court, her faded beauty set against the ravishing background of the Cuilcagh Hills over the border. The furthest west of the National Trust's big houses and domains, its sense of remoteness survives even today; in the 1970s, countryside beyond Enniskillen seemed like a lost world. With a strong vein of republicanism in Fermanagh and the border only six miles away, even at peaceful Florence Court the startling appearance of an occasional patrol of squaddies with rifles at the ready was a reminder of the Troubles. It seemed like 'bandit country'.

I was sent as part of a desperate bid to patch up relations between the Trust and the 6th Earl and Countess of Enniskillen. Unexpectedly inheriting the title, they had returned from Kenya to live at Florence Court as tenants of the Trust, as was their entitlement, and to open at least part of it, part of the time. In its wisdom the Trust had accepted the house with only 5.7 ha (14 acres) around it and only a meagre endowment from the Ulster Land Fund. The estate and much of the contents remained the property of the Cole family. The Trust's ownership did extend across the drive on the glorious east front but astonishingly only one foot beyond the edge of the gravel where a barbed-wire fence (usually) kept the cattle in the park.

Unsurprisingly, this tenancy arrangement proved to be disastrous, with a string of problems becoming more and more acute, culminating eventually in litigation. The Trust reluctantly and as a last resort had to ask the Earl and Countess to quit the Court, and they moved to the Dower House on the estate, just west of the house. Their first action was to plant a screen of trees to blot out the view of the big house; also any glimpse of the west parkland from Florence Court! The estate remained substantially outside the Trust's ownership until it was eventually acquired in two stages, the west park in 1985 and the east park two years later.

I was taken to Florence Court on my first Northern Ireland visit in 1971 at an early stage in this sad saga and I can confidently say that I achieved nothing. Lady Enniskillen, an American who had lived for years in tropical Africa, had bizarrely assumed the role of 'garden manager' although there seemed to be no one to do any gardening and she clearly knew nothing. I was charged with attempting to guide the Countess in her 'management' and persuade her to arrange some sort of improvement in the state of the grounds.

The pleasure grounds south of the house were fundamentally beautiful with a stream running through and a backdrop of woods and hills. But the tail-end of a hurricane five years earlier had blown down many of the larger trees and the stumps remained. The valley was a quagmire, the grass being cut annually where it was dry enough. Huge mounds of rhododendron, some 'Cornish Red' but mostly *Rh. ponticum*, were the main features along with some specimen trees of outstanding quality.

Met at the front door (and not invited in before or after), we walked in procession – Lady Enniskillen and me; Lord Enniskillen and the Regional Director (John Lewis Crosby); the Land Agent (Nigel Hughes) and the handyman/jack-of-all-trades, George. The experience was unreal. As I endeavoured to talk about the garden, the Countess would continue walking, dream-like, making polite conversation about how pretty everything looked. I confess to having been utterly ineffective in engaging her about the need for the removal of stumps and the clearance of accumulated undergrowth and brambles growing out of the rhododendrons. She never asked a single question until right at the end. Then suddenly emerging into the real world – 'can you tell me the name of this pretty bush', pointing at one of the vast mounds of *Rhododendron ponticum*! Defeat.

Now surrounded by an unsympathetic land owner, the prospect for poor, stranded Florence Court and its garden did not seem bright. However, we were equally concerned about the future of its estate and park, especially the main views from the east front. Even a cursory glance was sufficient to reveal a well-designed park in the eighteenth-century English landscape style, still cattle-grazed amongst the patches of reeds. Although the park was clearly missing many original trees and devoid of young ones, after 200 years the designer's intentions were clear. Only the spiky background of over-mature silver firs, and a ribbon of self-sown alders masking the stream, seriously marred the scene.

Sale of the park to the Northern Ireland Department of Forestry was no doubt intended as a threat to the park and an affront to the National Trust. A vision reared up of it being filled with conifers up to the front door. But the Trust was already on good terms with the foresters and a meeting was arranged by Nigel Hughes with John Philips, head of the Forestry Service in County Fermanagh. As an enlightened forester who understood historic landscape and conservation, John Philips was entirely sympathetic and proposed a management agreement between the Trust and the Forestry Department, which in effect leased the park and the extensive walled gardens alongside to the Trust. To do this, however, he needed to convince his senior management of the significance of the place and indicate the Trust's plans for its future conservation and renewal. Fine, except that he needed to have our considered scheme for their next meeting in less than a month's time.

There was no time for extensive survey or research but the opportunity had to be grasped. Having walked the site and listened to everyone concerned I went back and did the best I could with the evidence available. I could not believe my luck: to be charged with planning the restoration of a late-eighteenth-century park designed, as it turned out later, by William King, clearly a competent practitioner of the Lancelot Brown style.

I worked principally from OS maps, past and present, and aerial photographs which we managed to obtain 'unofficially'. For obvious reasons the terrain had been the subject of intensive aerial survey! We were particularly lucky that one batch of photographs was taken late on a sunny day in winter, and these showed precisely every undulation and tree stump, including former woodland boundaries. It was easy to distinguish the sites of lost tree clumps and specimens; the line of the eighteenth-century drive curving across from the eastern entrance

Florence Court. An aerial photograph taken late on a (rare?) sunny day in the early 1970s. After centuries of grazing almost every former feature of the park can be discerned, including the lines of an early avenue leading to the house on the right; also areas of woodland marked by shallow ditches and many tree stumps. The 18th-century drive loops along the bottom of this picture passing through a narrow neck of woodland to give variety to the route.

gates was also clear. In my legible but, by modern standards, unprofessional style I produced a workable plan in time for the meeting, necessarily without reference to any of my colleagues in the Trust. Success.

Bearing in mind the uneasy proximity of the park to the front door, I decided to take a chance and propose an extension to the pleasure grounds by taking in part

View from the front door of Florence Court showing the then boundary fence of the National Trust's ownership 0.5 m from the edge of the drive. Beyond is the 18th-century, designed landscape park: soggy pasture. (1973)

of the park. To lose the intimidating fence and allow visitors to step away to view the east front, I hopefully proposed a curving ha-ha of ambitious length set well back. It was carefully contrived so that the transition from garden to park would be invisible, especially from the Venetian windows of the piano nobile. Astonishingly, this daunting scheme for perhaps the longest new eighteenth-century-style ha-ha in Ireland was accepted without comment and the National Trust acquired the land up to it – 1 ha (2.5 acres) – in 1981. It was built slowly but to a remarkably high standard through an unemployment relief programme, well supervised by the Property Manager who was always complaining about the idleness of the workers who were forever 'breastfeeding their spades'!

Being able to reopen the eighteenth-century drive from the east lodges across the park was deeply satisfying – contriving a varied sequence of views of the park and the hills beyond, with glimpses of the house from different angles, closer and closer, dark and light; like travelling through a Claudian landscape. From the house I could not help putting myself in Mr King's shoes and wondering whether he proposed a lake. To me the gleam of water across the park in the middle distance was an obvious opportunity; perhaps the family ran out of money. Although the Trust later acquired the park and walled gardens, the woodlands remain in the hands of the Forest Service, but with their changing objectives it seems at least possible that the spiky old conifers on the horizon may eventually be replaced by the rounded outlines of oaks, limes and beeches? But maybe it is a sprinkling of decrepit old Douglas firs that makes an Irish landscape park Irish.

View from the front door of Florence Court over the hardly-visible new ha-ha and after some planting, still very immature. (1985)

One of the joys of Florence Court was that there was never any danger of anyone from the mainland interfering in what was going on; indeed, even the Northern Ireland Regional Office seemed semi-detached in the 1970s. Resources of any kind were almost entirely absent and there was a real sense of being on a new frontier.

On the fringe of the park is the first Irish yew (*Taxus baccata* 'Fastigiata'), one of two seedlings brought down from the hills by a local farmer in the eighteenth century at around the time the park was being laid out; there are more in the pleasure ground. Every fastigiate (Florence Court) yew owes its origin to this plant, which became ubiquitous in British gardens and churchyards in the second half of the nineteenth century, mainly in an attempt to convey the idea of the Italianate (see pp.237 and 239).

When the Enniskillens departed the big house, Anthony Hamilton, of noble birth, helped out the Trust by taking on the role of Custodian, with only the faithful George to assist. An IRA bomb was an obvious danger at a time when public buildings were under attack throughout Northern Ireland, but you would never have known this, with everyone being so friendly and helpful. I never encountered a problem during any of my visits, usually twice a year for twenty-seven years. Anthony did much more than 'fill the breach', gradually sorting out the remaining contents, running the garden and above all being a symbol of the Trust's presence in the area. He ran a happy household and I stayed with him in the house many times, usually sleeping in the old nursery, sparsely furnished and always cold but comfortable enough; a real sense of old-fashioned country house living. I would sometimes drive there alone from the airport at Aldergrove, calling in at different properties on the way. On one occasion I arrived just after dark in late winter in the rain and left my hired Morris Mini Minor on the drive. Breakfast was always rather a late and chancy affair with Anthony so I would get my own, searching as usual for a missing vital ingredient – marmalade, milk, tea, bread? I was interrupted by George shouting from below for me to throw my car keys out of the window. His brother, who was the postman, had noticed a flat

Aerial view of the south front of Florence Court.

The restored summerhouse, facing west, affords lovely views out over the pleasure ground to the Cuilcagh Hills and the republic border.

tyre on the car. With George's help he removed the wheel and took it with him on his post round to the local garage. In every way that incident typified the local culture of kindness and concern, each person becoming involved in what others are doing.

Not that it was easy to get anything done in the garden. I quickly learned to disregard every desperate reassurance from afar, trusting only in what I saw for myself. With willing but untrained people on unemployment relief schemes, the process of obtaining shrubs and planting and protecting them was fraught with difficulties. Having staked out a plantation and labelled each position, I went away wondering what could go wrong. I heard nothing until my next visit, then – 'och, Meesterr Sales, the very day after you left there was a terrible blaast and all your little labels blew away, indeed they did!' A sense of humour should have been on my job description.

However, step by step things improved, especially when the head gardener from Rowallane agreed to take on responsibility for supervising the garden. The garden and park are now in better order than they have been for at least three-quarters of a century.

WEST WYCOMBE PARK

BUCKINGHAMSHIRE

One of my earliest memories as a child in the late 1930s is of visiting West Wycombe to see the caves, and climb to the church with its famous golden dome. Thirty-five years later with a different perspective I saw the dome again, now as an eye-catcher of the eighteenth-century landscape garden and park. My role was to attempt to influence the mercurial Sir Francis Dashwood in managing and conserving this (now) Grade I historic landscape. My predecessor, Graham Thomas, had never been invited and it seems that as a newcomer in the early 1970s I was sent more in hope than expectation: a notoriously tricky place for any adviser.

The house and park were given to the National Trust in 1943 by Francis Dashwood's father, Sir John, without the church, mausoleum and caves, and crucially the gift did not include the house contents. The fixed endowment agreed then would not now cover the cost of a good holiday, management was to remain in the hands of the family, and the immutable opening arrangements reflected the level of pre-war interest in visiting country houses (i.e. seldom). As a result, Sir Francis was not much troubled by visitors and had a free hand in the house. However, like the National Trust, the property was perennially short of money and largely dependent on his good will for its conservation. Relationships with the Trust's regional staff at nearby Hughenden were predictably uneasy, as Sir Francis was liable to act on impulse according to his current obsession, and fail to consult. My briefing on the subject included a lot of hand-wringing, especially from the Historic Buildings Representative, Christopher Wall, whose aesthetic and historic sensibilities were frequently upset. 'One never knows what to expect.'

Historic research in those early days of historic garden conservation usually consisted of a paper exercise combined with visual assessment. At West Wycombe there was a wealth of data, including fascinating maps and plans covering the eighteenth century, clearly the most significant period. On meeting Sir Francis, I was immediately struck by his resemblance, as I saw it, to his ancestor, the illustrious Sir Francis Dashwood of Hell Fire Club fame, who laid out the park and garden in the late eighteenth century. He adapted a predominantly formal layout of broad vistas to create a luxuriously picturesque pleasure ground with ornamental lake, cascade, temples, bridges, winding walks and even a menagerie; also an extensive park, now confined by the spread of High Wycombe and cut through by the main road. In manner and style the Francis Dashwood I met was how I imagined the first Sir Francis. Maybe this was the way he set the place up – as a series of creative enthusiasms and theatrical concepts, acted upon without delay for his immediate gratification and the enjoyment of his many friends? He was clearly an extrovert and a bit of an exhibitionist, seemingly always planning some sort of ambitious event or whimsical garden feature: energetic, impatient and restless but always creative.

The family had maintained most of the more important eighteenth-century garden buildings together with the general outlines of the designed landscape, but

It seems that West
Wycombe park
was created by Sir
Francis for *fêtes
champêtres*, as
an expensive way
of entertaining
his friends; here
recreated by the
National Trust in
1995.

in line with general attitudes to historic gardens before the Second World War, they did not seem to have taken seriously its long-term conservation. No doubt they enjoyed the pleasure ground but gradually it had lost its eighteenth-century detail along with some of the older trees. Furthermore, the distinction between pleasure ground and park had become blurred. With insufficient resources the park had been cared for at low ebb and much of it was under arable cultivation. This was the daunting prospect that Sir Francis met when he succeeded.

On my first visit with regional staff I quickly realised the challenge when he immediately took charge and, in accordance with his own unwritten agenda, charged off to expand on his latest series of ideas, talking non-stop with great good humour. It was enormous fun but exhausting for everyone, especially me as I tried to keep up mentally, on unfamiliar territory, and sort the occasional practical and acceptable proposal from the flood of what seemed to me half-baked ideas. All this was directed at me personally and I was expected to respond instantly. The only way was to enter into the spirit and enjoy the whole thing, politely ignoring what I thought inappropriate and making vaguely encouraging noises about what, to a newcomer, sounded sensible. Although he was impatient and quixotic, I really enjoyed Francis's enthusiasm and extrovert good humour, but his approach to historic garden conservation was unconventional to say the least, even by the standards of the day. I quickly realised that progress would have to be on his terms – probably erratic, imprecise and more in the spirit than according to the letter.

Taking my cue from him, I decided after much thought to be bold but highly selective, and in my report, after the usual pleasantries (I was genuinely bowled over by the place), I set out some limited, fairly straightforward and

West Wycombe seen across the lake after persuading Sir Francis Dashwood to remove some of the overgrown yews on the island.

uncontroversial proposals. These involved reopening one or two historic views and replanting some of the structural trees lost long ago and never replaced. I made specific proposals for replanting the diagonal allée of trees framing the view from the splendidly porticoed east front to the cascade, as recorded in historic maps and a painting by William Hannan. I also specified the trees and offered to come again and place them. Happily the reply was positive and, although it was far from a simple procedure, with many second thoughts, we eventually got them planted more or less according to plan.

This conspicuous result must have given Francis confidence in the process. Although his style remained maddeningly discursive and erratic, thenceforth he did sometimes listen to my counter-suggestions, if not fully to my proposals. To my pleasant surprise he began to treat me as his personal consultant, a role reinforced when I made friends immediately with his wife Victoria, a charming and beautiful lady, who sadly died within a few years. In a way he seemed to see me as someone separate from the National Trust, about which he would complain at length. Because advisory visits resulted in action, there was a tendency for three or four regional staff to want to join me and on one occasion I clearly remember Francis asking two or three of them why they were there and sending them off!.

This eventual breakthrough resulted partly from being invited regularly to lunch. These were splendid affairs with plenty of good wine. They provided the opportunity for some small talk with Victoria and a chance to learn more about Francis and his undoubtedly passionate love of the place. Over drinks we were shown the historic paintings and were able to talk from spectacular viewpoints in the house about aims and priorities. To the Trust's alarm Francis was for ever wheeling and dealing with the furniture and chattels but I was determined to avoid being caught up in controversy of this kind. On the other hand he told me he was 'down to my last quarter million (pounds)' at one time. He seems to have restored the family finances by speculation, much of it from buying and selling land in Australia. He said he told the Inland Revenue that he was an 'international farmer'!

We made progress with dredging the lake, major prunings, some fellings and a good deal of planting, but I too never knew quite what to expect on a visit. I learned to be philosophical and accept the rough edges of Francis, realising that the vital aim at West Wycombe should be to encourage and educate his enthusiasm for the unique qualities of the place. Single-minded pursuit of the authentic may be right in principle but not at West Wycombe where Francis was determined to make his mark. However, along with this a great deal was achieved, much of it at his expense, in restoring the spirit and the fabric of the eighteenth-century landscape both in the park and the pleasure ground. It was vital to avoid disillusion but cultivating Francis's enthusiasm sometimes had results that would be thought bizarre in some circles. His equestrian statue on the horizon south of the house raised many eyebrows and I still wonder how he got away with it. However, I believe it was just the sort of thing his illustrious predecessor would have done and he undoubtedly enjoyed the controversy.

As time went on, more and more of the pleasure ground was restored, and then the park. In 1982 Francis commissioned Quinlan Terry to replace the lost Temple of Venus, and for the Queen's sixtieth birthday a figure of Britannia on a column was erected, another innovation which seemed impossible for the National Trust to oppose in the circumstances. By this time I had handed on the privilege and pleasure of advising regularly at West Wycombe to Mike Calnan, my colleague and successor as Head of Gardens. With Richard Wheeler as Managing Agent, and later as Curator, the process of renewal was consolidated.

Sir Francis Dashwood's time at West Wycombe can be looked back upon as an unlikely early success for garden conservation. Few people took historic gardens and especially landscape parks seriously in the 1970s. It was a decade later that

The house was intended to be seen as a series of classical temples in the landscape by planting trees at the corners to frame each set-piece. This diagonal axis from the cascade was replanted in the mid-1970s.

A *fête champêtre* in full swing in front of West Wycombe in 1995, seen across the now cleared part of the island.

English Heritage began to compile the Register of gardens, according to their historic importance, like buildings. Today's much more academic and methodical approach is to be welcomed. A lot has been learned but with the comparative freedom of his time at West Wycombe Francis Dashwood created an aptly fresh contribution to the history of the place while generally respecting his inheritance.

In her always revealing and sometimes scurrilous book about the National Trust, *Gilding the Acorn* (1994), Paula Weideger quotes Francis as having said on succeeding to the estate, 'what was really the biggest damn nuisance was the landscape'. This was entirely in character. To solve his problems he first called in Lanning Roper. After this it was Russell Page, hotfoot from Longleat, who was 'absolutely wonderful' but predictably expensive. So there was no pressure on me when I arrived on his doorstep! Nevertheless, he gave me the only unsolicited, if over-generous, testimonial I ever received for my work in the Trust – 'John Sales has been absolutely brilliant. He comes once a year and walks around with me and the local National Trust agent. He produces a three or four page letter of the things we are going to do, and we've done them all. He's got a marvellous eye; he's a charming man. Extremely knowledgeable. In many ways he's better than Russell Page who was so grand and so difficult to handle.'

Pardon the puff but there were no half-measures with Francis Dashwood; it could so easily have gone the other way.

When I was lecturing at Writtle College in the 1960s, Anglesey Abbey already enjoyed an enviable reputation for high gardening standards. On joining the Trust's staff I soon came to realise that this horticultural admiration amongst the vast majority of visitors was tempered by a degree of covert disdain among aesthetes and designers. It was a comparatively modern garden by National Trust standards, and its design was thought to be expensively illogical and whimsical – 'rich man's plaything', 'avenues going nowhere', 'sculpture displayed out of context', etc. That these views are no longer heard is a testament to how taste changes. The garden is now widely regarded as a mid-twentieth century beacon of grandeur and optimism, made through periods of austerity and pessimism for gardens. Looked at with hindsight, its structure has much in common with the transitional gardens of the early eighteenth century, still formal in outline but with informal elements. It is the only post-modern garden I know.

On my first 'advisory' visit (a steep learning curve), the distinguished head gardener, Noel Ayres, who had been there since the beginning, greeted me with

A border in the herbaceous garden in July 1979, bursting with vigour and meticulously cared for. One of a series of secret gardens, it is set in a frame of clipped beech.

old-fashioned courtesy, and we had the best of gardeners' lunches at his home in Lode, enjoying full sight of his own lovely garden. I learned a lot and was allowed back despite putting my foot in it by suggesting that a huge pear tree on the side of the big house could do with summer pruning. When challenged I offered to get up there and have a go and this seemed to break the ice!

This garden of nearly 100 acres (40.4 ha) has been kept constantly to an exemplary standard by only five gardeners, an amazing achievement of intelligent organisation, precise timing, well-honed skills and consistent endeavour. This was also before the days of highly sophisticated turf equipment. Autumn was the best time to go. Spurning mechanical leaf sweepers ('not good enough'), all the fifty or sixty acres of lawns were swept with long-handled besom brooms, all five gardeners working together in echelon formation. Unhurriedly, they would sweep in unison, gobbling up the acres and depositing the leaves in neat wind-rows for immediate collection. It was poetry in motion, like a grand corps de ballet, choreographed with artistry and performed with athletic precision.

By all accounts Huttleston Broughton, the first Lord Fairhaven, was a man for whom only the best was good enough, and who demanded extraordinary levels of precision and attention to detail in all aspects of his life. The carpet had to be brushed as he went out to remove his footprints; the garage had to be heated so the Rolls Royce would always be at room temperature; when asked to arrive at a certain hour the chauffeur had to arrive exactly as the hour struck, not a minute before or a minute later. This almost obsessive attitude to order was reflected in the garden, where at least a façade of neatness had to be consistently maintained.

The garden consists of a series of bold strokes – crisp avenues across a flat landscape on the edge of the Fen. Occupying the spaces between are a succession of flower gardens, each aimed at a defined period of the year and designed with enviable clarity of purpose.

In bequeathing the property to the Trust, Lord Fairhaven devised an impossible condition if taken literally – i.e. that the garden should not be changed in any way. But of course the nature of gardens predetermines change: it is their unique quality, and in the final reckoning it is what we most enjoy about them. Nevertheless, this set the tone for an unusual degree of conservatism, until the natural processes of maturity, combined with accidents like storms and disasters like Dutch elm disease, decreed otherwise.

If they are to survive, gardens depend on continuity – of purpose, of care and of cultivation. At the critical point of transition to different ownership, this was provided by Ailwyn Broughton, the second Lord Fairhaven, who built his family house in the late 1960s adjacent to Anglesey Abbey. He provided that vital link, ensuring the permanence of his uncle's wishes as far as practicable. His intense interest was always constructive and helpful, making my advisory visits over twenty-seven years increasingly interesting, enjoyable and satisfying, resolving pragmatically all the many challenges.

All too soon Noel Ayres retired, to be succeeded by his son Richard, an extraordinarily able and totally positive person who was never daunted. For family reasons he had never worked elsewhere, but this possible disadvantage was far

LEFT Anglesey
Abbey house
seen from the
rose garden.

RIGHT Formal
'Hyacinth Garden'
in its summer
dahlia phase.

outweighed by his flexible intelligence, foresight and ability to lead from the front, making no concessions in the pursuit of excellence. Always optimistic, he was consistently ahead of the game mentally and physically, ready for the next project and immediately able to visualise what was proposed.

In the 1970s Dutch elm disease swept through Essex and Cambridgeshire, changing the landscape irrevocably – perhaps a foretaste of other pandemic tree diseases facilitated by international trade and tourism. Before it was gardened, the Abbey's 100 or so acres consisted of fields articulated by narrow, mixed shelterbelts. The first Lord Fairhaven planted more but was never concerned about their content, only that their external appearance should be trim and unbroken. Venturing inside most of these belts revealed an overcrowded mixture: clearly unsustainable as woodland without thinning and management. In these thickets were thousands of elms which had to be removed as they died, a huge task but a blessing in disguise.

It was Richard Todd, assistant to Richard Ayres and his eventual successor, who managed this immense operation so well that it was hardly noticed. Thereafter, these vital woodland shelterbelts were taken in hand to be managed sustainably, and new ones planted to temper the bitter East Anglian winds from the north-east.

The first Lord Fairhaven's most singular garden features were planted in the mid-1950s to display part of his important and ever-increasing collection of sculpture. Marble busts of Roman emperors determined the Emperors' Walk and two wooden warships' figureheads named the Warriors' Walk. Understandably intent on a quick effect, he created formal linear walks enclosed by close-planted groves of mainly Norway spruce with European larch among them. Not to everyone's taste, this unique plantation needed frequent thinning and pruning to retain the ideal setting for each bust. The feature had to be perceived as a long gallery

but each emperor had to be encountered separately with elegant spruce branches forming his setting. At its ideal the result was original and successful, a piece of mid-twentieth century mannerism. But it took twenty years to reach perfection and then it seemed impossible to sustain, obviously destined to become a dark conifer plantation vulnerable to the elements. The dilemma was short-lived, for in 1979 a freak storm all but destroyed the feature. We decided on total clearance and a new beginning. There were two competing proposals. The regional hierarchy was keen on a totally new planting of Stone Pines to create in time an Italianate 'Appian Way' effect of rugged stems and overarching umbrellas of foliage. Tempting though this imaginative concept may have been, it was opposed by those who knew the property more intimately because it did not conform to the garden's established style, which was hardly Italianate, and in any case would have taken nearly a century to achieve. Instead we opted for a modified version of the original scheme, accepting that it may have to be replanted every twenty-five to thirty years. The new scheme included an admixture of yews to give permanence, so that when the spruce had eventually to be replanted there would be a background core of evergreens to re-furnish the site quickly. However, on reflection I regret having failed to include some larch to lighten the effect or even the golden larch (*Pseudolarix amabilis*).

With such a comparatively young garden, development was predictably rapid, and many of the original features had to be renewed, adapted or replaced. Slavish replacement like-for-like everywhere is rarely a practicable proposition and its attempt at Anglesey Abbey would not have served the garden well, especially with the advent of mass visiting and a longer opening season. Nevertheless, as a significant historic garden it was essential to endeavour to retain the special character and the unique values of the place. Gardens must move on, but to retain their individuality every deliberate innovation and every reaction to inevitable change must be measured against particular criteria derived from a knowledge of the place, its history and the specific characteristics of its site.

Working eastwards, by the time the first Lord Fairhaven had planted the Warriors' and Emperors' Walks and the small pinetum nearby he had virtually run out of inspiration, although he continued planting elsewhere. This left an odd-shaped

The Temple Lawn contains an arrangement of classical columns around a marble copy of Bernini's *David*, with lead lions guarding the entrance to the yew-hedged enclosure.

area bounded by a smart beech hedge on its west side, and a bedraggled shelter-belt of unsuccessful Scots pines and Norway spruce near the eastern boundary. My first job at Anglesey Abbey in 1971 had been to design a new car park situated outside to the east beyond this shelterbelt, through which visitors had to be led to reach the main garden and house: hardly an ideal introduction but unavoidable. As well as a skeleton of London planes saved from thinning the 1937 Coronation Avenue (some of the others went to Swindon town centre), we planted an enclosed garden for the restaurant and tree belts by the roadside and along the car park boundaries. With the thought of eventually replacing the decrepit shelterbelt of Scots pine, we also inserted, next to the car park, a narrow plantation of red-twigged limes (a feature of the garden elsewhere), with field maples as fillers and common yews as underplanting. Twenty years later this foresight proved useful.

Having given a lot of consideration to it over the years and looked at a few possibilities for this awkward eastern tag-end of the garden, the only definite conclusion was that the old shelterbelt should go. The ideal solution seemed elusive.

But the garden was developing and being enriched as each area came under scrutiny for renewal and detailed improvement. Although the garden was never open in winter, one shallow, wooded ditch was spectacular in January and February, first with masses of winter aconite which sow themselves freely in the sandy soil, and subsequently with snowdrops. By the 1980s Richard Ayres had pondered over this for some time. This area turned out to be a former dumping ground, presumably when Huttleston Broughton cleared the site of his predecessor's garden. The Reverend John Hailstone, the owner of the property from 1860, had clearly had a collection of snowdrops, which had their first period of intense popularity in the 1890s, with new species being introduced from the Greek islands, the Caucasus, the Dardanelles, the Crimea and the Balkans generally. Unlike archaeology,

Snowdrop cultivars and aconites surviving from the time of the Rev. John Hailstone were evidently discarded into one of the former drainage ditches after Lord Fairhaven acquired the property in the 1920s. Here they happily grew and multiplied until the several distinct hybrids were rescued and planted out in huge drifts by Richard Ayres in the 1970s and '80s; later identified and named.

bulbs are not necessarily destroyed by being dumped in a ditch: quite the reverse at Anglesey Abbey, where they evidently thrived and multiplied, creating new cultivars in an orgy of interbreeding. This is what Richard Ayres came across in the 1970s and with my encouragement (neither of us knew much about the genus *Galanthus*) he separated out the obviously distinct kinds and planted them in grass around trees and on the banks of the shallow depressions which were the Abbey's stewponds. Gradually the snowdrop gurus found their way to Anglesey Abbey and Richard Nutt was especially helpful in attempting to distinguish and name the species and cultivars revealed. A green-leafed *G. nivalis* was called 'Anglesey Abbey'; 'Richard Ayres' and 'Ailwyn' are neat doubles derived from the common double *G. nivalis* × *G. elwesii*,

Galanthus 'Richard Ayres'.

a broad-leafed species from the Caucasus. So it developed, with more cultivars being named and many more accumulated by exchange. With local 'snowdrop lunches' in the Cotswolds, I too became interested, and we developed a collection in our own garden near Cirencester, with friendly rivalry and much swapping. Galanthophilia is strongly contagious and demand for the garden at Anglesey Abbey to be open regularly in winter was impossible to resist. Apart from snowdrops, a garden of this scale and diversity has much to offer the winter visitor.

Unfortunately the grass was becoming damaged by footfall on wet or frosty ground and the need for a dry circuit route became all too obvious. The idea of a Winter Walk from the car park entrance arose out of this need, and Richard Ayres suggested that it should be made to mark the centenary of the birth of the first Lord Fairhaven. Eventually we decided on boldly turning the removal of the derelict eastern shelterbelt to advantage by using the cleared central strip as our Winter Walk, while crucially retaining the lines of yews planted on either side twenty years earlier for enclosure and background. An essential element of any successful winter garden is to be able to view it with the sun behind you and

The serpentine Winter Walk was my concept, much helped in the planting design by the resourceful Richard Ayres and his hard-working gardeners. It is arranged to give a developing succession of winter colour and interest.

To conclude the Winter Walk we needed something theatrical but simple after all that plantsmanship and Richard Ayres came up with this solution, a grove of the Kashmir form of the Himalayan birch var. *jacquemontii*.

with the plantings seen against a dark evergreen background, which also gives shelter.

I was happy that this bold stroke would echo the asymmetric structure of the garden as a whole, and that its decisive intent would reinforce the garden's character and values. Echoing the kind of serpentine walks seen in the early 18th century transitional gardens like those conceived by Stephen Switzer and Batty Langley, I drew a wiggly line in my notebook, the essence of which was agreed by Lord Fairhaven and Richard Ayres – and eventually, thanks to the Regional Director, Merlin Waterson, by the regional hierarchy of the National Trust as well. With Richard Ayres and one of my colleagues at Cirencester, Isabelle van Groeningen, we worked up the scheme as a progressive series of colourful winter-effect plant combinations involving shrubs, herbaceous perennials and bulbs, with a circular 'decompression zone' halfway, as a place to linger, where calmness and restrained planting would prevail. Later it was extended into a young piece of shelterbelt woodland, planted in the late 1970s, but the end of the first phase was marked by a typically Anglesey Abbey-style flourish – a grove of more than one hundred white-stemmed birch (*Betula utilis* var. *jacquemontii*), which are still pressure-washed annually.

Despite the virtual certainty of the Winter Walk's success and the obvious likelihood of it being able to generate substantial income, the Trust with its usual parsimony towards gardens seemed unable to find meaningful funds centrally. It was left largely to the property to raise funds and to glean what it could locally and from the Trust's Gardens Fund. Almost immediately it attracted tens of thousands of visitors in February and early March, giving a great deal of pleasure and generating substantial funds for the property, although little of it seems to have been invested in extra staff to compensate for the additional costs of upkeep. Much of its original and continuing success has to be attributed to the high standards set and constantly maintained by Richard Ayres and his successor as head gardener, Richard Todd. As with any garden, it is the day-to-day striving for excellence in everything that counts – plant selection, pruning, cultivation, development and substitution when needed. Great gardens depend on process as well as product.

HINTON AMPNER

Ralph Dutton was an unsung hero of the developing interest in historic gardens that began after the Second World War, leading to the formation of the Garden History Society in 1965. His book *The English Garden*, first published in 1937 and revised in 1950, was highly influential both in drawing attention to the wealth of historic gardens in England and in hinting strongly at the way they had been undervalued for generations. Although the English had been for centuries a nation of gardeners, there was no measure of the quantity, quality and diversity of our gardens until regisration began in the 1980s. A friend since school days of Christopher Hussey, architectural editor of *Country Life* for many years, Dutton shared his interest in country houses and gardens. He wrote knowledgeably about architecture throughout Europe and was able to relate this scholarship to a deep interest in gardens and gardening. As with others of my generation, his book, a companion to *The English Country House*, was the first book on garden history I read and possessed.

Ralph Dutton eventually succeeded his brother, who bequeathed Sherborne Park and Lodge Park (Gloucestershire) to the National Trust, to become for a few years the 8th and last Lord Sherborne, but he lived all his life at Hinton Ampner. The house, garden and park there were almost entirely his creation. In the English tradition he was rebuilding on the legacy of previous generations, the Georgian house having been extensively remodelled in the 1860s, when the garden terraces south of the house were formed as a grand Victorian foreground to the park and

The flower garden below the house leads down through an old lime avenue to a view of an obelisk set on the edge of the park.

A variety of clipped yew topiary shapes provide the structure of the main terrace walk where the borders are bedded out annually with colourful bulbs, annuals and tender perennials.

estate. He told me that before he inherited in 1937 he was not permitted to make his mark in any way in the house or the garden. However, he was allowed to practice his interest in the park, where in the 1920s and '30s he planted extensively in the English Landscape style. After half a century, when I first saw the park, the tree groups were already realising Ralph Dutton's intentions, and now the Trust owns a remarkable twentieth-century revival of the style, perhaps more Repton than Brown in character. After 1937 he gave the house neo-Georgian interiors, refurnishing throughout, and an unfortunate fire in 1960 was treated only as a temporary set-back. While retaining the nineteenth-century structure of terraces and trees, Dutton completely replanted the garden, indulging his love of ornamental shrubs in abundance, especially shrub roses, but also including a wide range of bulbs and herbaceous plants. His love of Sissinghurst shows in both his choice of plants and in the subtle way he created separate spaces of different character and impact, all cleverly incorporated into what at first glance seems to be a simple series of terraces. The garden represents the best in garden style of the third quarter of the twentieth century and should be conserved as such.

He was in his mid-seventies when I first met him, as a member of the Trust's Gardens Panel. I recognised Ralph Dutton as a man of great erudition and gentle manners. Without forcing his opinions, he gave me wise guidance and opened my eyes to much that I would otherwise have missed. Unfortunately my first visit to Hinton Ampner, to have lunch and see his garden (which one assumed might come to the Trust), was a total washout but we talked at length and ventured out for as long as possible despite the torrential rain. Clearly the garden had become his great passion and I believe it was, like the house, always underrated, being considered 'twentieth-century pastiche' by the purists of the National Trust. In fact, all gardens owe something to the past, Sissinghurst and Hidcote as much

as Hinton Ampner. At the same time the garden contains many original and imaginative touches and a strong sense of gradual revelation.

Gardens like Hinton Ampner, which are predominantly of a single era, are often overcrowded and over-mature by the time they are passed on to their next owner. After the Trust's acquisition in 1986, Hinton Ampner was in need of fundamental renovation and renewal throughout – hard pruning, replanting, weedkilling, manuring – to ensure its sustainability under a different regime. With the house and walled garden leased to a private tenant, the garden was now open to visitors, who have come to love it for the qualities that Ralph Dutton valued – its setting, design and diverse planting. The transition from private to public involved difficult adjustments and the necessary renovation caused unsightly scars, neither of which effects is understood either by those who knew the garden in Ralph Dutton's time nor by those whose interest in gardens is entirely temporal. However, the complaints, both internal and external, soon died down and I only hope that the garden will continue to be conserved with courage and consistency, always aiming towards Ralph Dutton's ideals.

The formal south-facing terraces, containing a fine assembly of shrubs and plants, give way to the park, planted with great skill and vision by Ralph Dutton in the English landscape style.

To me Glendurgan represents the archetype of Cornish valley gardens, combining long views with intimate corners and grassy banks with jungly hollows. However, it exceeds all others in heightening these contrasts by providing a series of deliberate surprises for the new visitor. My first visit in 1971 was spent following the Fox family procession, headed by Cuthbert and negotiated by Graham Thomas, each member politely disagreeing with the other. Luckily I was able to enjoy the luxury of being an observer, plunging into an exotic profusion of fascinating plants, a different excitement at every turn, unfamiliar trees towering around; to a mere Englishman everything seemingly larger than plant life as I knew it. Having avoided the Cornish snare of planting the whole place with an over-rich diet of tender rarities, Glendurgan retains its breathing spaces. The journey leads past streams and ponds, banks of wild and naturalised flowers and a vast laurel maze, to Durgan village with its bracing seaside brightness; then back past the rebuilt 'old' school room and the 'Giant Stride' in case anyone has the energy to exploit this grown-up maypole swing.

Apart from a minimum of regular upkeep, not much got done in the 1970s, despite the natural processes of growth, development and decay being disconcertingly rapid in the south-west. Although generally free of hard frosts and usually well watered, coastal gardens in Cornwall have frequent gales to contend with, as well as the occasional freak drought or arctic winter. Hence the 'turnover' of plants of all kinds is quick and Cornish gardens need to be continually renewed and regenerated by deliberate reworking. The many trees planted for shelter by Alfred Fox, who started the garden almost two centuries ago, and even those added later, were old by Cornish standards by the 1970s, but remained vital to the well-being of the garden. Time was running out.

After Cuthbert Fox inherited in 1931, the family's attitude seems to have been steadily more conservative, perhaps intoxicated by the beauty of the place and by what they had collectively created. Although Cuthbert and his wife Moyra continued to plant according to tradition and whim, longer-term conservation measures were perhaps understandably overlooked. Furthermore, the familiar story of rising costs and reduced resources meant that less could be done. However, as it matured, the garden was always loved and cherished by the family and admired by the few visitors lucky enough to see it.

Following the Trust's acquisition in 1962, Graham Thomas's advisory visits seem to have been agreeably sociable but largely ineffectual when seen from the standpoint of long-term garden conservation. His advice on roses for the walled garden was eagerly sought by Moyra, and Cuthbert enjoyed talking plants. But it was difficult to get agreement, not only for fresh planting but also for measures of adaptation and improvement. As always, fellings and prunings to reopen views and relieve congestion were particularly controversial. Everyone had a different opinion. An advisory tour would sometimes involve as many as twelve to fourteen people, including several family members, gardener, adviser and local National Trust staff. The inevitable fragmentation of the group and subsequent repetition of every discussion greatly irritated Graham but he seldom showed it.

In their wisdom the Trust had accepted Glendurgan on the understanding that the family's senior member would continue to manage the garden. This arrangement seemed reasonable with few visitors, but became a burden after Cuthbert died and his son Philip, who was not a gardener by training or inclination, took over. Philip assumed the role at a time when the Trust was asking for increased opening, under pressure for better access and increased income. Car parking, lavatories, refreshments, paths, drainage, etc., had all become increasingly inadequate and the depleted garden staff found it difficult to raise standards to meet expectations. Although his mother was unable to join the advisory crocodile in the garden, my impression was that she still ruled and Philip always seemed to have one eye on the house.

When I took over routinely advising, this regime was still stuttering along. Gentle decline, however charming, cannot last in gardens and there was an increasing backlog, especially of tree work; the maze was in conspicuous need of renovation. Frustratingly, jobs readily agreed on my visits were forgotten and the purchase and care of agreed new plants listed in my reports became increasingly problematic. Meanwhile, the increasingly severe and more frequent storms of the 1980s continued to take their toll. It became clear to all that radical change would be necessary to enable the garden to survive and prosper into the next century. Conserving the Fox family's garden and their connection with it remained the principal aim, along with increased access, improved facilities for visitors, more resources and full-time dynamic management.

At this time Peter Mansfield, who subsequently became Regional Director, was managing agent. Crucially in the mid-1980s he gained possession of a strip of land along the south side of the garden to extend the narrow shelterbelt which was already falling about; then he arranged for the redundant kitchen garden

A new entrance path had to be devised from the car park to circumvent the area close to the house. This was arranged to join the existing Camellia Walk. (1992)

By 2006 the new entrance path and planting had matured to create an appropriate welcome for visitors. Spring-flowering bulbs, camellias and other exotic shrubs are supplemented by summer-flowering perennials.

on the north side to be planted similarly for shelter. As though we had tempted providence, the great south-west storms of 1990 soon justified all this effort and expense but still left the garden in a mess. With a disabled gardener, and fallen trees and broken branches everywhere, emergency help was called for, and Robert James was seconded from Trelissick to take charge of the clear up. Peter then devised a remarkably imaginative and ingenious scheme which has saved the garden and enabled its total renovation, while retaining the family connection. Through patient, exhaustive and constructive negotiation with the next generation, Charles (Philip's son) and his wife Caroline, it was agreed that access would be rearranged to separate visitors entirely from the house, although crucially retaining an early view of it. In return for the family's completely private use of the garden around the house, the drive and the walled garden, the Trust would take over day-to-day management and increased visitor access in line with other gardens in the area. There would be a new car park (already hardly adequate) and improved facilities, including refreshments and the inevitable shop. All this was planned to pay for renovation and renewal.

The great challenge for the garden was to assimilate an acceptable route across the valley below the house but invisible from it, while retaining the traditional view down to the Helford River. In 1989 we began cautiously to explore the route of the valley head path – gently curving with the contour, revealing the valley but avoiding the feeling of teetering uncomfortably on the edge of a steep drop. To seem right from all viewpoints, the planting would need to echo adjacent shrub groups while taking advantage of the brightness and good drainage. Above all I was resolved to avoid any hint of a hedge above the new path, which would emphasise its line across the valley. I am now entirely happy with the outcome, the path leading to a little pre-existing pond and trickling waterfall surrounded now by exotic, almost tropical, planting with tree ferns and bananas. Although by no means universally welcomed at the time, this fundamental change of management and organisation was amicably negotiated, leading to as near an ideal relationship between donor family and owner as could be conceived in the

circumstances. It left the Trust to do what arguably it does best – manage, adapt and conserve the garden for the long term, taking into account public benefit and the need to maximise income. The Fox family are able to live as tenants with privacy and a degree of independence. Meanwhile, Charles takes a welcome interest in the garden, influencing its development in an entirely constructive way. His book *Glendurgan* (2004) is an affectionate history and memoir. More than ever, in the twenty-first century the National Trust can benefit from this kind of questioning local influence, especially to restrain more extreme examples of trendy commercial exploitation, crack-pot environmentalism and obtrusive 'interpretation', all mercifully absent at Glendurgan.

Key to the garden's revival and renewal, as always, was the appointment of a competent and energetic hands-on head gardener. Robert James was the first of a succession since the late 1980s of outstanding head gardeners. Luckily he was ever eager for action on any scale, inspiring his meagre staff in major exploits – path making and renovation, drainage, pruning, felling and not least stump removal, a legacy of several generations, each stump contributing to the spread of honey fungus, a soil-borne and usually fatal tree disease. Nothing seemed too much for the gardeners to tackle and they contributed many positive suggestions. These included a splendid replacement for the two planks that constituted the 'Chinese bridge', consisting of an entirely original raised walkway constructed through a bamboo grove, made of mostly home-grown bamboo poles and secured by rope work inspired by the local fishing industry. They undertook a brave and fundamental renovation of the maze in the heart of the garden with great success. Made in the 1830s to copy a unique informal design once in Sydney Gardens, Bath, it had lost its defining characteristics. The cherry laurel hedges had become misshapen and infested with seedling trees and ivy, and the paths were eroded.

Another new path, across the head of the valley below the house, gives views down to the Helford river at Durgan. It culminates in an almost tropical arrangement of exotics around a little spring and pond, including tree ferns, bananas and arum lilies.

OPPOSITE TOP The Laurel Maze. (1992)

OPPOSITE BOTTOM The maze after restoration with a replaced central summerhouse and big palms at each of the false destinations.

Luckily the original plan had survived. To some consternation I advised cutting the laurel to ground level, thus allowing the paths to be drained and re-gravelled and the hedges retrained densely. Eventually big hardy palms were transplanted to terminate four blind alleys, and the thatched summer house was triumphantly restored at the centre.

Advising at Glendurgan had been transformed from a mildly frustrating amble,
repeatedly encountering similar problems,
to an invariably constructive and enjoyable adventure exceeding expectations.
There was almost always an exciting event
or a prank arranged for my diversion,
such as a bunch of real bananas attached
to their banana plants on April Fool's
Day, or a stump for me to blow out with a
pre-prepared dynamite charge! The serious
West-Country storms of 1990 brought
down hundreds of trees at Glendurgan, jus-
tifying our warnings two decades earlier,
and the process of renewing and extending
shelterbelts has continued. Improvements
included reopening the almost-forgotten
Manderson's Hill, a high walk on the
eastern side where a viewing platform was
made to overlook almost the whole garden.

The nineteenth-century tradition of plant
introduction from the wild was revived,
partly through association with the Edinburgh Botanic Garden's conifer conservation project, involving many rare and
tender species for which Glendurgan
was one of the few sites likely to be mild

A group of
tall palms
(*Trachycarpus
fortunei*) in the
valley.

enough; also through the Trust's own propagation nursery at Knightshayes,
where we were raising wild-collected seeds from all over the world. I was lucky
enough to go on a life-changing trek in Bhutan in 1990 with Tony Schilling, formerly curator at Wakehurst Place, and this sparked the idea of collecting a special
range of Bhutanese plants for part of the valley, a scheme that has been recently
revived. The Trust was presented separately with a collection of a dozen or so
cultivars (I did not know there were any!) of the olive, and Glendurgan, with its
mildness and history of fruit growing, seemed the ideal place for an olive grove.
This is now maturing well on the north side of Birch's Orchard.

Few gardens in the Trust have given me greater satisfaction than Glendurgan,
because its care seems assured through the Trust's established style of management and the beneficial influence of the family. However, I must confess to my part
in the move away of Steve Porter, its head gardener at the turn of the twenty-first
century. In my post-Trust role as adviser at Chatsworth I helped appoint him as
assistant, eventually to take charge of Chatsworth's garden and park: a worthy
successor to Joseph Paxton, probably England's greatest-ever head gardener.

Until the 1970s every visitor's first experience of the grandeur of this ancient and beautiful property was via the back drive, past a mean lodge and the kitchen garden wall, to the back of the great house. As the shortest route to Kendal it seems gradually to have taken precedence over two other former drives, central and south, the latter having been a winding route through Sizergh's undulating parkland. Nothing was ever simple at Sizergh but the advantages of restoring this drive, with Repton-style glimpses of the picturesque Pele Tower alternating with long views and groves of trees, was difficult to resist, even by the most conservative of families. However, the National Trust was made aware of the extra annual cost of driving to Kendal via the longer southern route! The new car park west of the house was open and rocky in parts, where it was impossible to dig holes for tree planting. Nevertheless, I was delighted to be able to prove the success of the technique of 'mound planting' of semi-mature trees (described above under Ickworth). Provided that the trees are kept completely free of grass and weeds for two years, this time-honoured technique is invariably successful, their roots soon finding a way through the rocky terrain.

Sizergh Castle's rock garden was built during the heyday of naturalistic alpine gardening, using locally-collected waterworn limestone, now no longer available. By the 1970s the stone had been largely obscured by profuse planting, including Japanese maples and many ferns.

Overshadowed for centuries by the magnificence of the house and estate, the garden enjoyed a remarkable resurgence between the wars, an unprecedented burst of horticultural innovation, now captured as a period piece. The garden's principal feature of this time is its extensive waterworn limestone rock garden, designed, built and planted to the highest possible standard by T.R. Hayes,

whose nursery continues at Ambleside to the present day, at a time when plundering limestone pavement was not yet regarded as a conservation crime. Being anachronistic and never-to-be-repeated adds to its heritage value, and certainly should not prevent us from appreciating its qualities to the full, even though it can no longer be given all the skilled attention it once enjoyed. Unfortunately it was never managed with a view to retaining the open aspect we associate with alpine gardening; indeed, after half a century it was on the way to becoming dense woodland. As well as the intentionally large trees on its fringes, many of the 'dwarf' conifers (which proved to be merely slow-growing) had become small trees, many of them leggy and unkempt. Neglect of any programme of renovation and renewal had resulted in Stygian gloom in all but a central glade.

In the picturesque tradition, the first view of the house is from a distance across the park, then to be lost from view and recurring later.

Angela Hornyold-Strickland, the family member taking most interest in the garden, was not easily convinced of the need for change in any form, and the Trust quite rightly was always anxious to share decisions with the donor family if possible. Decision-making of this kind at Sizergh proved a painfully slow process as I played cat-and-mouse with Angela over the removal of this or that scraggy conifer (I confess we sometimes took out three or four without her noticing). Nevertheless, thanks to the patient and loyal head gardener, Malcolm Hutcheson, the rock garden was gradually renovated, section by section, at least one year spent exterminating the backlog of perennial weeds in each area before replanting. Malcolm proved to be an outstanding plantsman and naturalist, and he needed little encouragement to establish and sustain National Collections of hardy ferns, which grow exceptionally well at Sizergh with its lime-free soil and plenty of rain.

Angela was particularly proud of her flower arrangements in the house where she worked to ensure the highest standards. We tried to provide cut flowers and

The grand flight of steps into the garden is populated by masses of *Erinus alpinus* from the Pyrenees.

foliage in sufficient quantity and variety from the kitchen garden but there was always some (unspecified) deficiency compared with Arley Hall, her sister's home in Cheshire. This resulted in the mainly herbaceous border near the kitchen garden being 'raided' for cut flowers, a common habit in country house gardens. The extent to which this is acceptable depends on your point of view but the flowers cannot be in both places at the same time! This little local difficulty was gradually overcome by better communication and more sophisticated provision. I also completely redesigned the long herbaceous border, in consultation with Angela, so as to emphasise to her its importance to the garden's summer display (also using many plants that are unsuitable as cut flowers!).

Like the rock garden, the garden's ambitious extensions east of the house were designed in the 1920s with more gardeners in mind than either the family post-war or the National Trust could afford. As with many, if not most, of the Trust's gardens, retrenchment was a constant necessity; we were always looking for ways of simplifying labour-intensive layouts without unduly depleting interest and significance. Perhaps unwisely, gardening had been taken beyond the ha-ha into the park to create a formal Italianate flower garden with a summer house facing due north, all protected from the cattle by a thorn hedge. Formal bedding no longer being possible, it was a sad sight. My eventual solution (inspired by Grey's Court in Oxfordshire) was to convert it into a formal grove of flowering cherries, right for period and style, so that they could be appreciated from above the ha-ha and when walking through from below.

Far more successful, if a touch pompous, was the castellated viewing platform leading from the house via a grand stone staircase. This looks out over an enlarged pond and waterside planting of dogwoods and willows, but was diminished by being much too rigidly bordered by a clipped thorn hedge enclosing an unduly mean area from the park. The result was an unhappily stark division between park and garden, and muddy grass where visitors were unnecessarily channelled through narrow openings. Although we were able to improve the planting, extreme conservatism ruled at Sizergh and any sort of structural change was always a non-starter.

A visit of the Gardens Panel to Sizergh was a particular success in breaking the deadlock of immutable preservation that denied the need for any adjustments to meet the needs of changing circumstances. With The Lady Emma Tennant, daughter of the Duke and Duchess of Devonshire, as Chairman, the impact of the Panel's visit created a sea-change in the family's attitude at Sizergh, the Panel's recommendations solving or alleviating several difficulties, large and small, and making way for a major change around the lake. Tacit agreement was reached on a proposal by the late George Clive, an original-thinking landowner and forester from Shropshire, for removing the clipped thorn hedge and replacing it with a park rail fence (paid for from the Gardens Fund), set much further out. Combined with some tree and shrub planting, this would link park and garden less obtrusively. This breakthrough, engineered with her usual gracious charm by Lady Emma, resulted in a much more constructive relationship over the garden between the family and the Trust, a perfect example of how the Panel can be effective.

Almost the only uncontested feature of the garden, and arguably its most delightful, is the wild flower bank facing south above the lake. True to form as an all-round naturalist, it was Malcolm Hutcheson who developed the concept, beginning in 1970 with a very ordinary grass bank on thin soil over limestone, the classic ingredients of a flowery meadow. He began by cutting only once a year and removing the 'hay' after leaving it for a week or so to shed seed. As the meadow quickly became impoverished, the cutting date was delayed further and further, well into September. The result has been a spectacular increase in the range and diversity of wild flowers, all of which have arrived without assistance, including several species of orchid. I have never seen so many Greater Butterfly Orchids in one place. In June it is the great glory of the place.

After decades of cutting late, in September after seeds have set, the wildflower meadow is now a textbook example including a wealth of species including many Greater Butterfly Orchids (foreground).

The house occupies a spectacular site overlooking the Menai Strait and across to Snowdonia; the less gardening the better in the foreground of a view like this! However, from a gardener's standpoint Plas Newydd enjoys the advantages of lime-free soil of unusual depth and quality, and a remarkably mild climate with a moderate rainfall, well spread through the year. Wind and sometimes salt spray are the main enemies but the scope for plants is almost as wide as anywhere in Britain, given shelter.

The garden does indeed contain a wide variety and quantity of plants and an unusual range of features accumulated over two centuries, overlying the remnants of a Repton park, now hard to detect. Each generation has had its say and the result is fascinating, if a little disjointed. The site is further complicated by the fact that a large part of it, including the lovely eighteenth-century stable block, had been sold for the establishment of an outdoor pursuits school, complete with accommodation blocks and playing fields. The need to co-operate with Cheshire County Council gave the National Trust initial problems with access and car parking, which were resolved by the vision of Elizabeth Chesterton, who arranged the comparatively long walk to the house as a potentially enjoyable experience. Following her lead we were able to provide visitors with a varied series of views, culminating in a panorama of Snowdonia. This involved approaching the house from the north-west, looking directly at the less than attractive service wing and yard. We soon overcame this by planting a screening copse of quick-growing,

A view from Plas Newydd across the Menai Strait to Snowdonia.

wind-resistant trees including field maples, willows and alders, with holm oaks for the long term and shrubs in the foreground.

The late Henry, Marquess of Anglesey, was a keen and knowledgeable gardener, whose distinctive taste was rightly and successfully reflected in the garden and its plants. Clear in his opinions but never dogmatic, he was always willing to be persuaded, although he never seemed to give you much time to do so! With a strong sense of humour and a mischievous look in his eye, he was always a pleasure to be with, even to disagree with. He was invariably generous towards the better proposals of the Gardens Advisers. A great deal has been accomplished in restoring, developing and integrating the garden's contrasting features and in effecting the difficult transition from private house to tourist destination, while minimising the impact as far as possible.

On the occasion of their wedding in 1948, the Marquess and Marchioness received a wedding present remarkable for its originality and generosity from Henry, 2nd Lord Aberconway, of nearby Bodnant. It consisted of several lorry loads of choice rhododendrons, a typically robust gesture, as challenging as it was imaginative. Henry Anglesey found the ideal site for a rhododendron garden in the woodland about half a mile from the house along the Strait, sufficiently far into the trees to be well sheltered. Uneven enough to give variety and watered by trickling streams, it had all the ingredients. Here Henry created a paradise for plants and garden lovers, and never stopped developing, extending and diversifying the range of plants. I know of no better garden of its kind, the site being so similar to its Himalayan and Chinese counterparts that the rare large-leafed rhododendrons liberally self-sow. It was always a pleasure and privilege to visit with the immensely enthusiastic Henry, and a relief not to need to give advice

When the Marquess and Marchioness were married in 1948, their wedding present from Lord Aberconway of Bodnant consisted of several lorry loads of choice rhododendrons which formed the basis of Henry Anglesey's outstanding woodland garden at Plas Newydd.

of any kind. Now that this garden is accessible by a footpath, it gives pleasure to thousands of visitors every year.

The only formal garden feature at Plas Newydd is the Italianate terrace garden north-east of the house, originally constructed before the First World War and much developed and used by the family in the 1920s and '30s. The derelict Edwardian conservatory had never been replaced and a series of ad hoc changes had resulted in a pleasant enough flower garden with trickling water and nice views, but it lacked any kind of clear identity. Henry was always uncharacteristically pessimistic, pointing out that the garden was in shade after noon and gloomy on dull days. Eventually we persuaded him that something positive could be done, and sufficient funds were located locally and from the Trust's Gardens Fund for refurbishment and replanting. The scheme was arrived at by discussion between Henry Anglesey, Christopher Rowell (Historic Buildings Representative), and the Gardens Advisers – Mike Calnan (my eventual successor as Head of Gardens) and me. Precise restoration was neither possible nor desirable, but we followed the general precedent by opting for an Italianate scheme which was drawn up by Mike. This involved a trellis garden house on the upper level with a little fountain bubbling over a tufa pyramid thick with ferns, which gave the garden a focus and a destination, being the water source. The rest of the garden was replanted to give it a more formal and distinctly Italianate effect with clipped evergreens, fastigiate conifers and a chain of little fountains and pools.

The terraced, Italianate garden always rather sadly lacked a central feature, but this deficiency was satisfactorily resolved by a trellis pavilion, housing a fountain bubbling over tufa rock.

We saw eye-to-eye on most things but Henry Anglesey came from a famous military family and was a distinguished and well-known military historian. Maybe it was this background that influenced his approach to planting, which was unsubtle to say the least: more like a vegetable parade ground with shrubs and trees in lines

('up in threes, tallest at the back, shortest at the front') army fashion, even in an otherwise informal area! Gradually we reached a compromise.

On the other hand, we were entirely as one on a major project involving the cankerous old orchard that was too big to maintain, rarely producing any crop of value or interest. From the start Henry was adamant that it should be grubbed out and replanted as an extension to the already extensive west pleasure ground called (no one seems to remember why) 'The West Indies'. I was in full agreement but unfortunately this coincided with one of the Trust's periodic belt-tightening exercises – extreme economy being the order of the day. The Gardens Advisers were given strict instructions to avoid any kind of extension to gardens. We nevertheless got on and cleared the site of about 1 ha (2.5 acres) as soon as possible, before the nature conservationists had time to find potentially significant populations of rare beetles or lichens.

The adjacent part of the West Indies happened to contain some *Eucalyptus* species, mostly planted by Henry, including the comparatively tender *E. dalrympeana* with its spectacularly handsome striped bark, which had grown exceptionally quickly in ideal conditions. With the Sino-Himalayan and Italian gardens already present, it then occurred to me that if we had a 'West Indies' we could logically have an Australasian garden to complete the set. Henry liked the idea but we still had the problem of the Trust's no-expansion edict. By now the area was down to grass as a temporary measure to restore the soil's structure and fertility. My next thought was that if the need for a shelterbelt were to be met by using eucalyptus, no one would suspect that the plantation was intended as a garden feature, at least for a decade or so, by which time the Trust's economic imperatives were bound to have changed. With the regional staff and Henry Anglesey in on this covert afforestation, we went on to plan a *Eucalyptus* plantation comprising groups of

The pleasure ground west of the house has always been called, for no known reason, the West Indies; full of choice trees and shrubs on this favoured site. Alongside it we added an ornamental plantation of *Eucalyptus* species and Australian flora we called Australasia.

nine or ten species carefully chosen for being uncommon, diverse, decorative (as far as we knew) and just hardy enough to grow well at Plas Newydd.

Eucalyptus ('gums' in Australia) are notoriously difficult to establish in a way that allows them to become firmly anchored, with proper buttress roots. They move badly as field-grown specimens, and when planted from pots they remain unstable because their roots always coil around the inside of the pot. The conventional wisdom involved planting them in their final positions in spring as seedlings, when only a few inches high, so that their roots could develop freely and they would have time to grow large enough to survive the following winter. Our plantation had to be simple and easy to maintain once established, so we chose a generous but realistic planting distance to allow the tractor-mower to get through. Military precision was needed in timing the sowings and organising the planting, each plant going into a sprayed-off circle and given a minimum of protection, the whole area having been rabbit-fenced in advance. Thanks to the attention to detail of Jim Marshall, the recently-appointed Gardens Adviser, and John Dennis, the head gardener, the job was carried out successfully, although it took two seasons to complete.

Everyone, including Henry Anglesey, was mystified by the rows of little canes and tiny plants, invisible at that stage amongst the grass, but mercifully they soon grew. In fact they romped away and within a few years we were able to begin some surreptitious additions of Australasian shrubs, mainly around the edges. My vision, having seen native gum forests, was to allow any trees that fell to stay and regrow irregularly as they do in nature, pruning and thinning only for access and effect. After thirty years the maturing 'Australasia' has exceeded all my expectations to become a novel feature amongst British gardens, popular for its ornamental value and for its horticultural interest, even if not to everyone's taste.

Features of this kind need to begin with a clear vision, compatible with and complementary to the rest of the garden. Then this vision needs to be pursued with unwavering consistency but sufficient flexibility to take account of unavoidable changes and unexpected opportunities. In the case of Plas Newydd, the original intention was loyally and sensitively carried through by John Dennis for three decades as the plantation matured, and was further embellished with Australasian plants. One unexpected bonus came partly through this continuity and partly through observant management. Except on the main pathway the grass was from the beginning cut once a year and removed, thereby impoverishing the ground. This is the classic approach to encouraging wild flower diversity, in this case much aided by the eucalypts which are surface-rooting and greedy. The result was masses of native orchids together with other interesting and beautiful wild flora.

SCOTNEY CASTLE

Lanning Roper took me to Scotney a couple of times in the 1970s to meet Betty Hussey and join him on his advisory visits. He had been advising there since the 1950s and had continued after Christopher Hussey died in 1970: always as much a friendly relationship as a professional arrangement. This continuity suited the purposes of the National Trust as well as being support for Mrs Hussey, who became ever more keen on the garden. Lanning was sensibly anticipating the time when he would no longer be able to advise. Sadly he died in 1983, aged 71, and was much missed by his wide circle of friends and professional contacts (mostly synonyms in his case). His life and work are well recorded in Jane Brown's book *Lanning Roper and His Gardens* (1987). An American garden designer living in London, he first became known as a journalist and garden writer, following *Successful Town Gardens* (1957) and frequent articles in *Country Life*, and from 1962 as gardening correspondent to *The Sunday Times*. In the 1960s and '70s he became a dominant influence in British gardens through his many commissions, especially from the country house set, who have always tended jointly to anoint a single guru at any one time, whether for interiors or for gardens. He was universally loved and widely respected for riding the post-war wave of flower gardening and developing a post-Jekyll style created first by Norah Lindsay in the 1930s. Like Hidcote and Sissinghurst, his gardens were well structured with profuse planting, pretty and soft in contrast to the endeavours of new-town landscape architects for whom garden design seemed synonymous with hard surfaces and

When Edward Hussey decided to build a house overlooking Scotney Castle with William Sawry Gilpin's help, he created this classic scene, an archetype of the Picturesque.

The ferocious storm of October 1987 seriously damaged Scotney and even this 300-year old lime was uprooted. But by pollarding the tree's main crown it was possible to drop the root plate back into its hole.

massed shrubby ground cover. Above all, Lanning was a man of great charm who showed genuine interest in people of all ranks, whatever their background or role.

Lanning Roper was very accomplished within the parameters of his adopted style, which was instantly recognisable, depending strongly on silver foliage and pastel colours. This kind of conspicuous overlay is entirely acceptable in an historic garden as part of the continuing history of the place when it arises out of the taste of the former owner. On the other hand, should such a garden pass into institutional ownership, more careful consideration would be required to justify this kind of stylistic innovation. None of this mattered at Scotney where, after 1970, Betty Hussey relied even more on 'dear Lanning' for help and advice in the garden. They became close friends, Lanning frequently staying at Scotney for as long as he cared, invariably getting involved in making breakfast, washing up and generally helping out. Betty lived very simply with a minimum of help, with meals in the little kitchen cooked on the Aga, usually something prepared earlier by her daily helper. Attempting in some degree to assume Lanning's role after his death was a challenge. Betty was formidable both in presence and manner, partly because she was inclined in conversation to seemingly forceful proclamations. This I discovered had been her way of overcoming a speech defect – a stammer that persisted, she said, until her eightieth birthday when she was miraculously cured! As a result she adopted a curious habit of rolling her Rs in an exaggerated way and I never see any of those big Himalayan roses in bloom without hearing her saying 'Rrrrrambling Rrrrrrector'.

From the start we got on well. Recognising the limitations of my role at Scotney, I genuinely enjoyed her company, soon being invited to stay, usually twice a year.

Betty was a considerate and undemanding hostess, who in her time had entertained many interesting people, mostly in the worlds of literature, journalism and art, presumably through Christopher Hussey's long period as architectural editor of *Country Life*. These included John Piper (there were two of his watercolours in the kitchen) and Osbert Lancaster (some of his original cartoons hung in the cloakroom). On my retirement I was deeply touched when the National Trust presented me with a limited-edition print of Scotney Castle by John Piper.

I enjoyed staying at Scotney, especially for the privilege and pleasure of experiencing early morning views across that incomparable Picturesque landscape. Christopher Hussey had written the definitive work *The Picturesque* (1927), but the concept of the Picturesque in relation to gardens was not widely understood, especially in terms of conservation, until Sophie Piebenga's work in the 1980s. We know that William Sawrey Gilpin played an important part in siting the 'new' house and assembling the elements of the Picturesque views, by recommending the abandonment of the Castle as a stabilised ruin, and using it and the rugged quarry as parts of the carefully-composed picture. However Gilpin seemed never to draw precise plans or to write comprehensive reports, relying instead on sketches, descriptions and discussion to convey his ideas, leaving the owner to interpret these principles on the ground. No doubt he recommended the groups

The indomitable spirit of Betty Hussey during and after the storm was matched by the pollarded lime, another veteran; see picture on p.139.

of Scots pine and the other key trees and evergreens that provide the dominant structure of the views and frame the 'pictures', but much was left to the client, in this case Christopher's grandfather Edward Hussey. He and his successors planted a rich assembly of the exotic species which were pouring in, many from North America, including the now huge groups of *Kalmia latifolia* and various conifers in addition to the native yews and Scots pines, the rugged character emphasised by ferns and wild flowers. Much admired by the nineteenth-century lovers of 'the sublime' and 'the beautiful', the effect has been progressively softened and tamed by subsequent additions and by the natural processes of growth and development, 'the beautiful' winning out.

Betty Hussey loved the garden dearly but seemed to take its origins and structure for granted (at least until the great storm), concentrating always on the smaller-scale elements which she and Christopher had developed with Lanning Roper, especially plantings in and around the ruin, including the herb garden and the borders of shrub roses. By the late 1970s the garden had come to dominate her life as she walked around it morning and evening, followed by her cat. She took a great interest in every detail but her main passion was for flowers and she would constantly acquire new plants, sometimes gifts but also purchases arising out of her visits to the Chelsea Flower Show, usually with Anne Scott-James. Many of these whimsical treasures were unsuitable for the landscape garden and had to be tactfully ushered into the walled garden or into the little rose garden near the house. She frequently changed her mind and often insisted on some sort of minor development at the expense of the bigger issues. All this was mildly frustrating for the head gardener, Allan Champion, an energetic man of action who relished the big jobs. However, these were minor issues compared with the need to sustain the remarkable enthusiasm and optimism Betty invariably showed in relation to the garden.

The fact that Scotney is an icon of the Picturesque (and what this might demand of our gardening priorities) would never enter into our discussions, although it was always in my mind and in the collective thoughts of the regional staff, who were based at Scotney. Betty easily held her own in any test of will, always confiding in me about the alleged shortcomings of the National Trust as her landlord as though, like Lanning Roper, I was an independent consultant. It was a tricky path to tread but one where the long-term interest of the place needed to take precedence over short-term considerations, always of course attempting to steer a course towards the Picturesque ideal.

The great storm of 1987 struck Scotney with great ferocity overnight and by the morning of 17 October the house was without power and isolated by more than a hundred trees falling across the main drive from Lamberhurst. Betty had retreated from her bedroom after the windows blew in. Having already survived cancer and more recently a broken leg, she took the storm in her stride, soon coming to terms with the trauma of fallen trees and general devastation. I was in Devonshire at the time and drove to Sussex and Kent within a day or two, gaining access to Scotney via the back drive across the park. Predictably, the garden was an almost impassable shambles with trees of all kinds, including 250-year-old limes, lying on their sides. In some cases we were able to pull them back and

In calmer years, before the storm, autumn colour was always a great feature of Scotney.

successfully replant their root plates (after first pollarding them), but most had to be laboriously extracted along with mountains of brushwood.

I feared for Betty but need not have worried. On my arrival I met her in the garden; she was full of enthusiasm, insisting on joining me on as full a tour of the garden as was possible, stepping or climbing over fallen trees in an alarming way. As resilient as ever, she talked of the wonderful opportunities the storm would give us for replanting and how, aged over 80, she was looking forward to the future and seeing the new developments. Indeed she did live on for almost a decade to enjoy seeing the garden's rebirth until she began to lose her memory; a lesson to us all.

It took me three or four visits to Mount Stewart to get the hang of the place. Not only is it huge – 31.5 ha (78 acres) of garden – but it is also unusually diverse in style and content. Graham Thomas, my predecessor, continued to advise there as consultant until the early 1980s and I joined him from time to time, when he would engage immediately with the work in hand – detailed discussions with the extraordinarily capable head gardener Nigel Marshall. Graham declared it to be one of the National Trust's greatest gardens and I soon came to agree; also that it is perhaps the all-round best in the whole of Ireland. Under the often grey sky, the grey-stone early nineteenth-century house seemed a little too sober for me, saved by the massive profusion of climbers and wall shrubs which threatened to engulf it. In every way the garden had been highly developed by Edith, 7th Marchioness of Londonderry, and is full of wonderful plants both in the complex of formal gardens and in the gloriously spacious pleasure ground, arranged spectacularly around a vast lake.

It was the iconography that foxed me – features and sculptures, clearly interesting in themselves, but how did they relate to one another and to the garden as a whole? There was the elaborate Italianate parterre after the Villa Farnese at Caprarola; the Mairi garden after the nursery rhyme; the sunken garden attributed to Gertrude Jekyll; the shamrock garden with its legendary Red Hand of Ulster; a series of weird cement animals and birds commemorating First World War officers who convalesced in the family's London home; 'Tir nan Og', the family's elaborate cemetery; everywhere there was something significant, each with a story attached. I believe it is essential to define the unique character of any garden in order to devise a valid plan for its long-term conservation and almost inevitable adaptation, e.g. from private garden to one open frequently to

With their monkey finials the pillars in the Italian Garden are a jokey reference to the garden of the Villa Farnese at Caprarola near Viterbo.

The mythical animals and birds, crafted locally out of cement, represent officers of the first world war who convalesced in the family's London home.

many visitors. Mount Stewart has several features and qualities of outstanding value – site, design, plant collection – but (being a slow thinker) I eventually came to understand that the garden's unique value relates to its complex symbolism, almost every part having a different meaning and origin, sometimes easily explained but often more subtle and needing research and sensitive conservation.

None of this bothered Graham Thomas, who had visited the garden while the 7th Marchioness of Londonderry was still alive and before the worst phase of its decline in the 1950s and early 1960s. From Graham's remarkable memory he had retained a picture. The general structure and spatial layout of the garden derive from the first half of the nineteenth century just after the house was built: evidently a landscape scheme taking advantage of its commanding site facing south over the Strangford Lough to the Mourne Hills in the distance – trees, shelter and lake around the house with the walled garden well away. Lady Londonderry took on the garden after the First World War while the 7th Marquess was deeply involved in Ulster politics. Like many people, her interest in gardening grew exponentially out of having acquired a garden, in her case a big one well endowed with lugubrious evergreens but otherwise horticulturally barren. On the other hand, after a century, the structure of trees – holm oaks, Scots pines and many conifers, and woodlands of beech, oak, sycamore and Douglas fir – was already in place. She must have soon realised that, despite a remarkably equable climate, wind is the main limiting factor in Irish gardens.

Mount Stewart sits behind a promontory that juts out irregularly into the tidal Strangford Lough, which is famous for its wildlife, particularly overwintering waterfowl. This little wooded promontory contained the family's private swimming pool, fed at high tide by sea water. It also provides vital shelter for the garden – miscellaneous plantings of alders, willows, poplars and conifers – bunged in wherever there was sufficient depth of soil above the brackish groundwater and protected by a makeshift sea wall of boulders. Severe storms in the late 1980s led to serious erosion, flooding and death of many of the most vulnerable trees.

Repair of the sea defences would be costly and there was pressure from environmentalists to adopt a policy of non-intervention – i.e. what they called 'managed retreat', which I soon learned meant in fact unmanaged surrender! While this may well have contributed some interesting local wildlife habitat, it would almost certainly have led to progressive deforestation of perhaps the whole peninsula and a radical reduction in shelter for this world-class garden. Blinkered vision of this kind is all too common in the world of wildlife conservation, however honourable the intention. The cause of 'the environment' in their terms has begun to lose its broader objectivity and become almost a religious cause, never to be questioned. Luckily Paul Kendrick, the managing agent at the time, to the credit of the Trust, took a more balanced approach and repaired the sea defences, at considerable cost.

Thanks to an outstandingly capable and energetic head gardener in Nigel Marshall, over a period of about fifteen years from the late 1960s Graham Thomas was able to mastermind a remarkable renovation in most of the elements that make up this outstanding garden, despite a very tight budget. This was Graham at his best, left without interference to negotiate the transformation of a garden that mostly suited his talents – plantsmanship, colour sense, observation, foresight, boldness and attention to detail. Without him it would have lost most, if not all, its distinctive character and richness of detail. The garden had been stagnating – on the one hand becoming overgrown with fast-growing evergreens and, on the other, losing features through neglect of decisive renewal or timely replacement.

Wanting a quick effect, Lady Londonderry had relied for her topiary on Monterey cypress, *Cupressus macrocarpa*, cheap and fast-growing but notorious for dying out after close clipping, the young shoots thus stimulated being frost- and wind-tender. All the complicated topiary of the shamrock garden was dead. This portrayed the gruesome legend of the Stuarts racing across the Irish Sea. The first person to reach land would claim ownership of Ulster; seeing the likelihood of narrow defeat the leader cut off his hand and threw it on shore to be first to touch land. Hence the 'red hand of Ulster', which is featured as a flower bed inside a hedged enclosure in the shape of a shamrock. Graham promoted and guided the removal and storage of the mostly dead topiary pieces with their wire frameworks, and the total replacement of the cypresses with yew hedging. In my time as adviser we went further and trained back the topiary figures, but at two-thirds rather than full size, both for practical reasons and for consideration of scale. Similarly, in the Spanish garden the *Cupressus macrocarpa* hedges and arches were replaced, in this case with the now ubiquitous Leyland cypress, a hybrid between *Cupressus macrocarpa* and *Chamaecyparis nootkatensis*, quick growing and fine-textured if kept clipped.

Luckily (he may not have agreed!) Graham did not operate entirely without constraint other than cost. Lady Mairi Bury, daughter of Lord and Lady Bury, for whom the Mairi garden was named (her pram was parked there when she was a baby) continued to live in the house for much of each year, alternating with her house in Venice (what a life!). She took a deep, if passive, interest in the garden and of course remembered it well, even though her memory was probably coloured favourably by nostalgia for an idyllic childhood. In the convoluted fashion of

The Italian Garden parterre was a riot of exotic plants, strong colours on the east side, cooler tones on the west.

Northern Irish life, the garden had been transferred to the National Trust in 1955 through the Ulster Land Fund, separately from the estate and house, which remained with its contents in Lady Mairi's ownership until she eventually gave the house to the Trust in 1976. This illogical state of affairs was nevertheless made to work throughout the delicate negotiations that led eventually to the Trust's acquisition, and thereafter as Lady Mairi continued her plenteously smooth and seemingly untroubled occupation. As far as I am aware she never walked in the garden, her excursions being mainly limited to driving around the lake in her big old Rover car.

Early on in the restoration Graham Thomas would sometimes stay in the house, the sort of thing he enjoyed, but he found it a distraction from his incredible schedule. At Mount Stewart this involved spending the whole of two days in the garden, advising and discussing, taking detailed notes. After tea he would settle down and write his report (in longhand of course) with detailed recommendations of fellings, prunings, plantings, etc. There was a top copy for the managing agent and a carbon copy for the head gardener if approved. He would keep up this astonishing work rate for weeks at a time. Except for detailed work, only firm decisions (as he recalled them!) were recorded following discussion with all concerned; also with Lady Mairi for conspicuous proposals. In a climate as favourable as that at Mount Stewart, twenty years without decisive management results in a garden with overgrown vistas, trees blocking light, the absence of any young replacements to provide shelter, etc. Understandably, Lady Mairi, who had grown accustomed to decline by degrees over time, found it difficult to appreciate the need for radical change, especially tree fellings to admit light and give space for replanting. While this attitude to the garden is not uncommon among long-standing donors and family residents of Trust houses, it seemed more acute with Lady Mairi, who always seemed to enjoy living in an environment of unrelieved gloom with climbers and wall shrubs shutting out light, the sun hardly ever seeming to penetrate, even on the comparatively rare bright days of summer. Although sometimes frustrating for Graham (and later for me), this need to convince and to listen was always a good discipline for sometimes over-eager advisers, however right and logical their proposals.

If Graham had a failing (he would admit none!), it was that he was inclined to overdesign and overcomplicate where a simple solution was called for. The Shamrock Garden was a case in point. It had been laid out by Edith, Lady Londonderry, with the giant 'Red Hand' set in crazy paving, which does not ever seem to have been a success, being poor in quality and inclined to break up and become dangerously uneven – probably laid by locally unemployed labour in the early 1920s. The obvious alternative was gravel (beach), but rather than set out the 'hand' with a stone edge at its original size, Graham was intent on setting it at a much smaller scale within a shamrock-shaped area of crazy paving, and he ultimately got his way. The intention of emphasising the 'shamrock' intention, which is difficult at first to grasp from the shamrock shape of the outer hedges, was sound, but the result was altogether out of scale, overworked and unsubtle. After I took over advising, the hand was quietly converted to its original scale set simply in gravel. Lady Mairi never liked Graham's scheme, and she was right.

Due to the protracted nature of the acquisition, and the contents of the house remaining firmly in the hands of Lady Mairi, there was never anything approaching a full archive, the records being pieced together gradually, mainly after the early 1980s when I took over advising. My visits (if Lady Mairi was in residence) followed a pattern, which began with listening to her concerns, usually about tree work, and suggestions, usually about something unsuitable she had seen on the television and thought would be nice to have around the lake. She would

The extensive pleasure ground is full of rhododendrons and other choice trees and shrubs, many from seeds collected in the wild, often unique forms of rare species.

Geranium clarkei
'Mount Stewart'.

emerge in the gloom from a deep armchair with her little list and we would invariably have a very agreeable and interesting chat. Her defence against new proposals and any hint of change was to invoke the memory of her mother who 'would not have liked that'. She had an uncanny knack of producing photograph albums to support her view, a different one each time. Unfortunately she did not take kindly to Peter Marlow, the mild and charming Historic Buildings Representative (art historian), and it was some years before the Trust was able to borrow, catalogue and copy this important part of the archive. Every time she opened one of the albums it would spark memories as she showed me innumerable snaps of family holidays, excursions and events in the 1920s and '30s, between which there were pictures of the garden, usually associated with a special event. There was a small landing strip at Mount Stewart and Lady Mairi said she had had a licence to fly in the 1930s. She also told me about a flying visit from the German Foreign Minister Ribbentrop in 1938, presumably to hold discussions with her father and others as part of Hitler's scheme for a negotiated settlement aimed at preventing Britain becoming involved in any war in Europe.

Of even greater significance at Mount Stewart is the remarkable plant collection assembled by Lady Londonderry with increasing intensity as her plant knowledge increased. No doubt she learned by experience what a remarkably wide range of plants could be grown, and became increasingly bolder in her use of semi-tender plants, especially from South America, Australia, New Zealand and South Africa, as well as from China and the Himalaya. Despite being so far north, thanks to its position and to the Gulf Stream, the garden enjoys a uniquely even climate with comparatively little change from summer to winter, and with annually sufficient rainfall well spread out over the year. 'In winter the weather is mild and damp and in summer the weather is … mild and damp!'

Evidently, Lady Londonderry's enthusiasm for rare exotics developed quickly and she subscribed to many plant and seed-collecting expeditions in the 1920s and '30s, as well as obtaining plants through her high-level social circle throughout Great Britain. This was almost entirely different from that of Hugh Armytage Moore of Rowallane, less than twenty miles away in Co. Down. Eventually full catalogues of the plants in each garden revealed a very small overlap of less than 10 per cent, which is a credit to the National Trust after almost half a century of its ownership of both.

Michael Lear's diligent cataloguing and identification of the late 1980s was a turning point in plant conservation, both at Mount Stewart and probably throughout the Trust. Other than Bodnant, no other garden contains such unappreciated riches and botanical diversity. Because it contains so many separate introductions, genetic diversity has been found to be unsurpassed not only between species but also within species. This is of great scientific as well as aesthetic value now that natural habitat has become further degraded. As evidence of this kind is gathered, the Trust is perhaps at last beginning to understand that its collections of exotic plants represent at least as much value and meaning as the artworks and chattels of its houses or the wildlife and habitat of its open space properties.

KNIGHTSHAYES
DEVON

While in a sense all gardens constantly have to be made and remade if they are to survive, Knightshayes is unique in having been acquired by the National Trust while the donors were still creating the garden. Sir John and Lady Heathcoat-Amory took to gardening with great enthusiasm after the Second World War, and who would not on this gloriously breezy, fertile and frost-free site, with a structure of fine trees and hedges already in place from a century earlier? Luckily they began a decade or more before the Garden History Society was founded and a generation before the restoration of Biddulph Grange rekindled interest in Edward Kemp, who designed the 1870s garden at Knightshayes to complement Wiliam Burges's Gothic-style house. His garden was a formal layout of terraces with a flamboyant flower parterre in the foreground and hedged compartments east of the house. One of these, originally a bowling green, now contains the garden's iconic feature: a simple design of a circular lily pool, with a little statue, a carefully pruned weeping silver pear and two stone seats, an eloquent expression of disciplined English understatement best appreciated from a viewpoint above. This combination of restraint and exuberance continues around the skeleton of Kemp's parterre and now supplants his gorgeous colour, leaving the glorious view uncluttered. The whole of Kemp's formal scheme was converted

The pool garden created out of Edward Kemp's yew-hedged bowling green with irises, water lilies and a weeping silver pear.

One of Edward Kemp's yew-hedged enclosures was converted by the Heathcoat-Amorys into a formal set-piece containing small shrubs and choice alpines.

by the Heathcoat-Amorys to their distinctive taste, a discriminating plantsmanship that inspired a generation of gardeners and garden designers. It is tempting to speculate what would have been the reaction of English Heritage if the Heathcoat-Amorys were to have begun thirty years later to transform the work of such an important figure of nineteenth-century garden design?

However, the supreme achievement at Knightshayes was the 'Garden in the Wood' (never 'woodland garden'), created by thinning Kemp's one-hundred-year-old mixed woodland and progressively planting a huge collection of plants sensitively arranged according to the varied habitat thus provided. The idea arose out of gale

Lady Amory with John Sales on a regular gardens advisory visit in the 'Garden in the Wood'. Lady Amory (1901–97), under her maiden name Joyce Wethered, had had a celebrated career as a prize-winning golfer (English Ladies' champion for five consecutive years).

damage which revealed opportunities, a characteristic example of the way the British are inclined to go about garden-making – a combination of opportunism and inspiration. The gale damage of the mid-twentieth century was not only a key to realising the garden's potential but also a strong hint about the challenge for its long-term conservation. Single-age plantations like the garden wood at Knights-hayes are notoriously vulnerable but it is often difficult to convince people of their immediate responsibility to continue to find space for long-term structural tree planting. Such was the case at Knightshayes where planting was confined almost entirely to ornamental exotics until the late 1980s, although shelter planting was begun earlier below the garden.

Part of the 'Garden in the Wood' inspired by Sir Eric Savill's Savill Garden at Windsor: Japanese azaleas.

Graham Thomas, my predecessor, visited Knightshayes regularly from the mid-1950s, around the time he became the Trust's Gardens Adviser. As such, he was a consistent presence in the continuing development of the garden and parkland before and after they were given to the Trust in 1973, and up until I took over advising in the 1980s, well after the death of Sir John. My initial priority was to learn and record as much as possible from Lady Amory about the origins of their joint ideas for the garden and, as tactfully as possible, about the people and places that had most influenced their choice of plants and style of planting. In recording history, particularly garden history, there is no better way than to interrogate the main players, who so often in the past have gone to the grave without passing on any record of their motives, ideals, assumptions and constraints. Although reserved by nature, Lady Amory was always openly charming and ready to respond to my probing questions from her excellent memory of people and events. I was able to compile a useful list of the people involved but it was more difficult to assess their respective degree of influence. Of these Sir Eric Savill was obviously a key figure and Lanning Roper and Graham Thomas clearly influenced the early layout. As well as Graham Thomas, plantsmen included

Gentiana asclepiadea 'Knightshayes'.

Lionel Fortescue, Norman Hadden, Margery Fish and Nellie Britton who had an alpine nursery in Tiverton. The idea for using peat block walls to edge the beds, hardly politically correct these days, came from a visit to Branklyn in Scotland.

Graham used to enjoy his visits to Knightshayes hugely, and often proudly related the fact that his little car would be whisked away on arrival to be washed and valeted in time for his departure. He also loved staying overnight in the house while it still conformed to the Heathcoat-Amorys' taste and before it was restored to its Burges- and Crace-inspired Victorian splendour by Hugh Mellor for opening to visitors. While he had an excellent detailed memory for plants and generally for the development of the garden, Graham was not a good source of information on people, other than himself, who may have influenced the Heathcoat-Amorys, being usually reluctant to give credit to others in his peer group if he saw them in any way as competitors.

The steep bank behind the stone seat is furnished with Pfitzer juniper, now *Juniperus x pfitzeriana* 'Wilhelm Pfitzer'.

The Heathcoat-Amorys' long-serving head gardener, Michael Hickson, was recruited from Lionel Fortescue, creator of the well-known plantsman's garden at The Garden House, Buckland Monachorum, and became a close confidante and collaborator in everything to do with the garden and its development. Indeed, there is even one part of the garden in the wood that is named after him. An outstanding plantsman, Michael had a great influence on the garden's planting and was responsible for the establishment of the plant nursery in part of the walled garden. This supplied plants for sale and made a firm reputation as a source of uncommon plants at a time when nursery lists were shrinking and becoming

A shady border in the 'Garden in the Wood' with white foxgloves and greenish-yellow spurges.

more specialised. He has been an important element of continuity in passing on the Heathcoat-Amorys' way of gardening, especially after the death of Lady Amory. The 'Garden in the Wood' depends much on attention to detail – timely pruning, thinning and constant reworking to keep it fresh and free of aggressive colonising plants which spread quickly in the ideal conditions, gradually propelling the garden towards the commonplace. Lady Amory was acutely aware of this danger, for example of bluebells taking over. All too quickly gardens can become stale and cluttered if not constantly reworked and renewed.

Towards the end of her life Lady Amory lived in the east wing of the house while the main part was open to visitors. She continued into her nineties to take a welcome and critical interest, based on a tour of the garden in her electric buggy almost every day. On my advisory visits she would invariably have real issues to discuss, frequently expressing her frustration at not being able to carry out the tasks she thought overdue. Nor was she content with the status quo; the formal scheme on the wide border in front of the east wing was a product of this time. She said correctly that it had formerly lacked structure and eventually came up with the germ of an idea for a regular pattern of low hedges and topiary at the front, which she insisted must be of yew. After a good deal of discussion with all involved, we adopted a pattern derived from the reticulate tracery of Burges's Gothic fenestration to contain a pattern of low plants. Using yew was difficult but the outcome proved effective once the complex linear design had been established and an arrangement of plants of contrasting shape had been placed.

I was always acutely aware of the Trust's responsibility for conserving its huge plant collection. Taking all its gardens together, the Trust owns the greatest assembly of cultivated plants in the world. There had been no attempt to tackle the daunting task of cataloguing this unique collection and it did not even figure in the Trust's priorities in the 1970s. Whereas the Trust was meticulous in cataloguing and conserving the contents of houses and even the garden ornaments, it was unable to find funds even to begin listing and researching its garden plants, their rarity, sources, associations – an important national resource. We were able however to make a start with trees in twenty or so gardens, thanks to grants engineered by Lord Rosse from the Thomas Phillips Price Trust, through the Royal Botanic Gardens Kew. However, the National Trust had no nursery with the skills, resources and capacity for propagating its rare and unique plants, or for raising and growing on seeds and plants collected in the wild or from other known sources.

Eventually, with the encouragement of John Gaze, the Trust's Chief Agent, in the early 1980s, we were able to draw a small annual grant from the Gardens Fund for setting up a central nursery by adding to the existing facilities at Knightshayes. This was organised initially by Michael Hickson and proved its value as a source of new planting, especially at the time of the storms of 1987 and 1990 when so many rare trees fell and needed emergency propagation to save their unique genetic characteristics. Although inadequate to the task, the nursery carried on providing the Trust with special plants for twenty years or so until the Trust at last began to take plant cataloguing seriously and epidemic plant diseases, particularly *Phytopthora spp.*, made it necessary to establish a separate nursery with strict control of plant health.

Knightshayes now has a working kitchen garden, empty in the Heathcoat-Amorys' time, which fills a disappointing vacuum and completes the Victorian scheme. This has been an almost miraculous achievement and a credit to all involved. Values change but it should not be forgotten that, like the house, it was not the main reason for the Trust's acquisition. Nothing should be allowed to divert attention from maintaining exemplary standards of care and conservation in the garden bequeathed by the Heathcoat-Amorys, which ranks high among twentieth-century gardens of Britain and Europe.

Chapter 4

PROGRESSIVE RENEWAL

The valley and
stream below
the house
at Cragside,
showing Lord
Armstrong's
elegant
footbridge and
some of the
impressive
North American
conifers in the
pleasure ground.

As a family we used to visit Packwood in the 1960s when on holiday in the Cotswolds. We all enjoyed its romantic setting, eighteenth-century brick walls, gazebos and bee-boles, but most of all we were taken with the intriguing yew garden, which is supposed to represent the Sermon on the Mount. I was also impressed by the quality and impact of the flower borders, which were wonderfully flamboyant and not at all according to Gertrude Jekyll. They could be described as horticultural bling – great regiments of colour, predominantly yellow and orange – and a slight embarrassment to the National Trust's aesthetes, I guess. This was evidently according to the taste of Graham Baron Ash, son of a rich industrialist who gave him Packwood in 1905. Baron Ash devoted thirty-five years and his fortune to restoring it before presenting it to the National Trust, one of its earliest house and garden acquisitions.

My guess is that Baron Ash was interested principally in the house and its contents, together with the garden buildings – he reconstructed one of the corner gazebos – and was probably guided by his head gardener in the flower garden. After I joined the Trust and began to advise at Packwood, I realised that those unfashionable flower borders were intact survivals of a pre-Jekyll repetitively mingled style, consisting of single plants or small groups repeated along the border, graded evenly for height from front to back. This had been presumably passed down by gardening tradition from head gardener to head gardener and eventually to Mr E.D. Lindup (I never knew his first name).* Until his retirement in the late 1970s he was one of the Trust's first head gardeners and a great exponent of this then scarcely known or understood style. I have little doubt now that this kind of border was developed from the graduated arrangements of the late eighteenth century, illustrated by Mark Laird in his book *The Flowering of the English Landscape* (1999), Packwood being a rare survival. Significantly, the style was preserved not by attempting to freeze it but by constant repetition, as with a folk tune. The borders were regularly lifted, divided, manured and replanted, no doubt adjusting and supplementing the layout according to experience but always with the same ideal in mind. Success with sequential display was achieved by constant dead-heading and cutting back after flowering, in order to make space for vigorous neighbouring plants. The style lends a strong sense of unity to each border and is suitable for gardens of modest size, where repetition would not be in danger of becoming tedious.

While advising at Packwood in the 1960s, Graham Thomas wisely respected this traditional system, though it certainly was not to his taste. To my knowledge, he would not have fully appreciated its origins. He was content to avoid disturbing Mr Lindup's well-honed management regime which was of a very high standard, although there was only one assistant gardener. Predictably, this expert gardening was much admired by most visitors, if not always by some in the Trust. The sunk garden was made in the 1930s and Graham remembered Baron Ash buying the yew hedging from T. Hilling (the nursery where he then worked). It

* I can now confirm that his name was Dennis Lindup.

ABOVE The main garden court seen from the terrace with the house and associated buildings beyond. (2005)

Flanking the gates to the entrance court, the borders illustrate the planting tradition at Packwood since the 19th century, consisting of repeated small groups and single plants graded front to back. (1985)

was traditionally bedded out but Graham was responsible for introducing the herbaceous layout to save work. My minor contribution was the rose border with clipped yew buttresses against the roadside wall facing west.

Until I joined the Trust and was sent to advise at Packwood the origin of the wonderfully evocative topiary garden of clipped yews was accepted unquestionably as being a Carolean representation of the Sermon on the Mount, on the basis of a statement in Reginald Blomfield's *The Formal Garden in England* (1892), which described the 'multitude walk' of yew topiary, the terrace with its twelve Apostles and four Evangelists and the Mount with the 'Master' yew on top. I was obliged

LEFT Double borders on the terrace planted in mingled style, graded from front to back. (c.1985)

ABOVE A pair of new borders in the main flower garden, replacing some grassed over, presumably for economy.

to look more closely at the yew garden because some of the yews were unhealthy and others has already been replaced owing to their dying out. It seemed obvious from careful inspection that the twelve terrace yews are much older than the rest, dating probably from before the middle of the eighteenth century. The 'multitude' of yews is much younger and the 'Master' seemed by far the youngest of them all. A series of old maps exists in the house showing no sign of yews before 1756, when they appeared only on the terrace (i.e. the 'Apostles'?). Nineteenth-century photographs show an orchard where the 'multitude' now stands.

Looked at historically, the garden layout at Packwood is perhaps typical of the time after the Restoration when it was owned by John Fetherston, whose father remodelled the timber-framed house. It consisted of a walled flower garden near the house, beyond that a formal orchard rising to a terrace and then to a spiral mount for views out. The nineteenth-century orchard was presumably a replacement for the original, which would have had to be replaced after a century, with small clipped yews lining the four-square paths, exactly along the lines of the existing ones. By the end of the nineteenth century this second generation orchard would have been over-mature and when the fruit trees were removed the clipped yews, now larger, were evidently retained.

In his book *The Renaissance Garden in England*, Sir Roy Strong states confidently that while Packwood is 'in fact, a mid-Victorian re-creation of a Mannerist garden from before the Civil War', he includes it because 'this re-creation seems to capture the atmosphere of this type of religious emblematic horticulture … At Packwood we move in the world of the early Stuart symbolic garden …' Atmosphere is a matter of perception but evidence for this particular symbolism seems to stem entirely from a the yarn spun to Blomfield 'by the old gardener, who was pleaching the pinnacle of the temple', to lend the garden greater significance. No doubt he planted the 'Master' yew and would be delighted that his homespun legend has been accepted so readily – one up to the gardeners I say!

The problem with some of the yews (in summer) was diagnosed by Pershore College as 'water stress', and they recommended stripping off all the turf to reduce competition: clearly an unacceptable course of action at Packwood, where the soil and subsoil consist of heavy clay. Yews are notoriously susceptible to waterlogging. My hypothesis was that the reason for the water stress in summer was because the root systems were frequently damaged by winter waterlogging, making them shallow and susceptible to trampling, drought and grass competition. The answer lay in land drainage for the site as a whole and for each yew tree, together with spiking to aerate the topsoil and replanting on slight mounds to keep the crowns of the trees well drained. The outcome was eventually positive but slow and erratic.

The box hedges around the Yew Garden seen from the new orchard have been turned into living sculptures by many generations of clipping.

On this low-lying site and heavy soil, elm was the dominant tree, completely wiped out in the 1970s. Taking the hint from trees that were successful locally, we chose Turkey oak as a very hardy, quick-growing and wind-resistant tree for the main roadside avenue. It proved highly successful for the purpose but unpopular with nature conservationists because it turns out to be an alternative host to a gall which renders common oak acorns sterile, thereby preventing natural regeneration of oak in semi-natural woodland – luckily not a major problem in the area.

I was always keen to plant trees for shade, shelter, ornament and continuity. We found suitable sites for several in the car park across the road from the house – limes, Norway maple and Scots pine.

The Carolean mount at Packwood is a particularly good example of its kind but in the 1970s was in urgent need of renovation. Its spiral path was badly eroded; the clipped box covering the steep banks looked starved and was full of gaps, through which many visiting children would disappear to play wonderful games and make matters worse. We decided on total closure for a couple of years while the erosion was being repaired and a new generation of box was re-established densely overall. It was a major job but allowed us to provide robust protection for the roots and stem of the 'Master' yew which was suffering badly from trampling and 'person abrasion'. To deter the very tempting short cuts through the box we planted our secret weapon: butchers' broom, which is evergreen, tough, prickly and virtually indestructible even in dense shade – i.e. childproof. What spoil-sports we gardeners are!

A recent view of the Yew Garden. The second yew on the left, a replacement, is almost certainly *Taxus* x *media* 'Hicksii', an American-raised hybrid of great vigour and hardiness, coarser in texture than the native species but widely sold as common yew.

In 1938 Charles Barry's great house was demolished, thereby tearing the heart out of Clumber's park and its huge estate. Much remained, including an elaborate stable block, a 1.6 ha (4 acre) walled garden and, most strikingly, G.F. Bodley's 1880s Gothic chapel, big enough for any village community, which has now assumed the role of focal point. However, the void remains where the house should be and no historicist evocation of the past will suffice, other than to draw attention to its absence. I am convinced that only an imaginative innovation on a scale bold enough to match the surroundings will do.

By the 1970s the bones of a magnificent eighteenth-century park and estate were still easy enough to discern but the effects of decades of inadequate management were even more obvious. The National Trust had accepted this huge estate of the Dukes of Newcastle, bought by public subscription after the war. Joint management, including funding, was agreed with a consortium of local authorities, who rightly saw it as a precious local resource for recreation and conservation. The arrangement soon proved cumbersome and ineffective, and the local authorities were progressively less able to meet their obligations. Eventually, in 1980 the Trust assumed control but funding remained desperately tight, the local authorities' contribution having been withdrawn.

The famous lime avenue through Clumber Park, bordering the main drive from the entrance gates.

On my first visit in 1971, the famous three-mile lime avenue from the grand Apley Head entrance impressed me deeply but thereafter the experience declined. The house site and lakeside were wholly depressing, incorporating all the worst effects

of anarchic car parking, serious erosion and pathetically inadequate attempts at managing the many thousands of car-borne people who visited free at weekends. At that time the local authorities would not hear of any kind of charge, even for car parking, so there was no income and much expense.

Under management by the able and doggedly determined Regional Director, John Gaze, the place was taken in hand and, step by step, improved steadily in every way – car parking, visitor facilities, conservation, interpretation and security. He lived on site in the former parsonage, securely defended by a high fence against vandals and thieves. Along with mining subsidence, a hostile climate, poor soil and hopelessly inadequate resources, these were the principal challenges at Clumber in the 1970s: daunting by any standard. The place was also overrun by huge itinerant flocks of Canada Geese which consumed every blade of grass and left their offerings everywhere. But Clumber is an irresistible honeypot for people living in Worksop, Sheffield and Rotherham looking for somewhere to go at the weekend to sit in the sun or feed the geese.

Against much opposition, John Gaze gradually moved the cars away from the lakeside, and we were able to grass over or plant the squalid areas of eroded gravel, while providing congenial places for pedestrians to reach the lake edge. Income was raised by a shop and restaurant but not until 1980, when the Trust took full management control, was it possible to charge for entry to these popular parts of the park. Most of it remained free, the lime avenue bordering a public highway. As well as raising useful income, gate control improved security and made it possible to recruit members to the National Trust, who would thereafter be admitted free of charge. Slowly, as the place became more inviting and civilised, it also became more evenly populated, as visitors spread out from the sad-looking house site to enjoy Clumber's many pleasures.

The handsome classical bridge over the lake is a survivor of a great 18th-century landscape scheme covering more than 1500 ha (3,700 acres) created for the Dukes of Newcastle.

The great walled garden was totally abandoned but the Trust had managed to keep the walls in a reasonable state of repair. I regretted the clearance of the derelict melon yard. However, the impressive lean-to greenhouse range, which spanned the whole breadth of the main walled enclosure, with vineries and palm house on the verge of collapse, was saved by John Gaze, who successfully claimed compensation for mining subsidence. It was restored to working order apart from its heating system. However, there was only one gardener for the whole site of 10.5 ha (26 acres). Nothing concentrates the mind as much as poverty of resources on this scale.

Nowadays conventional professional wisdom dictates the immediate commissioning of a conservation/management plan, based upon a full assessment of the special qualities and significance of the whole place. This is fine in principle but in the 1970s it would have cost probably more than the Trust's entire budget for the property for several years. Furthermore, this approach would have involved researching the complete history of the landscape and garden, before looking more specifically at the estate's biology, archaeology, hydrology, etc.; indeed the range and extent of survey and research now required begins to look more and more like a recipe for delay rather than a call to action. It is perfectly possible and often necessary to take action without knowing everything about the place (if indeed that is ever possible), even though this is not ideal and prone to the occasional mistake. The simple principle here should be that the less you know, the more cautious you need to be especially with irreversible decisions like demolition and tree felling.

Most of the important historic gardens and great estates that have survived perfectly well for many years, even centuries, have done so without conservation plans. With these, each successive generation will have respected past achievements and provided continuity for the traditions of the place to be upheld while making their own mark. As with any impoverished owner, when resources are at the absolute minimum, as at Clumber Park in the 1970s, priority needs to be given to preventing further loss, to repairing progressive damage and concentrating renewal where it may be repaid with increased income and better morale.

It is vital to provide staff with a sense of progress, however gradual; they need to be motivated by a succession of challenges that they are capable of sustaining.

Luckily the Trust's gardener-in-charge at Clumber was Brian Wilde, a no-nonsense, down-to-earth, practical East Midlander who got on with it without complaint. As well as doing his bit he said his bit, keeping his end up admirably in competing for scarce resources.

This was our approach during those pioneering days at Clumber Park. The extensive Gilpin-style pleasure ground contained many fine trees and the pattern of informal spaces had generally survived. However, much of the detail had been lost or had become smothered by the steady progress of *Rhododendron ponticum*, probably never planted as such, most likely having developed from suckers where it was used as a rootstock for grafted cultivars. Hardy and successful on the poor acid soil at Clumber, this ubiquitous evergreen had spread everywhere by layering and seed. Since it was the main source of shelter, and undeniably beautiful in flower, the only sensible approach was to manage the *ponticum* with a view to its long-term replacement. We were able to recruit a variety of unskilled help for Brian, either as volunteers or more often from government schemes for unemployment relief. This made it possible, stage by stage, to take in and roughly renovate most of the pleasure ground. More difficult was to begin to establish trees and shrubs for ornament and greater diversity. Most of the early plantings were stolen, often within hours of being planted, so we established a small nursery, well protected from deer, rabbits and people. To foil the thieves, our approach was to plant larger plants through shallowly-buried wire netting to which the shrubs would be attached. For large shrubs this proved reasonably effective, and as the place began to look more cared-for, vandalism and theft gradually decreased.

On such a bleak, windswept site and on such poor soil, widening the range and restoring diversity was a challenge and we had to choose trees carefully. As well as establishing successors for the key trees like Lebanon, Atlas and incense cedars, we chose species and cultivars of *Sorbus* – mountain ash and whitebeams – to provide a variety of foliage and autumn colour from leaves and fruits. Every new tree represented a struggle in the face of the climate, the wildlife and the vandals, but success was cumulative and rewarding: what a contrast with Stourhead or Studley Royal!

After two centuries the northern belt, which encloses and shelters the pleasure ground, was over-mature with overgrown yews, some in danger of collapse, others too leggy to give effective shelter at human level; the wind whistled through. Furthermore, there had been no attempt at creating space for a new generation of large forest trees to replace in time the old oaks and big pines. This prompted a major clearance and pruning, leaving the best yews and cutting others back hard to let in light, encourage regrowth and allow replanting. We turned this into a woodland walk, with a variety of smaller trees and shrubs, as well as trees of the ultimately large species.

From time to time on advisory visits I had noticed a large, mature holly with yellow berries growing in what seems to have been the laundry yard of the great house. I had commented on it to Brian Wilde but only gradually did it dawn on us

This avenue of Atlas Cedars was planted to provide a grand, formal carriage route from the house (now demolished) to the walled garden. (c.1985)

that it might be something special. On inspection it clearly belonged to a grex of vigorous hybrid hollies, *Ilex × altaclarensis*, named after Highclere (of Downton Abbey fame), where the cross was first made. I did not know of a yellow-berried Highclere holly and arranged for it to be seen by the queen of hollies, Susyn Andrews, an expert taxonomist, who confirmed its singular pedigree. We had it propagated and planted in the garden and elsewhere in the Trust, but it was not until 2002 that I was able to take it to a flower show at Vincent Square where the Royal Horticultural Society conferred on it an Award of Merit as *Ilex × altaclerensis* 'Clumber Park' (see p.2).

Walled gardens are notoriously labour-intensive but the one at Clumber is probably the grandest in the National Trust. It deserved to be seen even when it contained nothing but rough-mown grass – four acres divided into linked enclosures with 'slips' and a gardeners' bothy alongside. Overlooking all this was the well-appointed house from which the head gardener, in the garden's heyday, presided over twenty-eight gardeners, three-quarters of whom worked in the walled garden. With no foreseeable prospect of restoration, our policy was to make use of the restored greenhouse range, in which we housed a collection of old garden tools and equipment, along with replanted vines and figs. By the early 1980s we could afford to do some planting to give a flavour of the original – after forty years to bring back some productivity.

On the one hand it was essential not to be overambitious, but on the other it was necessary to have a clear concept of possible future development. However limited, restoration needed both to respect precedent and to be part of a possible longer-term programme of renewal. Accordingly, we began to revive the grand formal approach to the walled garden via a remarkable avenue of Atlas cedars from the pleasure ground and chapel. In the main part of the walled garden we decided to leave space for restoring the massive double herbaceous borders that formed part of this ceremonial route with the Palm House as its goal. To give some sense of structure, the gravel paths were restored and a simple pattern of fruit trees planted in the quarters furthest from the impressive greenhouse range, so as to avoid screening it. The quarters nearest the greenhouses were further subdivided and reserved for growing vegetables, soft fruits and cut flowers. Gradually this skeleton was fleshed out – cultivated, planted and cared for – to restore at last some sense of the traditional purpose of the walled garden.

With increased resources the Trust was able eventually to expand the garden staff modestly and to deploy more and more volunteers, under the inspiring guidance of Neil Porteus who really brought the whole place back to life and recreated a flourishing kitchen garden. He went on to become a Gardens Adviser for the Trust and then to work in Ireland: a great talent.

The huge, double herbaceous borders through the walled garden have been replanted by the National Trust. They lead to the restored palm house and vinery range of greenhouses.

I began my education in Cornish gardening at Trelissick, meeting the legendary head gardener, Jack Lilly, at Truro railway station early one spring morning, after travelling overnight via London. Whilst not delighted to be getting up extra early, Jack treated this aspiring Gardens Adviser kindly; straight home to Trelissick for a full Cornish–English breakfast. Jack was an old-style head gardener, worldly-wise and slightly mischievous, who manipulated the Trust's presence with good humour and tactful acquiescence. As a manager his approach was pre-war authoritarian in style, but effective: both he and the garden received a lot of uncritical praise, perhaps too much for the good of the head gardener. But he had the ear of the all-powerful Regional Director Michael Trinick, who took a great personal interest in 'his' gardens and trusted Jack. Importantly, the garden always looked well and Jack was a good plantsman in the Cornish mould. This regional (some would say Cornish national) freemasonry of rival head gardeners watched one another like hawks and competed ferociously at the annual Cornish Garden Society spring shows.

At the time my experience of Cornish gardening was nil and my knowledge of rhododendrons confined mostly to those I had seen as a student at Kew. I was not prepared for the almost wholly different set of tender, locally-raised cultivars (I remember especially 'Gwillt King', glorious in the morning sun), including the 'Penjerrick' cultivar and a vast range of rare and unusual species and their forms. I was out of my depth and Jack Lilly knew it, tolerantly helping out but characteristically storing up a few quips to embarrass me later. He did not suffer fools or

Trelissick House seen over the ha-ha across the park from the tennis lawn. (1971)

slackers among his staff, in fact relying heavily on their qualities and enthusiasm. In his light-heartedly tyrannical way he inspired several to greater things, notably Peter Borlase, who managed the garden and park at Lanhydrock with great distinction for many years, and later Barry Champion, who succeeded him.

The curious thing about Trelissick for any visitor is that, like me on my first visit, you sneak in like a gardener going to work through the back entrance, past the walled garden, only later seeing a narrow diagonal glimpse of the house, the reason for the garden's existence. This was to a degree understandable because the current generation of the donor family, the Copelands, lived in the house and were jealous of their privacy. However, this route is frustrating for anyone, like me, who needs to begin by understanding the whole place and its relationship with the surrounding landscape before enjoying the garden and its plants. It seems to me an important principle that visitors to any property should as far as possible arrive as would guests of the family, if not entering the house then at least seeing it and understanding immediately why it was situated thus. The glorious view from Trelissick's south front across the park to the Carrick Roads makes this immediately obvious; could there be a better prospect? But in Cornwall good views are synonymous with damaging winds. Plunging into the garden from the house front makes clear the logic behind the garden's layout, straight from the breezy brightness of the terrace into the bosky lushness of the woodland, a perfect contrast.

Developed in the 1930s, the older part of the garden is situated mostly within an extended shelterbelt flanking the house. The woodland both breaks the blast and provides a vital canopy to carry the wind over the garden. A common misunderstanding of shelter planting is that a dense windproof belt is all that is required, but this on its own simply creates turbulence. In extreme exposure, especially with salt-laden winds, shelter planting should be arranged first to filter the wind; at Trelissick this is done partly by strategic park planting and deciduous trees along the fringe of the garden, backed up by wind-resistant evergreens, shrubs and trees. In addition, the garden needs to contain a continuous network of deciduous trees for shelter throughout the garden. It soon became obvious to me that this vital canopy was composed almost entirely of old trees, mostly beech, and that renewal had been neglected. My sole influence in the 1970s – rather too late, as it turned out – was to get some young forest trees planted, as distinct from the many ornamentals that had been popped in by generations of plant lovers, including Graham Thomas since 1959.

Trelissick was one of Graham's favourite gardens and, after I succeeded him as chief Gardens Adviser, he continued until the early 1980s as Garden Consultant for this garden, along with Lanhydrock and Trengwainton. Under his typically methodical influence the garden was renovated throughout and tidied up, removing large quantities of undergrowth and decrepit trees. He also enriched the main flower borders to give the garden more of a summer dimension, and expanded the already wide range of hydrangea cultivars for the same reason. Undoubtedly, however, his main contribution to Trelissick was the replanting of 'Carcadden', an area of former orchard and nursery across the sunken road that leads down to the King Harry ferry. This involved the expense of replacing the existing bridge,

A view across the
park to the Carrick
Roads.

entirely functional though it was, with something better looking and safe enough for pedestrians and strong enough for garden machinery. The managing agent Peter Mansfield's perspicacious idea was inspired by a wisteria-clad bridge he had seen at Wisley, and he managed to persuade the brilliant architect Philip Jebb to sketch a rustic structure, which was given a steel core to make it structurally sound. Evidently the area contained a few remnant fruit trees, which were removed, and some larger trees, the best of which were retained to give some sense of continuity and maturity. Using a refurbished rustic summer house as the first destination uphill, Graham created a typically prescriptive route anti-clockwise from the bridge with attractive views back here and there to the garden proper. Despite repeated hydrangea cultivars in large groups and an esoteric assembly of exciting plants, it was a long time before 'Carcadden' became the intended magnet for visitors, the planting at first seeming to be a thin scattering with little cohesion. The western part was more successful because of the presence of some established trees and shrubs and because Graham included Japanese cherries which are such useful pioneers, precocious in flower and quick in growth. After Graham retired I added a group of 'Tai Haku' at the eastern end for the same purpose. Cherries had always been important components of the garden.

In many ways Trelissick is a typical Cornish garden, a steep coombe descending to the Fal estuary, with a little stream to provide variety of habitat; in sheltered and generally frost-free, it boasts a remarkable collection of plants, all jostling for space in the well-watered Dell. But for any new visitor the garden also contains surprises such as suddenly looking down on big ships moored on the Fal or a glorious view of the gothick pile of Tregothnan being revealed.

Graham Thomas retired from advising at Trelissick at the end of the 1970s in the firm belief, I know, that the garden was well set up for the future. In some ways he was right but the next decade was a bad one for Cornish gardens, Trelissick in particular, much of it being situated on a rocky promontory open to easterly gales. After a decade or more of comparatively equable weather, the next decade brought extremes, culminating in serious winter storms in the south-west early in the 1990s. One summer brought a punishing drought, a real killer on the thin shillet that serves for topsoil. There were winters of unusually sharp frosts but most damaging was one in which freezing east winds persisted for weeks, causing serious damage to all tender plants and the demise of many. Suddenly the sub-tropical lushness was gone and we were replanting everywhere. I learned how ephemeral Cornish gardens can be. On the other hand many, if not most, plants are able to survive a temporary setback, often re-growing vigorously, and in Cornwall quickly. However, the rate of turnover is always rapid in Cornish gardens because of a tendency to experiment with semi-hardy plants, and because growth, development and decay are so much faster. Surveys of woody plants by Michael Lear for the Trust during these calamitous years indicated annual losses sometimes approaching 10 per cent. This, however, did include many wild-source new plants raised from seed at the Trust's nursery at Knightshayes and gifts of other known-source exotics, some from Edward Needham of nearby Tregye, now itself an outstanding plantsman's garden.

In effect the garden at Trelissick was made in the late 1930s by Ronald Copeland and his wife Ida, within its flanking belt of forest trees planted when the house was rebuilt *c.*1825. By then there was shelter enough to establish a modern plants-man's garden, extended and enriched after the Second World War. By the 1980s this planting in the Cornish climate was in need of renovation and renewal and many of the trees, now a century and a half old, were on the verge of collapse, apart from some planted by the Trust since 1955. The storms of the 1980s took a heavy toll and the 1990s storm was catastrophic within the garden. Crucially, the belt held more or less firm with just enough of the big trees surviving, together with the young ones of the 1960s, '70s and '80s to tide the garden over. Never again should the garden face such a crisis due to lack of long-term vision.

Salvia microphylla 'Trelissick'.

After the drudgery of the post-storm clear-up, the creative gain lay in the opportunity for replanting, faced with the challenge of preserving and revealing those qualities that make the garden unique. Under Peter Mansfield's management we were able to re-establish its connection with the Fal by building a summer house overlooking the river from where reputedly a local priest used to preach to the ships' crews. This seems far-fetched but there is an extraordinary acoustic at this point that makes the legend entirely feasible. The dell needed an entire new canopy of trees and as well as replanting the traditional sweet chestnuts and oaks, we planted quicker growers like Southern beeches (*Nothofagus spp.*) which in that climate are incredibly quick-growing without being coarse and unwieldy like most poplars, or disease-prone like many willows.

Jack Lilly was succeeded as head gardener in the early 1980s by Barry Champion, a Cornishman who had ventured out

of the county for training at Cannington College, Somerset, and had worked at nearby Tregothnan. He had already proved himself as a skilful gardener and outstanding plantsman and went on to dedicate himself practically and emotionally to the garden for over thirty years, seeing it through some difficult times. He prided himself on high standards of presentation and invariably arranged specially for the gravel paths to be raked and the edges cut for my advisory visits. As well as enthusiastically carrying out every single task set out in my reports (having been agreed on my visits), he would frequently bring forward valuable comments and suggestions, often derived from the keener members of his staff. He was perhaps inclined to feel disappointment too deeply for his own good but conversely was heart-warmingly proud of any successes. One of Barry's achievements was to put together a collection of traditional Cornish apple cultivars and plant a large orchard as an extension, westwards of 'Carcadden', a sunny spot far enough inland to evade the worst gales. Each tree has at its base one of a matching collection of the rather tender and strongly-scented *Narcissus tazetta* cultivars, once widely grown in Cornwall.

More mundane but no less important was the programme of narrowing the eroded margins of all the gravel paths in the old garden to restore their proper scale: also providing them with resilient steel edges to preserve their trim appearance. Although never noticed by visitors, it is this kind of unspectacular renewal that preserves values important to the special character of the place. Ever-increasing visitor numbers have inevitably compounded the challenge of presenting the garden to a creditable standard, which has been largely accomplished at Trelissick by the restrained use of hard surfacing materials as unobtrusively as possible.

HARDWICK HALL

A house as stupendously impressive and architecturally glorious as Hardwick Hall is bound to dominate, not only its immediate surroundings but also the whole district. This was after all Bess of Hardwick's intention. In the garden you can hardly escape its towering presence and the heavily-decorated garden walls provide a unifying architectural structure. When built it must have been a wondrous spectacle to people accustomed only to their humble dwellings and the modest churches of their locality. Laid out in its present form by Lady Louisa Egerton, daughter of the 7th Duke of Devonshire in the 1860s, the garden's design successfully pays tribute to the house whilst also providing hedged quarters in the south garden where the scale comes down sufficiently to make detailed gardening more rewarding.

The garden had been well cared for by the Devonshires before 1959. When it came to the National Trust, Evelyn, Duchess of Devonshire, who was widowed in 1938, was the last of the family to live there. She stayed on very effectively and amicably as custodian for the National Trust after its transfer as part of an estate duty settlement following the death of her son Eddie in 1950. Lady Emma Tennant, who served with great distinction as Chairman of the Gardens Panel for fifteen years, remembers staying in that big cold house as a child with her great-grandmother.

The Herb Garden at Hardwick Hall was planted in 1994 to a design by Paul Miles and later extended because of its popularity. All kinds of herbs, medicinal and cosmetic plants are grown, plus 'wigwams' of golden and brewers' hops.

She says that, although principally a needlewoman, the Dowager Duchess took a great interest in the garden, and the south-facing border in the main south garden is still substantially to her design with its shrub roses, silvery foliage and cool colours. Nevertheless, there was much to do by the 1960s and Graham Thomas immediately made his mark as Gardens Adviser on the hedged allées that divide the south garden into quarters. He directed the cutting back and remaking of the hornbeam and yew hedges, a radical reduction in their breadth that restored their proper scale at a stroke. At this time, when he was writing the rose books, he introduced many shrub roses to the south-east sector of the south garden.

Perhaps Graham's best and most enduring improvement was in converting a splendidly decrepit old orchard in the north-east quarter of the south garden. As well as retaining and augmenting the fine old apples and pears, he turned the grass into a meadow of wild flowers, naturalising bulbs to give a continuous display through spring and early summer, then again after grass-cutting from Colchicums. Mown paths divide the orchard into quarters bordered by avenues of perhaps the best of all the Chinese crab apples, *Malus hupehensis*. A consistent regime of late-summer 'hay making' and perceptive tree pruning and renewal has created one of the Trust's best flowery orchards.

The south-facing mixed border in the main garden in 1973, more or less as it was left by Evelyn, Duchess of Devonshire, who was widowed in 1938 and lived in the great house until it was acquired by the National Trust in 1959.

I took over advising at Hardwick in the early 1970s, quite cautiously because the regime was conservative and I was a new boy. The east court with its heavy-handed circular fire pond in the centre is particularly difficult for gardening because of the huge scale of the surroundings – house one side and open view on the other. My attempt at giving structure and summer colour to the borders involved creating a series of yew-buttressed sections containing repeat-flowering bush roses, with spring-flowering edgings.

A few years earlier a massive beech tree in the north-west quarter of the south garden had collapsed. After some discussion the consensus was that the relative simplicity here was a welcome counterpoint to the other quarters, so we planted a few specimen trees of large-growing species, enough to allow for accidents and plenty of choice for the future. Who knows what may be the next pandemic tree disease to strike?

Paul Miles joined the Trust as Assistant Gardens Adviser just before I officially succeeded Graham Thomas as Head of Gardens in 1973. His background, after training at Wisley, was in garden design and construction for Notcutts at Woodbridge. He was also interested in historic gardens and country house gardens in particular, modelling himself, he said, on Russell Page and Lanning Roper. While his contribution in the Trust was not inconsiderable, his underlying ambition was to set up as an independent consultant, which he did after a few years, to be succeeded by Jim Marshall. Paul was the ideal person to design the herb garden at Hardwick, originally an idea of Graham's for the south-west quarter of the south garden. The scheme was ambitious for the time it was made, and more so when it was doubled in size a couple of years later. Full of interest and variety and with a strong design, it has been an unqualified success, at last giving the garden a reputation independent of the great house.

As always the success of any feature of this kind, full of significant detail and needing careful cultivation, is dependent on the quality of its care and upkeep. Robin Allan succeeded John Jennings as head gardener at the right time. The whole of this large garden was becoming more complex, demanding an ever-higher standard of cultivation and attention to detail. Robin was the person for the job. Top class flower gardeners invariably set themselves high standards and (sometimes irritatingly) they may assume the same degree of meticulous attention to detail in others. The function of management should be to facilitate this expertise within reason, rather than to expect all employees to conform to some arbitrary norm. For example, employment objectives that ignore the horticultural imperatives of excellence that apply in the best flower gardens would condone mediocrity.

Convallaria majalis 'Hardwick Hall'.

Similarly, flower borders of the highest standards demand acute observation and critical appraisal from both within and without. Tony Lord came to the Trust (with a PhD in Chemistry) after training at Kew. He began as a technical assistant in the advisers' office in Cirencester and was appointed Assistant Gardens Adviser after a few years. He eventually left the Trust to take over editorship of *The Plant Finder*, and has written some outstanding books on flower gardening; he was honoured with the Victoria Medal of Honour from the Royal Horticultural Society in 2005.

The glorious west front of Hardwick Hall overlooks a green entrance court within which Bess of Hardwick's initials 'ES' can be discerned in the grass after drought, matching those on the house. The perimeter borders here, facing north, south and east towards the house are important both as a setting for the house

The flower
borders in the
west front court
were redesigned
by Gardens
Adviser Tony
Lord, according to
Gertrude Jekyll's
principles of
colour scheming
and plant
grouping; planted
and cared for by
Robin Allen with
all his painstaking
attention to detail.

and as a way of announcing the presence of an important garden. Although reasonably well cared-for, the more-or-less Gertrude Jekyll-style layout had become tired and weedy, with some of the larger subjects becoming over-dominant. The time had come for their progressive renovation and we agreed to develop a classic Jekyll series of borders with a linked colour scheme. Beginning with cool tints on the south-facing side, this would span the spectrum round to bright colours and strong contrasts opposite. Each border would need to be emptied, cleared of perennial weeds, manured and replanted with an augmented scheme. To stand up to the monumental scale of the space, larger species would need to predominate in bold groups. Working with Robin Allan, Tony Lord did an entirely successful job, using his considerable plant knowledge and understanding, now a textbook example of the genre and a fitting preamble to the great house.

The garden at Hardwick Hall, always on the grand scale, has been renovated during the Trust's ownership without radically altering its general layout. It has been developed and enriched with original features that have consistently respected what went before. While it is right that each feature should bear the imprint of one of several talented individuals, the important consideration is that each contribution should be subsumed into a satisfactory whole.

STANDEN

When I was appointed by the National Trust in 1971 there was little corporate enthusiasm for things Victorian, even though Wightwick Manor was one of its earlier acquisitions and Waddesdon Manor one of its grandest. Similarly, there was an unspoken assumption that Victorian gardens were either too close to vulgarity or too full of dreary conifers and meaninglessly obscure plants to be at the top of the Trust's wish list. When Standen, Philip Webb's last and arguably finest house, built in the 1890s, was bequeathed by Miss Helen Beale in 1973, the Trust had to be persuaded to open it to the public. There was a strong current of opinion that considered it and its garden unlikely to attract many visitors, despite the growing interest in the Arts and Crafts movement and a garden full of exotic plants. Webb was a close associate of William and Janie Morris, and ironically by the turn of the century the Trust was eagerly acquiring the Red House which Webb had designed for them in 1860, his first commission. Standen's immediate success and accelerating popularity say something about the taste of the Trust at the time and even more about the way it has tended to underrate gardens and landscape settings.

Arthur and Helen Grogan were distinguished historians of architecture and the fine arts, who had served the Historic Buildings Council, a predecessor of English Heritage, for many years. They were obviously ahead of their time in championing the Arts and Crafts, Philip Webb in particular, and had taken a great interest in Standen. Without Arthur Grogan it might not have been left to the Trust, and it would certainly never have been furnished and presented in its present form if they had not become its lessees. The Grogans not only greatly improved the range of furniture and chattels from their own collection, they also became the Trust's first lessees. Standen today in a real sense is their legacy as well as that of the Beales. But neither they nor the Trust were prepared for its burgeoning popularity and they were soon forced by circumstances to accept a different role, allowing the Trust to manage the property and its opening to meet demand.

The Grogans were a charming and gently determined couple who were desperately anxious to restore and refurbish Standen according to their meticulous standards and well-informed notion of Philip Webb's ideas. With their learned art-historical approach, nothing less than precise evidence and accurate precedent was good enough. Needless to say they had a good eye and a sure aesthetic judgement. I was lucky enough to visit many times both before and after they took the lease. They were very hospitable and I stayed in a bedroom now open to visitors. As a result I was able to learn about the Arts and Crafts at Standen and something of Philip Webb's attitude to the garden as seen through the eyes of Arthur Grogan.

Instead of arranging the house as one would expect along the steep contour, Philip Webb obeyed his principles of respecting the vernacular by relating the layout to the existing cottage and associated buildings. He cut into the hillside

at right angles to the cottage to create a walled courtyard behind the house and on the principal garden front made a terrace running into the hillside. The result is an awkward relationship with the landscape, the steep slopes cutting uncomfortably across the main prospect. Perhaps Webb foresaw the garden in architectural terms as a series of level platforms descending from the house, as indeed it became. However, there is no evidence that Webb took much interest in the garden other than by preserving the villagey Goose Green in front of the cottage and designing the courtyard and terraces immediately around the house. Here Arthur Grogan's knowledge was crucial and his judgement sound. We restored a version of Webb's formal terrace out to the little gazebo which anchors the corner of the main lawn, and repaired the square oak trellis under the terrace, along with the herbaceous border. Another Arts and Crafts touch is the square mulberry lawn bordered by lavender.

Surely the finest feature of the garden is the quarry adjacent to the house from which, according to principle, stone for the house was taken? Here in perfect contrast to the dry brightness of the terrace the atmosphere is all shade and humidity. This effect of calm melancholy is intensified by giant ferns and luxuriant planting among precipitous rocks around a central pool and drippy fountain. Luckily this tree-hung microclimate needed only gentle intervention and consistent care based on detailed observation, although managing the tree cover would be an important longer-term obligation.

In fact the garden was overwhelmingly the creation of Margaret Beale, who used the steep banks around the lawns to assemble a wide range of plants popular in the first half of the twentieth century, including many hardy hybrid rhododendrons and azaleas; also trees, both flowering species like cherries and magnolias

Looking down into the Quarry Garden. True to his principles, this is where Philip Webb obtained stone for the house, thereby creating perfect conditions for the ferns and other shade-loving perennials much loved in the 19th century. (1973)

and fine specimens of tulip tree and Monterey pine. Above the house she made densely-planted walks leading to a narrow upper terrace and gazebo, to take full advantage of the glorious views towards Crowborough Beacon.

It all added up to a substantial garden of great variety with lots of lovely plants and colourful effects, if a little thin on summer interest. The main conservation challenge, in common with many single-generation gardens, was with overcrowd-ing and lack of decisive management in recent years. It is one thing to make a garden in your own lifetime, gradually adding and developing, and quite another to consider its long-term conservation, while continuing to preserve its signifi-cant qualities, with reduced labour as a limiting factor. This invariably involves working through the whole garden, pruning, felling, grubbing and replanting to ensure sustainability.

None of this robust planting and heavy-handed horticulture was to Arthur Gro-gan's taste. His approach was always to simplify and his gardening sensibilities were affronted by colour en masse; exotic conifers were anathema. I soon realised that his judgement away from the house was suspect, in view of the fact that Margaret Beale, whose impact was consistently at odds with his taste, needed to be taken seriously as the garden's principal creator. That Standen's garden is never likely to be regarded among the country's greatest in design, content or significance is beside the point. It is typical of its time and of a garden, on a glorious site, created piecemeal by someone whose love for it shows throughout.

It was overplanted and in the 1970s partially neglected but it possessed excellent qualities, fine plants and features related to its history that needed to be revealed and redeveloped with some degree of humility. Arguably the garden at Standen appeals to visitors at least as much as does the house.

The counterbalance to Arthur Grogan, the aesthete, was Robert Ludman, the gardener, a remarkably fortunate appointment. In character, physique and inclination he was Arthur's opposite number; no job was impossible for him, however intimidating. He learned his gardening under the legendary Jack Lilly, head gardener at Trelissick, but his firm ambition was always to run his own show, being temperamentally what used to be called a 'single-handed' gardener. (Certainly Robert could do with one hand what most gardeners manage with difficulty to do with two!). A big chap, Robert had enormous energy and never-failing drive. He enjoyed being set seemingly superhuman tasks and programmes of work that most gardeners would find daunting even with someone to help. But the Trust had decided that for 4.8 ha (12 acres) one gardener was all that could be afforded.

Although neither seemed quite to appreciate the point, Arthur and Robert were exactly complementary in their abilities and understanding of gardens. It was an almost impossible partnership, Robert always feeling that Arthur was fussing too much and holding him back, Arthur constantly fearful of Robert's robustly masculine approach and almost aggressive pride in what he thought was right. In fact a great deal was accomplished in a short time. With help, the relationship proved constructive and effective through the crucial early years after acquisition. It was left to me both to plot the course for the garden and to arbitrate. In my mind much depended on preventing a total breakdown in the relationship between Arthur and Robert, so I needed to tread warily. There was plenty of creative tension but not much harmonious dialogue. My visits soon fell into a predictable pattern. Knowing of my expected time of arrival, Robert, who lived in a sort of gatehouse along the drive, would watch out and waylay me 'accidentally'. He would quickly pour out his pent-up concerns and horticultural disappointments. We got on well and he was always loyal to what I had written, after careful consideration, in the reports of my visits. The trick was to release his frustrations without committing myself, having not yet heard the Arthur's version of events.

The next stage was to arrive for coffee with the Grogans, and possibly with the managing land agent, without mentioning the encounter with Robert, although I guess Arthur suspected something. Anyway, it was invaluable to know the scandal before our usually long discussion over coffee, during which I would get the other side of the story together with Arthur's often acute observations about the garden and our priorities as he saw them. These meetings were always enjoyable but it was tricky to avoid committing to anything before Robert joined us. The subsequent garden tour was a further negotiation, attempting to keep things moving forward with agreement or at least acquiescence from everyone. My reports were similarly circumspect: careful judgements aimed at giving everyone some sense of achievement, not least me on behalf of the Trust. In those days my loyalties as an adviser or consultant were clear. I invariably guided events along lines that I believed right in the interests of the property, taking account of its history and traditions, and of the existing circumstances of ownership and management.

Following his winter 'hibernation' writing books, my predecessor Graham Thomas used to arrange his advisory visits so as to start after Easter in the south (preferably Cornwall), reaching Northumbria last. In this way he claimed he could experience spring several times. After his initial visit back in January 1958, you would never have caught him at Wallington before June or after September. My first visit in 1971 was as part of Graham's annual progress north via the Lake District to visit his friend and colleague Cuthbert (Cubby) Acland at Stagshaw, then on to Acorn Bank and eventually Wallington. My experience of gardens and gardening in Northumbria was non-existent and I knew I had a lot to learn. I soon observed that although winter is consistently cold with days depressingly short, the climate at Wallington seems to lack the rapid temperature changes that catch out plants, especially evergreens, inland further south. Hence, given shelter and a favourable aspect, it is surprising what flourishes. Spring comes late but after the spring equinox growth accelerates rapidly through the lengthening days to create a burst of summer luxuriance not experienced in the 'soft south'. Similarly, trees, especially conifers, grow with extraordinary freedom through the peak of the year.

Wallington is a great estate, involved with every major development in garden style and landscape fashion since the seventeenth century when the mansion was built. In the following century the splendid early formal layout was adapted by the Trevelyan family to the English landscape style with extensive ornamental

A flower border on the terrace of the walled garden in 1981 showing Graham Thomas's great expertise with colour-schemed planting in the Gertrude Jekyll style; a Surrey border in Northumberland?

woodlands and a pleasure ground near the house. Appropriately, Capability Brown went to school in Cambo village on the Wallington estate, presumably walking there daily from Kirkharle a couple of miles away. In common with other great houses situated in sparse landscapes, Wallington was largely self-sufficient and no doubt its nineteenth-century economy could teach us something about local sourcing and recycling, especially in the garden. Wallington even had its own surface coal mine.

As a convinced socialist, Sir Charles Trevelyan was ahead of his time in bequeathing the whole estate and its contents to the National Trust during the darkest days of the Second World War. However, he was to remain in total control of Wallington until he died in 1958. His unconventional style of management, coupled with declining resources, left a legacy of contraction and decline. This was most noticeable in the walled garden, situated a little way east of the house, in a sheltered valley above the river, with views out over the park. This had been the fount and focus of the garden for two centuries, sloping mainly south to catch the sun, and set snug within its high walls and sheltering woodland. It was obviously no mere kitchen garden, entirely for production and utility; it was clearly intended also as a source of pleasure and recreation, a destination for short walks from the house, enjoying the contrived informality of the pleasure ground woodland on the way. In times of hunger and deprivation, stepping through the gate must have seemed like entering paradise, surrounded by all that horticultural abundance and luxuriant colour. In the middle of the greenhouse range stands the conservatory, an indispensable haven from rain and cold winds in this climate. Towering above all is the Owl House, the head gardener's domain from which he could see everything, a sharp reminder of the authoritarian power wielded by these minor martinets of nineteenth-century gardening.

In 1958 Graham Thomas found the garden weedy and semi-derelict, entirely beyond the capabilities of the much-reduced, post-war garden staff. While labour and skills had evaporated and buildings had deteriorated over two decades, no

The conservatory at Wallington is both a welcome refuge and a flowery feature in its own right with pot plants on the benches and big fuchsias, pelargoniums and other tender subjects in big pots and in the borders.

attempt had been made to come to terms with the changing situation. With Ben Proud, the Trust's capable and firmly objective agent for the north-east (and a keen amateur gardener), Graham decided upon a common-sense programme of radical simplification and transformation. Logically this would aim at discarding all inessentials and labour-intensive activities unless they were thought to be part of the garden's unique qualities and attractions, bearing in mind that the Trust needed to bring visitors in large numbers to this isolated spot.

The first steps were to grass over the now weedy former vegetable and soft fruit plots in the terraced western half and begin to repair the structure of paths, walls and buildings, including crucially the main greenhouse range with its now iconic conservatory. Accumulated perennial weeds were painstakingly eradicated by the head gardener, Geoffrey Moon, and his meagre band of assistants, and one by one the borders were cultivated, manured and replanted according to Graham's direction. Geoffrey was dedicated to his task and later emphasised to me how much he had learnt from 'Mr Thomas' despite early misgivings: how Graham had become his mentor, his visits and reports anticipated with great excitement and some apprehension. Geoffrey was a gentle soul, a plantsman who acquired plants for their own sake and his own interest, usually through gifts or exchanges, without regard for their eventual use or compatibility within the scheme of things. Graham had a remarkable memory for plants and I soon came to appreciate the game played between them in the context of Graham's characteristically precise ideas of what was appropriate for every part of the garden. Geoffrey would 'pop in' his treasured new acquisitions here and there, vainly hoping that they would not be noticed by the eagle-eyed adviser. Graham always spotted them, taking a mercifully relaxed view, but nevertheless pointing out the transgressors and 'tactfully' advising their relocation.

The grandest garden office in the National Trust occupies the upper storey of the pedimented Owl House, where the all-powerful head gardener would be able to keep a keen eye on his gardeners.

The walled garden's main distinguishing feature is a little stream coming from the pleasure ground pond just above the walled garden to the west. This had been piped through a decorative stone niche and paved terrace to be caught in a pool, all designed in 1938 by Mary, Lady Trevelyan. This is a lovely place to sit and enjoy the morning sun looking out over the garden. Formerly in a conduit (locally a 'cundy') for most of its descent downhill, the little stream was uncovered along two lengths and made into a rocky stream bordered with a variety of little plants. The big wall borders on either side were given Jekyll-style mixed borders with generous groupings of herbaceous plants and climbers on the walls. Altogether it was a transformation, much appreciated by visitors: a stylish piece of Surrey gardening transplanted to Northumbria.

Less successful was a yew-hedged rectangle, formerly used as a vegetable plot, which Graham grassed over and planted with a mixture of choice small trees, orchard-style. To me they were a sad sight struggling in the grass, constantly wind-blown in this strangely exposed position. Few visitors were tempted in and I eventually interplanted them with hazels to give a sense of continuity, to be coppiced to allow underplanting with small bulbs and wildflowers. I hope one day it will revert entirely to vegetables to put productivity back into the garden.

On my first visit the lowest third of the garden contained little other than derelict greenhouses, melon pits and cold frames. However, Graham came armed with a plan for its rebirth as an informal arrangement of trees and shrubs with

The borders contain a catholic collection of uncommon plants, providing the walled garden with an exotic contrast to the landscape park over the garden wall.

a plastic-lined fish pond at its lowest point. In contrast to the colourfully rich plantings elsewhere, the arrangement was based on the use of predominantly bold-leafed subjects with contrasting texture and form, an imaginative concept which was fully realised in subsequent years. However, this was not achieved without mishap. The conduit ran under the site and Graham utilised it to feed the pond via a little stepped waterfall, draining into a saucer in the centre of the pond and back into the conduit. Unfortunately occasional blockages, which occurred when the stream was in spate, were not taken into account. After the pond was filled and stocked, a blockage below the pond created a powerful head of water upstream that blew out under the pond, the 'fountain' inflating the plastic liner like a bouncy castle balloon and emptying the pond of its contents. The sight caused great amusement to everyone except Graham, who unsurprisingly did not seem to see the funny side of the situation! He insisted on trying again, with the same eventual result. Eventually, when I took over advising, we installed an emerging overflow pipe to prevent further disasters, and the whole place settled down to mature much as intended.

In *Ancestral Voices* (1975), James Lees-Milne writes eloquently of visiting Wallington in 1942 and finding the Trevelyans 'overpowering' and the two married daughters Patricia and Pauline 'abrupt and rather terrifying' with their mental agility; there is no mention of the garden. Both daughters continued to live on the estate and took a judicious interest in what the Trust did; Patricia ran the tea room for some years, where she regularly played the Northumbrian pipes to visitors over lunch. Although as Forestry Adviser John Workman did a lot of necessary, mainly utilitarian tree felling and mixed planting in the woodlands, not much was done in the pleasure ground woods near the house and between it and the walled garden. These were the areas most frequented by the family who were all keen on wildlife. Graham Thomas had unwittingly provoked fury for cutting back a ramshackle 'arch' of yew to regrow and soon learned that, if not about politics, the sisters were certainly conservative about change in the pleasure ground.

This reluctance to disturb the status quo inevitably leads in garden woodlands to stultifying gloom, as tall trees compete for light and the understorey of evergreens

With a blue and yellow colour theme, designed by Graham Stuart Thomas, these double borders are lined by arches of honeysuckle.

blankets the earth and smothers all. By the 1970s Wallington was in desperate need of a programme of progressive pruning, felling and replanting in the garden woodlands, aimed at augmenting diversity, restoring ornament and improving wild life habitat. Despite this traditional negativity, and thanks to the occasional need to fell dangerous trees, a good deal was achieved in making the grounds more dynamic, but much more needs to be done, even now.

There is a problem in the north-east with hard-pruning evergreens, especially yews, to regrow. Evergreens were almost always planted in woodlands to provide understorey and low shelter among forest-type trees. Yews live longer than most big trees and leave no space or light for regeneration or replanting. Whereas many broad-leaved evergreens respond well and regrow quickly after hard pruning, in the north yews are much trickier. In most of England and Wales healthy yew hedges regrow readily after cutting back. Yew trees respond more slowly, depending upon their age and whether they have any basal or epicormic growth on the main stems (which is encouraged by light). In the north yews are nearer the limit of their climatic zone and respond more slowly, if at all. The process needs to be gradual and spread over several years, persistently pruning out branches to admit light and encourage regrowth. There is much more of this to be done at Wallington. If left untouched, surface-rooted yews can easily be bowled over by storms or broken up by heavy snows. In gardens there is no such thing as preserving the status quo or 'minimum intervention' as architectural conservationists put it.

Another frequently neglected process in garden woodlands and pleasure grounds involves the judicious removal of lower branches to admit light to the understorey and other plants beneath. Arborists call this 'crown-raising', a puzzling term for non-professionals: 'branching up' to gardeners. This is always a matter of judgement because specimen trees often look best clothed to the ground. On the other hand, most mixed planting of the informal pleasure-ground type with trees, shrubs and other plants growing together as a community, needs to be given enough light and space if plants are to prosper and perhaps flower. The impact of careful tree pruning of this kind over a couple of years can be a revelation, with shrubs and plants suddenly liberated from years of increasing depression bursting into growth and flower. In my experience it is the most frequently neglected job in gardens because the problem develops gradually without gardeners or owners noticing. It is a classic case calling for the fresh eye of the outsider – an observant adviser willing and able to ask the right questions and supply the right answers from experience.

CRAGSIDE

NORTHUMBERLAND

When Laurence Harwood, Regional Director in Northumbria, first took me to Cragside in 1977, I found it quite impossible to comprehend the magnitude of the National Trust's acquisition. From the road on the other side of Rothbury, Laurence pointed out the house, almost engulfed by the million or more conifers with which Lord Armstrong surrounded himself and transformed the open fell into pleasure ground and woodland. From a distance it looked like a forestry plantation. We entered the estate from the east, much the best way to approach the house (but impractical for visitors generally) through a grove of Douglas firs soaring to incredible heights. As a mere gardener I admit to mixed feelings on my first view of the house through the trees: not beautiful, though I took to it later when arriving in a thunderstorm – a dramatically Wagnerian scene as the lightning struck.

Attention had been focussed primarily on the extraordinary house built for Sir William (later Lord) Armstrong in 1864 by Richard Norman Shaw in his romantic 'Old English' style. This was early days for any objective assessment of our Victorian heritage, but the tide was turning thanks to Mark Girouard's *The Victorian Country House* (1971). Cragside was obviously highly significant of its time in so many ways, but not to everyone's taste. Thanks largely, I feel sure, to the enthusiasm of Sheila Pettit, Historic Buildings Representative in Northumbria, the Trust committed itself to a major restoration of the house and its fascinating contents and decoration. She directed the whole operation and it remains now much as she recreated it, a testament to her professional expertise and fine judgement.

It seemed that little thought had been given to the grounds before acquisition, even though they provided such an impressive setting. Indeed, it would have been difficult for anyone to grasp that, far from being simple forestry or even mixed woodland, the whole vast estate was laid out primarily for ornament, i.e. garden and pleasure ground on the grandest possible scale, containing exotic trees and shrubs throughout. I realised that, with hardly a native tree in sight, Cragside represents the epitome of high-Victorian gardening in which art was to triumph over nature, the ideal being to transform whole landscapes with trees and flowering shrubs from around the world, recreating an entirely exotic 'naturalism'. At Cragside abundant use had been made of the fashionable conifers collected by David Douglas and others in the Americas earlier in the century. Along with rhododendrons, gaultherias and other shrubs, Cragside had established its own special ecosystem, now blanketing the whole landscape with a limited range of trees and aggressive shrubs even better suited to this piece of Northumberland than to their natural habitat.

The bad news was that, because it was a Treasury Transfer in lieu of estate duty, I was calmly informed for the first time in my career with the Trust that there would be no funds for gardening or gardeners. The Trust had taken on Cragside with inadequate funding and without the closely associated stable block or the walled formal garden, rightly as it turned out in the hope of visitor-generated income and the expectation of further acquisitions. Gradually the estate was put back together, the stable block being bought in 1980, and eventually the formal garden in 1991 through several generous bequests.

Having been until the twentieth century a place from which to enjoy open views of the surrounding fells, the house was now almost entirely enclosed by magnificent conifers which had grown at prodigious rates. Investigation revealed a wide range of mostly western North American species, all of course collected from the wild, including many superb specimens and impressive groves of conifers as good as anything you can find, even in Scotland, the home of champion conifers. Although the panoramic views were gone for good, after careful deliberation we agreed on the need for removing two of the largest western hemlocks situated just below the house, to give light and preserve at least a glimpse out. On such a steep slope this was a huge operation, causing inevitable damage despite every effort, and there was no way of removing the stumps.

With only a forester to organise things for the whole estate and a car park for the house to construct on the steep slope, not much gardening was going to be done. Pictures in the house and in the accumulating archive showed the area around the house as a giant rock garden, composed of massive weathered rocks evidently

The huge rock garden at Cragside after clearance. It was made in the Victorian 'tumbled' style using rocks collected from the surrounding fells. (1993)

collected locally from the fells and arranged to indicate a tumbled effect, as though they had slipped, or been tipped, down the slope in fact carefully arranged. Here and there they were still visible but most of the rocks were covered densely with evergreen vegetation, mostly *Gaultheria shallon*, a leathery-leaved, vigorously spreading, ericaceous shrub with little pinkish flowers and dark purple fruits. Like the best of the conifers this species comes from western North America but seems to have taken to Northumberland, forming over the years extensive mats of compressed stems covering everything. Clearance was slow and laborious and needed to be followed up by spraying with Roundup (glyphosate) to prevent regrowth and to kill seedlings. Young volunteer groups were heroic in their application but the place had a narrow squeak when a bonfire was left to burn and came close to igniting the whole hillside. Nearly impossible to extinguish, it had crept through the compacted brushwood and peaty accumulations to create an inferno which threatened trees and damaged rocks. That was a lesson and a warning.

At first we had no idea of the extent of the rock garden around and below the house but as it was gradually revealed we began to realise its hitherto unknown significance: it was not only stylistically unique but also perhaps the largest ever made in Britain. It was a highly sophisticated piece of work arranged in keeping with the massive scale of the place to provide a series of cameo features and varied habitats for plants. We found plenty of clues from photographs and paintings as to the range of plants grown before the gaultheria smothered everything. There were hardy hybrid rhododendrons and azaleas around the fringes of the rock garden (we replanted *Rh*. 'Norman Shaw') and many heathers and related ericaceous plants among the rocks, smaller conifers, golden yews and big *Berberis spp*. A heather garden of the modern suburban kind with dwarf conifers and contrasting foliage colours would not do, and the Trust's Gardens Panel (especially

Victorian carpet bedding has been expertly revived in the formal garden alongside the surviving orchard house. (1994)

An early 20th century postcard showing Lord Armstong's extensive carpet bedding in the formal garden, when all the greenhouses were intact.

its Chairman, Lady Emma Tennant) was understandably suspicious of our intentions. Nevertheless, we agreed that for once heathers were right and decided to plant mostly summer-flowering cultivars of heather or ling (*Calluna vulgaris*) and the bell heather (*Erica cinerea*), always keeping to the older, vigorous and less stridently coloured forms. Following the same train of thought we planted cranberries, blueberries and related ericaceous species individually to give interest and variety. Once established, the heather garden would suppress weeds and minimise work, which was important with so large a garden. Eventually we were able to widen the range to encompass the garden's original diversity. However, this is a garden made decades before the 'rage for rock gardening' kicked off in earnest with Reginald Farrer's *My Rock Garden* of 1907 and has no connection with the twentieth-century passion for little plants or recreating distant alpine scenery.

As part of the acquisition of the stable block in 1980 some gardening help was squeezed out of the negotiation, and modestly encouraging rock garden clearances and plantings were made in time for the opening of the house. However, it was not until 1991 when the Trust was able to acquire Lord Armstrong's impressive formal garden that gardening in the full sense returned to Cragside. With its fascinating assembly of kitchen garden, 'Italian' terraces, flower garden, carpet bedding, fern grotto, orchard house and clock tower, this had always been the creative mainspring of the garden. The Trust was fortunate to be able to recruit Andrew Sawyer as head gardener, a Geordie of exceptional ability and plant knowledge, whose drive and high standards soon put Cragside back on the horticultural map of Britain. From a standing start he and his enthusiastic staff have recreated both a flower garden of rare quality and significance and restored largely the idiosyncratic pleasure ground near the house with its unique rock garden.

CALKE ABBEY

DERBYSHIRE

When the National Trust was acquiring Calke Abbey in the mid-1980s I had to ask to go there to see the garden, no one having thought a visit by the Chief Gardens Adviser relevant. 'Oh yes, do come but there is no garden' was the kind of reply I received, which surely indicated that there would be no money for the garden if indeed there was one! Like the house, the whole estate had been slumbering for a century, but whereas houses can remain more or less embalmed, gardens and parks inevitably go on changing and being changed. For the nature conservationists an ancient neglected park with splendid old trees is grist to the mill, although at Calke even they would point out the need for young trees. In fact Calke is also a significant, designed park improved by William Emes for the Harpur Crewes in the English landscape style of the late eighteenth century. It would eventually have a conservation management plan, endeavouring to reconcile these differing values.

At first sight it seems that the parkland rolls right up to the house, backed by woodland, otherwise sitting in grassland. However, you cross a cattle grid and ha-ha and realise that this huge meadow is pleasure ground into which the deer and sheep have been admitted for so many years that hardly any shrubs or young trees had survived their grazing. On the bank opposite the house are the remains of the pleasure ground shrub planting among trees which still shelter the extensive walled gardens and screen them completely. This area was roughly fenced, and our first priority was to renew this barrier to exclude sheep and deer, neither of which are compatible with young trees and evergreens. After that we were able to replant.

Of course it was nonsense to say there was no garden. Even then the gardener, an ex-miner, was still growing vegetables, a basket of which he would take to the house every day. He simply supplied what he had grown and never, he said, did he ever receive any comment about quantity, quality or content. When we stepped into his 'bothy' (in fact the office of the grand head gardeners of the past), we were awestruck. Along with a scrap-heap settee in front of the fire, presumably for the gardener's cosy lunches, there was the intact set-up of a nineteenth-century tool shed, high desk, range of seed cabinets, racks of tools and clutter, including the yellowing show certificates for prizes won many years before. As with the great house, here was a case for preservation and repair in the architectural sense – 'as much as necessary and as little as possible'.

Luckily the walled gardens are arranged in three main sections. The largest was a 1.6 ha (4 acre) sheep-grazed space with two derelict lean-to greenhouses, flanking a splendid but ruinous orangery (since repaired). Apart from doing its best to save and eventually restore the buildings, the Trust's slender resources at that time were best spent elsewhere on achievable and sustainable horticultural objectives.

The small, walled flower garden was truly a revelation, although at the time it contained little more than one lean-to greenhouse (usable if you ignored health

The formal flower garden, part of the walled gardens, during restoration. In the left far corner is the surviving Auricula theatre flanked alongside by the aviary and the conservatory. (1988)

and safety regulations), an attached aviary and a derelict feature in the corner facing south-east. I could not believe my eyes as I gradually realised that this was something I had only ever seen in books. It was, as far as I know, then the only surviving auricula theatre, still recognisable with the remains of its 'proscenium arch' and tiered benches for setting out pots.

Without the need for any archaeology it was comparatively easy to find the flower bed edges in the rough grass and to draw up the slightly eccentric layout of Lady Crewe's early nineteenth-century flower garden with its central fountain pool, now again surrounded with basket-weave ironwork in Regency style.

The flower garden with the borders replanted and the geometric flower beds set out with an authentic Victorian bedding scheme of contrasting colours. (1996)

The Auricula theatre in the Calke walled garden after restoration in 1996, with its summer show of pelargoniums.

No Jekyll-style borders and subtle colour schemes here; we decided on strong contrasting colours according to nineteenth-century theory and practice. Similarly, this was an opportunity to replant the perimeter borders with a Loudon-style 'mingled' border of repetitive single plants and small groups graded evenly from front to back. Together with the restored auricula theatre this is now a startling period piece, not to everyone's taste but as true as possible to its unique history.

In the first summer after the flower garden's restoration I had an indignant letter from a National Trust member who lived in East Sussex, whose garden-visiting experience seemed to have been confined to the genteel 'soft south'. She said how much she admired the National Trust's gardens, especially Sissinghurst, but that she was shocked on her visit to Calke Abbey. She wrote to say that she 'did not think the Trust did that sort of thing'. In my reply I did my best politely to explain that it was the Trust's job to do what seems right for the place, to retain and restore historic individuality even if the style was not to everyone's liking. In fact, I found her letter rather encouraging and a useful one to quote to people who lazily imply that the Trust made all their gardens look alike. I should have said that if she did not like it there are plenty more that she would like!

We were fortunate to be able to recruit Steve Biggins as (sole) gardener-in-charge at this crucial stage of restoration and renewal. Energetic and well-trained, he had worked previously for the Trust at Ickworth, so we knew his capabilities. With his down-to-earth approach Steve developed just the right style for Calke where, apart from the flower garden, the place needed to reflect in some way the faded grandeur of the house with its haphazard contents. This was no place for the prissy potager or the twentieth-century obsession with exotic foliage and subtle colours. Rugged practicality was our aim.

Erysimum cheiri 'Harpur Crewe'.

The third section of the walled garden, still substantially under cultivation on my first visit, is called the physic garden, presumably to distinguish it from the main kitchen garden which would have been a major show piece as well as a productive garden for top quality fruit, vegetables and flowers. The physic garden seems to have been partly herb garden, partly nursery, partly frameyard (for melons, seakale, marrows, etc.), partly greenhouse and partly for the production of cut flowers and foliage for the house; all in the days when abundant produce was demanded at all seasons for a largely self-sufficient community. By the late twentieth century it had become the sole productive space, with a mainly derelict frameyard, although the melon pit (sunken greenhouse) was still (sort of) functioning for the production of cucumbers. Most of the acre-and-a-half was given over to soft fruit and vegetables, petering out at the eastern end with fruit trees, mostly old apples.

Bearing in mind that even Steve was no superman, and the flower garden was to be labour-intensive, we decided on a policy of gradual renewal in the hope and expectation that some further funding for gardeners would be forthcoming (as indeed it was) when the Trust and the visitors realised the full significance of the garden. The tricky philosophy would be to attempt to retain an air of gentle decline, combined with evidence of productive revival, notionally to match the reduced demands of the house and its changed function. In gardens ambition is constricted by the availability of labour, especially the employment of skilled gardeners with energy, drive and mature judgement. Steve had all of these and also called a spade a spade, manfully defending his inevitably limited gardening time from those who would use the gardener as handyman or messenger.

Throughout my time in the Trust I sought to protect gardeners from this insidious and frustrating diversion of their time and effort, i.e. using them for unskilled work generated by activities not in any way related to the garden. If this arises from minor or major crises or because of accident or for special occasions, it is entirely acceptable that everyone should pull together. However, too often gardeners are used as a source of uncosted labour to support regular events and to carry out predictable maintenance work without being credited in any way. Every time labour is lost to a garden it inevitably results in a decline in standards unless replaced in kind.

ROWALLANE

Until 1973, when the IRA put a fire-bomb into the regional office on the edge of Belfast, Rowallane was the home of the Regional Director, John Lewis-Crosby, and his wife Diana. They were a charismatic couple with a deep knowledge of Irish houses and their contents and a special understanding of Northern Irish affairs. During my first visit to the province with my predecessor Graham Thomas, we stayed as guests of the Lewis-Crosbys, a wonderful opportunity to experience the garden in relation to the house as a private dwelling, before it became institutionalised as the regional office. With visitor numbers in the low thousands, mostly in April and May for the azaleas and rhododendrons, the impact of the Trust had been delightfully slight and on waking for an early walk in the garden it was easy to imagine oneself in the shoes of Hugh Armytage-Moore in the 1930s. Our short stay at Rowallane on that occasion coincided with one of the Lewis-Crosby's big dinner parties that they frequently gave for the great and the good (and not so good?) of Northern Ireland society and politics. Principal among the guests was Sir Terence O'Neill, Chairman of the Regional Committee, who soon became Prime Minister of Northern Ireland for a short time, before the more hard-line Unionists took charge and internment was implemented. With him was Lady O'Neill, the strongest single influence in the Trust's gardens in Northern Ireland and a knowledgeable plantswoman.

Jean O'Neill had in effect assumed, part-time, the role of the former owner of the garden at Rowallane, visiting often enough to sustain a relationship with it and the head gardener, John Hanvey senior, who had of course served Hugh Armytage-Moore and was able to carry on the traditions of the place as a respected figure in the comparatively small world of Ulster gardening. Mainly, I gathered, because it seemed to be the most convenient solution, his son, another John Hanvey, was appointed to succeed his father, with the agreement of Jean and Graham Thomas. Jean was charming and gracious and was devoted to the garden but, almost to the exclusion of all else, she was a plantswoman with extensive knowledge of flowering shrubs and a special interest in Australasian woody plants. Although subsequently she would occasionally conduct me round the garden with John Hanvey junior and ask my views on some issues, she was clearly in charge. Her enthusiasm led her to donate to the garden many new shrubs and trees provided from her many gardening connections and enthusiasms, some from Australia. While this did carry forward the garden's traditions for plant collecting from the wild, sources were never properly recorded and labels were often lost; indeed, many young plants never found a home and in the then obviously lax regime at Rowallane were wasted.

This indiscriminate approach to plant collecting frustrated me, but as yet no one outside the botanic gardens had attempted to establish any sort of objective approach to the conservation of historic plant collections which aimed at retaining the special character and spectrum of each. Clearly the Trust's principal responsibility was to identify, record and conserve the existing plant collection, but there was not even a complete catalogue at Rowallane, let alone any method-ical approach. On the other hand, totally to freeze the existing range of plants would be stultifying and would fail to continue the garden's enlivening tradition of plant collecting from the wild together with their subsequent evaluation and cultivation. It was a long time before the Trust began to take its plant collections seriously enough to spend significant resources on their critical identification, cataloguing and propagation. In contrast, the Trust's collections of the contents of houses have always been quite rightly catalogued, described, photographed and conserved with meticulous care, whatever the cost and however humble the object.

A consequence of Lady O'Neill's plant-orientated approach to the conservation of the garden was that she rather ignored the subtle value of its progression of spaces and views, in favour of filling most vacant pieces of grass with trees or large shrubs, usually spaced out orchard-like according to whim. It was not until Lady O'Neill gave up her chairmanship of the Northern Ireland Gardens Committee and retired to Hampshire in the late 1970s that I took over advising regularly twice a year at Rowallane. I was faced with the tricky challenge of having to grad-ually unpick what Jean had done – leaving appropriate trees where we judged them to be right and removing many that seemed to have no relevance, cluttering views and threatening in time to spoil valuable features. Although she went back from time to time, Lady O'Neill always graciously commented on the condition of the garden and never once reproached me for removing her introductions; saintly restraint by any standard.

Rhododendrons and azaleas in the Old Wood part of Rowallane, collected, propagated and planted by Hugh Armytage-Moore. (2001)

It was not until 1980 that the Trust began seriously to catalogue its incomparable collection of plants, and we were able to set up a scheme called the Woody Plant Catalogue. Through the influence of the Earl of Rosse, funding from the Thomas Phillips Price Trust was channelled via the Royal Botanic Gardens, Kew into a joint project with the National Trust aimed at cataloguing woody plants in twenty large gardens and arboreta. Although limited in extent, the aim was to catalogue and as far as possible critically identify every woody plant along with known details, especially origin and date of planting. Following a pilot study by Michael Zander, Michael Lear was employed part-time by the Trust under my general supervision to begin this time-consuming and expensive exercise. With commendable energy and flexibility he quickly developed his expertise in garden-based recording, identification and research in gardens and arboreta as far removed as Cornwall, Northumbria, Kent, Wales and Northern Ireland. At Rowallane this resulted at last in a proper analysis of Armytage-Moore's precious diaries and annotated notebooks, and a huge effort to link these with contemporary plant collectors known to have provided plants or seeds. This raised the significance of many individual plants from being merely interesting or decorative to being important scientifically and historically, sometimes as the first of a species to be grown in the UK, occasionally as a unique survivor of a rare species. It allowed us subsequently to formulate objective policies for the conservation of plant collections and for the accession of appropriate new introductions to carry on the process.

The main challenge for the Woody Plant catalogue was to formulate a system of recording that was simple enough to be practicable but full enough to be sufficient; vitally it should be one that could and would be easily updated, without which it

Rowallane house seen from the walled garden with the long tile-edged formal beds, replanted with a scheme of blue and yellow including *Hypericum* 'Rowallane' behind *Agapanthus* 'Headbourne Hybrids'; in front is massed *Geranium wallichianum* 'Buxton's Variety'. (1988)

would soon become solely an historical 'snapshot'. Botanic garden systems were far too complex and labour-intensive, bearing in mind that head gardeners were unlikely to receive additional help. At the time the Royal Botanic Gardens, Kew had more gardeners than all of the National Trust gardens put together, while the Trust was responsible for the world's greatest collection of cultivated plants under single ownership! The Chairman of the informal committee that ran the Woody Plant Catalogue was George Clive, a member of the Trust's advisory Gardens Panel who, in his quiet and effective way, was a tower of strength and support on behalf of the Trust's gardens.

As soon as I began regularly advising at Rowallane, it became apparent that in almost every respect the garden had been steadily deteriorating for a generation, first under the ageing John Hanvey senior and latterly under his son, neither of whom had the energy needed constantly to renovate and refresh the place. Especially with old gardens of high reputation, it is all too easy to allow growth and development of the more vigorous plants unobtrusively to overwhelm the choice plants and to obscure the qualities that gave the place its original reputation. It takes a new eye and a different approach, based on an in-depth study of the garden and how it was made and developed, to stimulate a valid plan for a garden's long-term conservation. At Rowallane, where the garden had stagnated for many years, there needed to be a clear strategy for renovation based on priority and driven with energy and enthusiasm. It was time for new leadership and John Hanvey junior, who was not a fit man, readily agreed to move on to a different garden.

With the Northern Ireland regional office moving to Rowallane, and with increased visiting in the early 1980s, the garden came under heavier pressure, mainly from staff and visitors who all wished to park or deliver as close to the front door as possible, threatening to erode the character of the place still further. In Northern Ireland, even more so than in England, most people are usually indignant about having to walk more than a few steps from their cars, and the ubiquitous 'white van man' will often drive over lawns and plants to reach his goal! We decided on a bold move, strongly and crucially supported by the new Regional Director, Tony Lord, to grass over the tarmacadam forecourt, leaving only footpaths, and channelling all vehicles into a new, screened car park. As well as protecting the garden, this was conveniently justified on security grounds. Furthermore, there had always been a back drive through the arboretum/pleasure ground, which had become a short cut for locals and a security risk. Closure of this in favour of slightly widening the front drive and eventually a new return drive was a huge improvement.

None of this could have been accomplished without a new head gardener with exceptional leadership qualities and proven experience. To the enormous benefit of Rowallane, Mike Snowden, after seven years of outstanding service at Erddig, accepted our invitation to take on this new challenge and move into the stable yard accommodation with his wife June and daughter Penny. Despite the continuing political unrest and insecurity in the Province, they never regretted this brave and imaginative move, staying on in Saintfield happily after retirement despite their Yorkshire roots.

Within a few weeks of their arrival the morale at Rowallane was transformed; staff regarded merely as reluctant operatives had each been assigned responsible roles to which they responded positively. Plans were made for new machinery, improved staff facilities and renovation of the nursery, with its hundreds of stranded plants in pots. Much of what needed to be done was obvious – pruning, tidying up, removal of self-sown trees and seedling laurels, etc. Little real gardening had been done for years and the whole of the walled garden needed progressive renovation, section by section, to remove perennial weeds, rescue precious plants, prune shrubs, divide overgrown perennials and propagate plants under threat. Hugh Armytage-Moore seems to have inherited a conventional kitchen garden and, as is the way of plantsmen, proceeded to fill it with new introductions obtained through his friends and contacts, until fruit and vegetables became totally redundant. Some original introductions from the wild and unique cultivars were there, including the *Viburnum, Chaeonomeles, Hypericum, Primula* and *Crocosmia* named for Rowallane.

Armytage-Moore had inherited the place with a long ornamental drive, a walled garden near the house, and beyond it a conventional Victorian pleasure ground/ arboretum with a pond, all sheltered by beech, Scots pines and laurels. Alongside this, to the east and north, lay a series of little rocky paddocks typical of the small-scale landscape of Co. Down with its relentless drumlins (hillocks) and picturesque outcrops of rock covered with whin (gorse). As the need for grazing land had decreased and the walled garden overflowed with horticultural and botanical treasures, Armytage-Moore proceeded gradually to take over these stone-walled enclosures for gardening, planting many newly-raised rhododendrons, azaleas and other rare trees and shrubs. However, none of this was done indiscriminately, as is often the case with plantsmen (who are inclined only to see one specimen at a time). His touch was light and he must have given careful thought to preserving the character of the landscape and revealing and enhancing its unique features. The separate enclosures even retained their traditional names – old wood, paddock, hospital, etc., and each was given a separate character in the planting. The rock garden is an impressive natural stone outcrop with a boggy stream alongside. The terrain is locally very variable, with wet and dry areas, thin lime-free soil predominating but with more fertile areas occasionally. All this and the equable climate made it possible to find successful places to grow a hitherto unfamiliar range of plants from China, the Himalaya, Australasia and South America.

With the new head gardener we devised a plan for comprehensive renewal, based upon precedent but not entirely governed by it, where changed circumstances and new demands dictated. Each part of the programme of work was assigned a priority to be met flexibly as resources and opportunity allowed. Over the ensuing fifteen years or so Mike Snowden and his staff totally renovated the whole place, removing or pruning and reducing vast areas of overgrown laurels and common rhododendrons to reveal long-lost features, re-open views and recreate long-gone spaces, especially along the landscaped drive and in the pleasure ground/ arboretum. This gave room to extend and enrich the collection of trees and shrubs with known-source introductions

Crocosmia masoniorum 'Rowallane Yellow'.

from the wild, now properly recorded. Also in the pleasure ground/arboretum, the silted-up pond was dredged and given a new setting of trees and shrubs.

One remarkable innovation in the spirit of Rowallane came about through the long-established garden practice of collecting up big-surface stones and building cairns, low walls or simply heaps. One of these was built whimsically to form, for no known reason, a large circular platform which we always called 'the bandstand'. Through great perception and good fortune, the Historic Buildings Representative, Peter Marlow, came upon a derelict but structurally sound listed Victorian bandstand, then redundant, in Newcastle, Co. Down. He was offered the caste-iron superstructure and accepted it. Well recorded by contemporary photographs, it turned out to fit the exact proportions of Rowallane's stone platform. Its removal and reconstruction, supervised by Mike Snowden, was a triumph of enterprise team work and not a little skill. Innovation in historic gardens should never be ruled out, especially in a case like this where the bandstand's destiny seemed pre-ordained.

The other important innovation at Rowallane was a long-term programme aimed at improving the diversity of its wildlife. Most gardens are at least as rich as an equivalent area of rainforest in wildlife habitat and food sources. Extensive areas of native plants and nettles are neither necessary or desirable. Management is the key – pruning and grass-cutting at the most advantageous times, retention of long grass and dead wood where it does not prejudice the garden's character, some ponds and marshy areas free of voracious fish, etc. At Rowallane spectacular success was achieved in the pleasure ground/arboretum, which had been traditionally mown (when dry enough) with gang mowers, thereby retaining fertility and lush grass. This was changed to an annual 'hay-making' regime of long grass with mown footpaths, and within a few years the wild flowers returned in abundance, including masses of orchids, accompanied inevitably by insects and small mammals to sustain larger creatures and birds. However rewarding, these measures are not appropriate everywhere and would be totally at odds with most flower gardens, which rely for their aesthetic effect and historic significance on being manicured.

CHASTLETON HOUSE

OXFORDSHIRE

The notion of romantic decay as desirable and worthy of preservation has gathered strength in the consciousness of the British, especially the English, during the twentieth century. This taste seems to have originated in the eighteenth century with ideas of the Picturesque arising in response to Lancelot Brown's smooth idealism: taking the form of carefully preserved (or constructed) ruins surrounded by rugged scenes of craggy rock, tufty grass and half-dead trees. For different reasons this style is now much to the taste of the nature conservation lobby, some of whom would have us turn all parks into wood pasture and protect every ruined wall from repair for fear of disturbing the lichens. How often, when hearing that I was the Trust's Head of Gardens, have people sought me out to pronounce, thinking it an original observation, that they much preferred this or that garden before restoration, implying that we should have frozen it thus?

In the Trust I learned to pick up hints, and always assumed that Chastleton would be acquired because of it being an allegedly unaltered Jacobean house of great beauty. Visiting it in the 1980s was a memorable experience, Mrs Clutton-Brock emerging between curtains of draught-defeating clear plastic. She would wave an arm in the direction of a non-stop guide, whom one found by listening hard for a distant voice, and joining the party for as long as necessary. After repairs by English Heritage and subsequent lengthy negotiations, it came to the Trust in 1991 via the National Heritage Memorial Fund. By then the Trust had become expert at a style of historic buildings conservation that aimed at preserving strictly the

The north front of Chastleton house under repair while the garden was still largely derelict. Near the house were croquet lawns where the rules of the game were regularised.

status quo on acquisition, without any attempt at restoring to an earlier condition. With great skill and meticulous attention to detail, Calke Abbey, for example, was faithfully recorded, emptied, repaired and reinstated in an attempt at preserving the appearance of benign neglect and romantic disrepair. Even the impression of accumulated grime and generations of wear and tear was reproduced.

Such was the Trust's obsession with the supposed untouched historic veracity of Chastleton House and its contents that this policy of 'preserve as found' was extended to the garden, much to my despair. Clearly I had failed to demonstrate, even after Calke Abbey, that this approach is both philosophically and practically unsound in gardens, except in relation to buildings and artefacts. Every plant has a finite life expectancy and, like people, cannot be revived when dead, merely preserved or embalmed.

A contributory fallacy in this decision was the legend that the garden was contemporary with the house, an overlooked survivor of early seventeenth-century gardening. There was no evidence of this, although the main axial enclosures south, east and north of the house correspond with what one would expect, and they may well have been survivals. In his book, *The Renaissance Garden in England* (1979), Sir Roy Strong firmly implied (without evidence) that the circular layout of the 'Best Garden' on the south side is 'a distant reflection of the original layout', adding perhaps spurious weight to the fable. It is not unknown for owners or gardeners to invent some history to give their garden greater significance.

In fact, I soon handed over advising at Chastleton to my colleague, and eventual successor, Mike Calnan, but not before the Trust had determined its mistaken policy. The only solid evidence I was aware of is that H. Inigo Triggs recorded that in 1828 there was a replanting on the lines of an earlier arrangement, no doubt part of the romantic fashion for 'historical' re-creation at that time. There is

evidence that the garden was subsequently redeveloped and that lawns were laid for croquet because it is known that the official rules of the sport were regularised at Chastleton. Furthermore, in style and planting, the Wilderness Walk, which survived the post-war dereliction, seems to have come straight out of the illustrations in William Robinson's *The Wild Garden* (1894). A succession of photographs shows clearly that the garden, far from being relict, was in good order between the wars and reasonably well kept even after the Second World War. The 'romantic decay' seems to have set in only as a result of neglect during the forty years or so leading up to the Trust's acquisition.

So the Trust blundered on for twenty years with an erroneous policy based, it seems, on little other than romantic hearsay, leaving the garden tidy but blandly meaningless and with nowhere to go. One could reasonably enquire on what basis the Trust has restored the croquet lawns and cultivated the walled garden for vegetable production while the 'Best Garden' remains an empty relic of its pre-war splendour? The history of Chastleton's garden seems to have been one of a series of re-creations, always perhaps with a nod to the past but clearly in the style of the day. Why not another one?

Chapter 5

STORM

Before the storm
this Cedar of
Lebanon at
Petworth was a
champion tree,
the tallest of its
kind in Britain;
on 17th October
1987 it was the
longest.

NYMANS

WEST SUSSEX

At the time I succeeded Graham Thomas as Gardens Adviser, Lord Rosse was a tower of strength in the Trust, being the Chairman of the influential Properties Committee and of the putative Gardens Panel. Among his many interests he was passionate about gardens; since then the Trust has lacked an influential gardens champion of his standing. Lord Rosse was knowledgeable, well-connected and able to manipulate events with sheer charm. His judgement was infallible until it came to his own property Nymans, where subjectivity and Lady Rosse (who was the garden's 'Director') held sway.

My first encounter with the Countess of Rosse was on a day when she and the Earl of Rosse had invited (one did not say 'no') all the great and the good of the Trust, including the Director General Jack Boles, along with the regional hierarchy, to Nymans to resolve management and financial problems, mainly involving the house. The main part of Leonard Messels' 1920s house had been destroyed by fire in 1947, leaving only the western part with a roof and the rest preserved as a shell. Consequent problems of waterproofing and maintenance were costly and Lady Rosse was determined that the Trust should meet the bills, although the property was always deeply 'in the red'. Uncertain of my role in the tricky negotiations, I nevertheless hung about making polite conversation until Lord Rosse took me to one side: 'You may think my wife is difficult, John,' he said, 'but you should have met her mother.'

Graham Thomas was never welcome and my visits to Nymans in the 1970s were few. Although I admired the remarkable quality and diversity of the plant collection, the place always seemed dank and over-mature, with only a few glimpses of

Nymans is primarily a garden of rare, interesting and beautiful plants collected by Leonard Messel and his family. It surrounds the stabilised ruins of the house mostly destroyed by fire in 1947.

the superb landscape of the Sussex Downs. As Lady Rosse would say, 'one's parents felt it slightly indecent to see out'. Starting with an unremarkable late-Victorian layout, the Messels had enriched the plant collection and embellished the garden in their lavish style for three generations. Since Leonard Messel's time they had subscribed to almost every notable plant hunting expedition, from Ernest Wilson onwards, including those of Harold Comber, son of Nymans's legendary head gardener James Comber. Being perched high, the garden is comparatively frost-free, the lime-free soil deep and fertile, and only shelter is needed to grow an astonishing range of plants, especially trees and shrubs. Until the 1987 storm, the garden contained no fewer than twenty-eight national champion trees (i.e. the tallest of their kind in Britain); after the storm only eight.

The garden had been marking time since it was accepted by the National Trust with an inadequate endowment in 1954 on the death of Leonard Messel, his wife Maud remaining in charge until 1960. The traditions of acquiring plants from the wild and showing at the Vincent Square RHS shows had continued unabated. However, little consideration had been given by the Rosses either to the renewal of the garden's structure or to the continuity of the gardens staff. The garden was full of spindly overgrown conifers, originally planted for shelter, together with overcrowded evergreens and exotics: an accident waiting to happen. Similarly, in the late 1970s there was only one person under sixty-five among the garden staff; most were in their seventies and one part-timer was over eighty. To a gentle suggestion that a new head gardener should be sought, Lady Rosse's reply was that 'Nice [the head gardener then] has at least ten years in him', which would have made Cecil nearly eighty before being allowed to retire! I was charged with finding a successor suitable to Lord and Lady Rosse who would be capable of picking up the threads and acquiring the garden's, as yet, unrecorded history and traditions. The excellent Philip Holmes (the only young gardener) had no ambition to take charge but remained as a valuable bridge between generations.

David Masters started his horticultural training at Sheffield Park after a successful but unrewarding former career. Highly intelligent, he learned quickly and before long was appointed head gardener at Beningbrough Hall, near York, where he distinguished himself by leading a small team in transforming the garden from near dereliction to a place of which the Trust could be proud. Knowing his background and abilities, I was sure David was the right person, but there had to be a leap of faith. First he had to be introduced and vetted by Cecil Nice, then the Rosses had to be persuaded. When eventually they agreed to see him their reaction was predictably non-committal, but favourable. Luckily Cecil Nice liked David, who had to be carefully briefed about understanding the need to learn from his predecessor. Nymans's third head gardener of the century, David played the game and was accepted as Assistant Head Gardener 'on probation'. However, to be fair to him the Trust had to give an informal verbal undertaking that he would not be cast aside if the Rosses took a dislike. We need not have worried because they soon came to rely on David, and Cecil Nice was only too happy to pass on his knowledge and retire. But it was a close-run thing.

After Lord Rosse died it was agreed that I should visit regularly, as with other gardens, to advise Lady Rosse who repeatedly reminded me of her title of

Director. She was always charming but I well understood that she had no intention of accepting any initiative proposed by me, representing the Trust, which had to be manipulated to her ends. So began an entirely insincere game in which she held all the trump cards. Her way was to command me 'dear John, come at noon' when she would be ready to receive me, full of her latest idea, often something comparatively minor. She must have realised that, having driven from Cirencester, I would be able to have an hour with David Masters, who by then enjoyed her confidence. This enabled me to agree a joint response and a way forward on important issues already broached by David. I never mentioned having already seen him and she never enquired.

Her tactics were to insist on giving me a large drink, which I was not allowed to refuse – because it was 'Michael's [Lord Rosse's] special cocktail' (highly alcoholic) – obviously to soften me up. Sometimes I was able to dispose of much of it while she was not looking, but this depended on the 'phone ringing, after which she would tell me who it had been: perhaps her son, maybe Lord Snowdon, and on one occasion the Queen Mother. She then talked about the garden for a while, relating her concerns. (Latterly these focused on replacing the Japanese Garden structure, which had to be taken down when the weeping elm died of Dutch elm disease – what to replant? She insisted on raising the height of the mound and the structure, and eventually chose, from a series of alternatives, a weeping hornbeam, now unaccountably removed despite its intimate association with this remarkable lady, a key figure in the history of a great garden.)

Then it would be lunch with wine during which she would relate some of her philosophy as Garden Director. Very proud of understanding 'the common visitor from Croydon', she would point out that 'the common people never look up; if I ask them whether they have seen the Handkerchief Tree they think I am talking about a stall at Selfridges. So I put my little vulgar flowers [by this she meant dwarf Japanese azaleas] low on the ground for them.' She said that she often spoke to 'her public', always regally asking where they came from, but she was disconcerted one day when I heard the reply, 'I come from Surbiton dear, where do you come from?' No doubt surprised but unabashed, Lady Rosse replied politely, 'I live here and I am the garden's Director.'

David Masters would be instructed to appear at 2 pm, and by about 2.30 pm Lady Rosse would announce the need to 'venture forth' for an hour or so, never getting further than the Rock Garden, where her concerns were invariably centred.

Although the reports of my visits tended to be full of evasions and generalities, bearing in mind Anne Rosse's extreme conservatism, with David Masters much was done covertly. Through Michael Lear we were cataloguing the plant collection, beginning the process of propagating its rare and endangered plants and planting trees for shelter, albeit too late. All this went on at a level outside Lady Rosse's consciousness, or at least she never let on. Jim Lees-Milne had her exactly summed up in his obituary of her in *The Times* when he said words to the effect that 'Anne Rosse raised the practice of insincerity to the level of an art form'.

Providentially, by the time of the great storm of 1987 Anne Rosse was too far advanced into dementia to be fully aware. She had been a great beauty in her

BELOW LEFT
An aerial view of the Pinetum immediately after the storm of 16th October 1987 when 95% of the trees were lost or irrevocably damaged.

BELOW RIGHT
A similar view in October 1988 after extracting hundreds of tons of rare timber.

youth; it was sad to witness her decline, although she was able to find the strength of will to help her granddaughter, Lady Frances Armstrong-Jones, to reopen the extended and redesigned rose garden in 1990, as well as to plant a replacement for the giant monkey puzzle tree lost in the storm. Sadly this young tree was allowed to die through neglect of watering.

Taking everyone by surprise, the great storm of October 1987 devastated Nymans. After almost a century most of the original structural planting and many of the larger trees, especially conifers, had been maturing. The ferocious storm caused havoc throughout, but particularly in the densely planted pinetum and the Top Garden, with 90 per cent of larger trees either uprooted or shaken and broken beyond recall. Incredibly, David Masters slept through it, drawing the curtains in the morning to unbelievable devastation, perhaps the worst in any of the National

The mixed flower borders in the Wall Garden after the effect of the great storm which resulted in less shelter but more light.

Trust's great gardens. The shock was numbing to all concerned, especially to the gardeners, whose life's work had gone. Then there was the depressing prospect of many months of clearance without any reward: all drudgery and not much real gardening. After a year hundreds of tons of timber had been removed. It reflects great credit on the whole garden staff that they remained positive. But the first sign of their positive attitude was shown ten days after the storm, when Nymans staged an exhibit at the RHS Tree and Shrub Show at Vincent Square, demonstrating the former wealth of the tree collection by a tremendous display of severed branches and crowns of trees.

At the time of the storm the new rose garden was being prepared for replanting to my design, an extended version of the original. Most of Maud Messel's stock of old shrub roses, guarded by her for decades, had been propagated for their new home in fresh soil treated against replant disease. With so much clearance to do, it was tempting to delay this work but we decided to proceed as quickly as possible, knowing that roses give an almost immediate impact; the gardeners could thereby work towards at least one part of the garden looking well in the immediate future. There was much to be seen as early as 1989 and by the official opening in June 1990 it was full of colour, a real psychological boost.

All the fallen trees had been recently catalogued and critically identified by Michael Lear and, along with unique trees from other gardens, an emergency propagation programme was put in hand. This resulted in over 60 per cent of the

RIGHT The great Monkey Puzzle, *Araucaria araucana*, before the storm.

The site ready for the redesigned and extended rose garden at Nymans. Despite the massive clear-up after the storm we decided to go ahead immediatelyed so as to raise morale and allow visitors to experience the restoration.

genetic stock being saved for replanting, along with others already in stock, plus new introductions being acquired from the wild, in the tradition of Nymans. It was a rare privilege to design the new pinetum along the lines of the original – though inevitably and rightly not the same. For mutual shelter and quick effect, the pinetum was densely planted with quick-growing fillers, e.g. birches and *Nothofagus*, to nurse the longer-term trees. (Timely thinning and replacement are vital for gardens, especially arboreta.)

Before the storm one of the problems for visitors was circulation, the garden being narrow and linear with the only site for a car park at its extreme western end. Comprehensive destruction and replanting made it possible to point visitors on arrival through the pinetum onto a new path which gives fine views to the north. The idea was that this would curve round towards the house, thereby encouraging visitors to see more and relieve congestion. To this end the pinetum was given more of the flowering shrubs already present, e.g. hydrangeas, eucryphias, rhododendrons, etc.

As Lady Rosse faded, Alastair Buchanan, a grandson of the garden's founder, Leonard Messel, took on the role of family representative only a few days before the great storm. Already known to David Masters and the other gardeners, he played an important part in restoring morale and a positive role in the garden's revival thereafter.

The task of clearance, reconstruction and replanting was daunting, but it was a privilege beyond compare to be involved. In the case of Nymans the time scale of renewal had to be much faster than the ideal, and this made it more exciting. Rather than an attempt to stick slavishly to precedent, the conservation of

The extended Rose Garden in 1990 about three years after the storm, containing most of Maud Messell's collection of historic cultivars which she had saved.

plantsmen's gardens like Nymans is about renewing the historic structure and then contriving a unique ecosystem in which the processes are natural but the plants are mostly exotic, associated together as never before towards an aesthetic ideal derived from the former owners.

The Countess of Rosse with her grand-daughter Lady Frances Armstrong-Jones (von Hofmannsthal) opening the replanted Rose Garden in June 1990.

Constant change and development are both inevitable and desirable – that is what we enjoy about gardens. Significantly, almost from the day of the storm (after which people were admitted once it was safe), visitor numbers increased rapidly year on year, with people enjoying the transformation. Gardens like Nymans are as much about management as maintenance; propagation as repair; plants as precedent. Above all Nymans is about people.

Ten years after that cataclysmic storm the garden was both presentable and dynamic, containing a better collection of well-documented plants than at any other time in its history: a remarkable achievement by a devoted team. Restoration is hardly the right term because the process should be continuous, as the history of Nymans over the past century has demonstrated.

The great storm of October 1987 was a turning point for historic parks and gardens in Britain. Perhaps because it hit the south-east principally, including Hampshire, Sussex, Surrey and London, extending north-east as far as Norfolk, it had a profound effect on the consciousness of the country's most influential citizens. For the first time, it seems, people began to understand that trees, however mighty, were not immovable fixtures and that our landscape is not an immutable backdrop, to be taken for granted like the air we breathe. Although enlightened owners and organisations like the National Trust had been planning and planting for the future, too few people in Britain had given thought to renewal or succession in their gardens and parks, the richest and most diverse collection in the world. Furthermore, as swaths of overcrowded conifers fell like matchsticks, the storm also gave support to the move for change in forestry policy and practice.

Most gardens and parks were due for a cull, many of them having accumulated fine old trees dating both from the eighteenth-century English landscape planting

Part of the pleasure ground at Petworth immediately after the great storm of October 1987.

boom and our nineteenth-century obsession with planting exotic trees from all over the temperate world. Although trees obviously vary greatly in their longevity, it is reasonable to assume that the turnover of trees, for various reasons deliberate and natural, can be expected to average a century or so. After many years without serious storms, there was a backlog of vulnerable trees in most well-established estates. Although seemingly disastrous, the loss of around 10 per cent experienced at Kew and several other well-known gardens and parks could have been expected. This was the order of loss in the park at Petworth. While obviously traumatic at the time, the storm created no long-term problem. John Workman, the Trust's Forestry Adviser, had been instigating steady renewal planting throughout Brown's parkland for at least two decades, based simply on first edition Ordnance Survey maps, which proved a reliable and accurate record of nineteenth-century tree positions.

The storm showed up how little serious historic landscape research had been carried out in England, including at Petworth, and how far behind it was compared with historic houses in this respect. Fortunately, some four years before the storm, English Heritage had been formed, part of whose remit was to create for the first time a register of historic parks and gardens and to advise on their conservation. The huge wave of emotion arising from the storm resulted in funding for an English Heritage scheme for grant-aiding historic sites covering replanting plans and repair, based crucially on proper research and surveys undertaken by approved contractors. Following the National Trust's pioneering conservation plans of the late 1970s and further surveys and researches carried out by the Royal Parks in the early 1980s, these English Heritage grants had the effect of consolidating and expanding the new profession of historic parks and gardens surveyor, and of formulating conservation plans, based on approved techniques of survey and research. This was a tremendous step forward, not least in informing landowners about the significance of what they owned, as well as promoting evidence-based replanting.

With no one at English Heritage fully understanding the fundamental differences between the conservation and repair of buildings on the one hand and the restoration and renewal of designed landscape on the other, a rigid structure of like-for-like replanting was put in place. In essence, if you could prove something was once part of the scene you could claim to put it back. In many ways this simple philosophy served its purpose for post-storm replanting and worked perfectly well for the repair of buildings, which are often the most expensive elements of any restoration. However, it ignored the fact that gardens and parks arise out of a series of interlinked processes, beginning with buildings, land form and planting, followed by growth and development – i.e. thinning, protection, cultivation, pruning and adjustment. To take a simple example, a park clump of say twenty-five forest trees, interplanted with a 'nurse' of short-lived trees, may eventually become five trees standing alone after half a century. In gardens this kind of process is likely to be much more complex and dependent on many more judgements.

In the first decade of the eighteenth century there was by all accounts the worst storm ever recorded in England. It caused a 'tsunami' up the Severn estuary,

An aerial view of the pleasure ground and part of the park after catastrophic damage from the great storm.

serious flooding, many trees blown down across the south of England and much upheaval and loss of life. No doubt this promoted a surge of replanting afterwards, especially in the great estates, and the pleasure ground at Petworth was first planted at this time. It began as a close-planted formal plantation, probably designed by George London, described as 'birchen walks' and clearly intended as pleasure ground from the outset. By the time Lancelot Brown arrived in the 1750s, this plantation would have been semi-mature, and no doubt the short-lived birches were already being phased out to favour the mixture of forest-type trees, some of which survived until the 1987 storm. Contrary to established prejudice about Brown, he retained this large formal plantation as the core of his expanded pleasure ground, which he designed in his recognisably informal style with two temples and a wide range of trees and shrubs. This expansion involved demolishing part of the town to allow for a shelterbelt of trees and a screen of evergreens for privacy, Petworth always having had a reputation for turning its back on the town and its inhabitants.

The pleasure ground at Petworth was noted in the nineteenth century for the quality and height of its trees, soaring up on impressively tall stems to create a high canopy, as on the continent of Europe. Growing in close company on fertile greensand, they were the product of their style of cultivation over a century and a half, gradually becoming fewer as occasional trees fell. Moreover, few had been added since Brown's time, apart from smaller ornamental trees and shrubs. An even-aged plantation of exceptional height is liable to fall together and this is what happened in October 1987, the central pleasure ground being almost completely destroyed, including England's tallest-ever Lebanon cedar which that night became the longest! It was impossible to cross the pleasure ground on foot next morning.

We were left with the massive task of clearing hundreds of tons of mostly useless timber and disposing of a huge number of stumps mostly weighing several tons each. However, the Trust's highly intelligent head gardener, Trevor Seddon, was undaunted once the initial shock had worn off, and he took an admirably philosophical view, soon coming to realise that this was an historic opportunity as well as a lot of work. We were of a single mind in believing that replanting would be a privilege on such an historic site; there is nothing more satisfying than planting trees.

We were delighted when the Trust decided not to seek an English Heritage grant for replanting because this would have hampered our actions. Taking account of the history of the pleasure ground and its trees, we decided on the need for a radical approach which took into account the fact that we had only two gardeners for 12 ha (30 acres): hardly sufficient when everything was mature, hopelessly inadequate while young trees and shrubs required maximum attention and constant care. Had we opted for an English Heritage grant at the time they would no doubt have insisted on replanting as exactly as possible what had fallen, a thin scattering of trees reflecting only the survivors of the original plantation. Nor would young trees planted at this density have any prospect of re-creating the pre-storm effect of tall stems and high canopy, instead inevitably developing as broad-crowned trees of totally different character and appearance. Furthermore, we judged they would appear meaninglessly forlorn scattered thinly across the site. A piece of former woodland would have been transformed into open grassland containing young trees, with all the unsustainable demands of upkeep associated with tree establishment and protection and grass management.

Ultimately we managed to convince all concerned that the best approach, both historically and practically, would be to start the 280-year long process over again. Only a dense plantation, gradually thinned over a century or two, could possibly recreate the effect of the trees that fell. A dense piece of woodland, forestry-style, would also be cheaper to establish and easier to care for, creating an immediate impact if carefully designed. This approach was accepted with enthusiasm by hardly anyone, including garden historians, even if they fully understood the (historical) point that gardens are about process and cannot be re-created at a stroke. We kept our heads down, and within a year or two most people began to enjoy the visible evidence of growth and development.

Reflecting the early-eighteenth-century term 'birchen walks', we decided to use silver birch as the quick-growing common denominator and short- to medium-term interplant in order to create an attractive quick effect. At 2 m (6 ft 6 in) spacing, this mixture of birch and longer-term forest trees soon created a canopy to suppress ground vegetation. Although we tried black plastic 'spats' for weed control, they proved no more successful than spraying with glyphosate for the first two to three years. Despite dry seasons, growth rates on all trees were nothing short of phenomenal, due to the fertile soil, the total absence of weed and grass competition and the provision of impenetrable rabbit fencing. From 0.5 m (1 ft 8 in) seedlings planted in 1989, we had birches over 3 m (9 ft 10 in) high in

The great house
at Petworth seen
from Lancelot
(Capability)
Brown's park.

two years and after a mere four years of growth they were up to 6 m (19 ft 8 in), already creating a strikingly decorative effect with their white stems. Thereafter it was important at this dense spacing to favour the best of the longer-term trees – sweet chestnuts, oaks, limes, beech, etc. – ensuring a diverse range of species, bearing in mind the constant threat of epidemic disease such as had already taken the elm.

The joy of this style of planting, although not suitable for every situation, lies in being able to enjoy the process and the consistent manipulation of the plantation by thinning and selection while retaining the canopy. The important thing is to provide plenty of options for our successors, an important consideration in historic garden conservation. I only hope that they will honour their obligation to care for the future by consistent timely thinning, protection and renewal.

We enjoy Killerton's garden and estate today because of an extraordinary act of generosity by the Aclands which included giving the National Trust the huge Holnicote estate in Somerset. The tortuous story is told in Merlin Waterson's *A Noble Thing: the National Trust and its Benefactors* (2011). However, whatever the family machinations and the political manoeuvres, the outcome is unquestionably of lasting benefit to the Trust and the nation.

For once the garden arguably eclipses the house because of its historic importance and botanical significance. Although formal and flowery near the house, it is the pleasure ground/arboretum that counts most in any assessment of the importance of the place. Associated with the golden age of plant hunting, the tree and shrub collection is outstanding in quality, diversity and significance. In 1808, at the time he set up what would become Britain's most important plant nursery of the nineteenth century, John Veitch was agent for 'the great' Sir Thomas Acland. They are credited with establishing the pleasure ground, beginning with the beech avenue, which has been consistently renewed. The Veitch connection was sustained through John Veitch's son James, who developed the nursery while it remained on the estate, and his grandsons James and Robert, who moved the nursery to Exeter. Eventually James Jr left the Exeter branch to develop its famous London base. Beginning in the 1840s, the firm sponsored plant hunting expeditions, from the Lobb brothers in the Americas and the Far East, to Ernest Wilson and William Purdom in China at the end of the century.

This emphasis on exotic plant introduction and on cultivating an ever-increasing collection of choice and uncommon plants has been sustained by the Aclands ever since, despite the need for economy in the 1930s. The property came to the Trust as a gift from Sir Richard Acland in 1944, evidently after he had lost a lot of money through the defunct Common Wealth political party that he set up with J.B. Priestley in 1943 during the war time national government. Sir Richard and Lady Anne moved out of the house but continued to live on the estate and to take an interest in the garden. I remember with great pleasure our occasional walks through the garden in the 1980s during which, with some diffidence, they would ask pertinent questions and make always constructive suggestions. Their recollections were valuable and illuminating and they were accepting of the need for change, an understandably rare quality in former owners.

The garden contains many important trees and some outstanding specimens of early introduction, including magnificent tulip trees (*Liriodendron tulipifera*), western red cedars and wellingtonias, probably from the first of their seeds raised in Europe. Gardens of this kind are often overcrowded and in need of sensitive renewal involving looking ahead, firstly by identifying and evaluating the plant collection and then by ensuring its propagation and replanting ahead of its inevitable eventual demise. As with cattle and royalty, it is the original 'bloodline' that counts; but for plants the exact genetic imprint can only be passed on by vegetative propagation – cuttings or grafts from the original plants. The huge task had never been tackled systematically and in the 1980s Killerton was high on our list of woody plant collections to be critically identified and catalogued by Michael Lear, so as to create a database which had then to be consistently updated. However, aiming simply to replant the same genetic form of the same species on the same spot in perpetuity would be neither biologically nor strategically practicable, nor is it necessary in order to retain the significance of the collection. In a plant collection the precise positioning of a plant is much less significant than perpetuating its exact genetic identity, provided that the garden retains its special planting style and character. Furthermore, to allow for accident, it is essential to propagate several cuttings from a specimen before its demise to ensure survival and to plant the progeny in several locations. This continuing task will never be complete but thanks to the Trust's new propagating nursery, the work is well underway.

Good lime-free soil and a favourable microclimate, due to being on a south slope, have made it possible to grow a wide range of less hardy plants, especially evergreens, and there is almost always something of interest and beauty to be found whatever the time of year. Spring and early summer are the peak times for enjoying Killerton's garden as the rhododendrons, azaleas, magnolias, camellias, etc., come into their own. Wind is the limiting consideration for growing plants and for enjoying them, shelter from the south-westerlies being vital at Killerton. Equally important is the glorious succession of views from the hillside in contrast to the cosy sheltered spaces.

Shelter was created originally by a belt of trees and evergreens beyond the ha-ha on the west side of the garden, an area eventually taken in as a bracing walk with glimpses here and there across the lovely parkland. Yews were used as

Magnolia kobus at Killerton. Storm damage was severe on the exposed western flank of the garden but the more sheltered east side mostly escaped. In Devon the worst storm occurred in January 1990.

understorey for a variety of trees, including the quick-growing and wind-tolerant Monterey pine (*Pinus radiata*) which grows even better in Devon than on the coast of California. By the 1980s these were over-mature and top-heavy with their masses of retained cones. Some had already fallen but the ferocious storms of 1990 and 1991 brought down most of those remaining, causing great damage; in retrospect we learned the need to take out Monterey pines after a century or so, long before they become liabilities. In contrast, a group of magnificent specimens of the Lucombe oak (*Quercus* × *hispanica* 'Lucombeana'), a hybrid between the evergreen Cork oak and the quick-growing Turkey oak raised in Exeter, survived without any damage in the full force of the wind.

By that time Andrew Mudge had succeeded the long-serving and distinguished Arthur Godfrey as head gardener, and was faced with the laborious but ultimately rewarding task of re-establishing the shelterbelt. We used a deliberately resilient mixture of deciduous trees and evergreens, including tough short-term species like cherries and thorns and longer-term beeches, oaks and limes with evergreens including yews and hollies, for the important understorey, all to be progressively thinned and managed.

Andrew took to the task with energy and enthusiasm, soon revealing a remarkable ability to organise work and inspire his staff. Within a few years he had accomplished several renovations of important parts of the garden as well as taking the renewal of the shelterbelt in his stride. He was always impatient for improvement, in a head gardener a quality so much preferable to someone, however knowledgeable and experienced, who needs to be pushed forward.

High on my list for total renovation was the old quarry behind the Bear's Hut, turned into a rock garden by the famous former head gardener, John Coutts,

The rock garden in the old quarry behind the Bear's Hut had been totally renovated and replanted. It was untouched by the storms of 1990.

before 1909 when he left to become Assistant Curator at Kew. Its style of construction would have been described by Reginald Farrer, in his *My Rock Garden* (1907), as of the 'almond pudding style' with the rocks stood on end like dragon's teeth and no attempt at simulating natural rock formations. This is not a place for his kind of meticulous alpine gardening with its miniature landscapes and time-consuming attention to plantsmanship. Nor is it an easy site, half of it being

One of the over-mature and top-heavy Monterey Pines that were uprooted by the storms, causing a great deal of damage.

situated on a steep slope exposed to the baking sun, the southern part being in deep gloom but barren and dry. By far the most successful plant was hart's-tongue fern, which had spread everywhere, sun and shade, tolerated even by Graham Thomas as a ground cover. However, in my experience this fern looks well only in humid shade; it survives in sun but the foliage invariably bleaches to an anaemic yellow with brown edges in times of drought. Our first step was total eradication of this 'weed' along with many other real ones: i.e. total 'scorched earth' treatment for a whole year. Bearing in mind the need for economy of labour, we decided on mostly low-growing, sun-loving shrubs and dwarf perennials for the hot banks. However, the crucial improvement was to introduce water by means of a plastic pipe laid by the gardeners across the garden. At all costs we were determined to avoid the Chelsea Flower Show gushing stream, preferring instead a cool trickle from a mossy corner via a marshy area to a quiet little pond. With primulas and other waterside plants on the quarry floor, this has created an ideal contrast, always needing care and attention but sustainable with Killerton's dedicated staff and volunteers.

On the dust jacket of *Plants for Ground Cover* by Graham Stuart Thomas (1970) is an historic photograph showing two important features. Uncomfortably close to the house was a large Tulip Tree which had been a worry since at least John Coutts's time because if it fell it would hit the house. After seventy years the Trust caved in to pressure and removed it for safety reasons, the last of several big trees that once populated the area west of the house and linked it visually with the pleasure ground landscape. Simple research revealed how many trees had been lost and never replaced, not an uncommon occurrence in old gardens. There is often a reluctance to replant big trees anywhere near the mansion despite historic precedent and aesthetic considerations in relating the buildings to the landscape.

Cyclamen coum and *C. repandum* from Italy naturalise freely with snowdrops in the grass at Killerton. (Early spring 1990)

The rustic bridge over the old ha-ha ditch is overhung with magnolias.

Now there are several young trees around the main lawns and at last, against some opposition, we were able to replant the historic tulip tree, Killerton's talisman.

The foreground of Graham Thomas's *Ground Cover* dusk jacket is occupied by his planting scheme for the former rose garden occupying a level terrace set out originally by none other than William Robinson, famously the author of *The Wild Garden!* The wisdom of this innovation between park and informal pleasure ground is debatable and by all accounts the formal rose garden of interwar bush roses was never a success in the soft Devon climate. No doubt fired by his researches in the late 1960s for the *Ground Cover* book, Graham designed an effective arrangement of dwarf shrubs, including skilful contrasts of foliage, colour and texture, a much imitated model of its kind. Twenty years later it had reached the end of its useful life and, with more resources, the consensus was that a more intensive and colourful layout, aimed at a long period of display, would be appropriate. This involved another total renovation to raise fertility and eliminate perennial weeds. My scheme was designed to begin with dwarf bulbs and early-flowering plants along the edges of the borders followed by herbaceous plants and shrubs, including repeat-flowering shrub roses and evergreens to give form and texture. Thanks to thoughtful cultivation and a meticulous pruning regime the outcome was much admired, being just high enough to give a sense of enclosure and strong enough visually to stand up to the broad scale of the surroundings. After another twenty years, after the turn of the century, the scheme was ready for another full renovation. Each part of every garden involves a separate time-scale of renewal and needs to be planted as part of a long-term conservation plan for the place.

BLICKLING HALL

Having lived then for a decade or so in Essex, I found Norfolk a stiffly conservative place at first. However, I soon came to admire the common-sense values, solid craftsmanship and local pride of the gardening community. I was familiar with the challenges of cold east winds and summer drought but not with the paternal, if not slightly feudal, approach to management that still prevailed in the 1970s. Blickling then was a well-run estate with an immaculate garden which had remained superficially static since the 1930s, although of course inevitably it was changing and decaying. In common with most large country house gardens, the whole enterprise had contracted in line with greatly reduced resources, the number of gardeners (mostly middle-aged) being by then just sufficient for the flower garden and pleasure ground. The extensive walled gardens, once the dynamic heart of the place, were now becalmed under a fall-back regime of grass and fruit trees. The National Trust had managed the fundamental change from private to public and from relative wealth to cautious parsimony with dedicated professionalism. The ship was still very much afloat despite creaking a bit below decks.

Thirty years of retrenchment is liable to encourage a defensive and unadventurous approach, but with advice from Graham Thomas, and under the regional management of Nicolas de Bazille Corbin, the most significant elements of the garden had been wisely cared for and steadily renovated as far as financially possible. The

The formal, 19th-century garden at Blickling and the 18th-century landscape park beyond.

garden is one of great historic importance in the English tradition: three centuries of precious continuity during which the garden and park were laid out, extended, developed and altered in line with current needs, taste and resources. At Blickling this was done in a way that preserves both evidence of every period of the garden's history and the most significant features of its recent past. No one ever set out to design the garden as it is today. This place of outstanding beauty, interest and international importance has come about from a series of deliberate and accidental changes arising from its history and those who have owned it. These are the unique qualities of the greatest of historic gardens in Britain.

Between the wars, Norah Lindsay was by far the most influential flower gardener in Britain. She made gardens for royalty, for the gentry and for what Vita Sackville-West called 'the filthy rich'. A self-made garden designer and plantsman, she came to the fore with energy and good contacts as Gertrude Jekyll became less and less active. However, unlike Jekyll, she did not write books or even draw proper plans, preferring usually to order her own palette of plants and set them out directly onto the ground. She was an artist, painting with colour and texture, used with a combination of controlled flamboyance and luxuriant abundance. Her style was a freer and more relaxed development of Jekyll and equally subtle – 'tone on tone' she would say. Her life and work are well described by Allyson Hayward in *Norah Lindsay: The Life and Art of a Garden Designer* (2007), but perhaps there is another book to be written about her gardening. The flower garden at Blickling is arguably her masterpiece and is certainly the best preserved

The great herbaceous borders at Blickling are a unique survival of Norah Lindsay's luxuriant planting style. During the 1930s she transformed the Victorian parterre using herbaceous perennials. (1990)

of any of her works. However, typically for an English garden, it was not designed from scratch, arising instead from the need to simplify for economy a complex and labour-intensive 1870s parterre by Markham Nesfield, which was also too gaudy for twentieth-century upper class taste. She seems to have been something of a nomad, staying as a house guest wherever she worked for however long it took: not at all in the mould of the modern consultant garden designer.

Looking past the lily pond in formal garden up the main vista from the house.

Effective conservation of the flower garden at Blickling is a special challenge, since it is such an important period piece. The colour schemes were obviously carefully contrived and the plant content still precisely matches the period c.1930, but no doubt Norah Lindsay would have used many plants already being grown, omitting only the labour-intensive bedding plants, along with the many little beds in which they were grown. While it is perfectly acceptable and necessary in such circumstances to adjust and gently rearrange according to experience and horticultural necessity, exactly as she would have done, plant substitution should be avoided even to the extent of retaining what may now be regarded as inferior forms. A horticulturally robust but conservative approach is required, at which Jim Marshall, who advised at Blickling during the 1980s and '90s, excelled. He patiently had the characteristic, but tired, period roses propagated and replanted in fresh soil, giving the whole parterre a new lease of life.

The pleasure ground beyond the flower garden parterre was set out for the 8th Marquis of Lothian in the middle of the nineteenth century, replacing in part a seventeenth-century formal wilderness with a more extensive baroque-style scheme of close-planted, formal avenues centred on a delightful eighteenth-century Doric temple. In the 1970s the immediate aim was to prune back the evergreens, which furnished the various segments of the Union Jack pattern of

The great storm of 1987 caused a swaithe of serious damage even as far north-east as Blickling in Norfolk, creating havoc among the close-planted trees of the formal woodland.

avenues, to reveal the stems of the deciduous trees and emphasise their formality, Versailles-style. After a century, close-planted forest trees on this scale are inevitably vulnerable to wind-blow, and a few had already suffered. Aware of this possibility, we felled the remnants of one avenue and replanted it with common oak on the same pattern as before. This was a considerable step in the right direction but a subsequent freak storm, during which ice formed on tree branches, caused a lot of damage especially to the tallest trees, Turkey oaks, some of which fell while others began to break up. We planted replacements where practicable, while fearing that there was more trouble on the way, and so there was, in the late 1980s, when storms brought down or seriously damaged most of the formal avenues. By then Jim Marshall was advising and we jointly pressed for a radical approach, attempting to retain only the one or two substantially intact avenues. The remnants of the rest of the avenues were felled, enabling the stumps to be chipped out, and replanted each with a separate species as before, to retain the vital rigid formality. After twenty-five years this approach has been vindicated but the time will come for all of it to be done again, something that is sadly unavoidable for a plantation of this intensity and character: a huge task and deeply disruptive.

Historic garden conservation is about setting up, sustaining and guiding cycles of growth, development and decay; some for a hundred days, others for a hundred years.

Chapter 6

RESTORATION

Biddulph Grange, looking over the Italian Garden across the meticulously clipped pattern of yew hedges of the Dahlia Walk.

ERDDIG

WREXHAM

The story of Erddig's miraculous revival from the edge of dereliction has been admirably recounted in *The Servants' Hall* by Merlin Waterson (Historic Buildings Representative), who masterminded the whole remarkable exercise, something entirely unprecedented in the Trust and beyond. The book's foreword by the Marquess of Anglesey perfectly encapsulates the tortuous endeavours and the delicate negotiations leading to the Trust's acquisition of the Hall and 810 ha (2,000 acres) from Philip Yorke in 1973. With its irreplaceable collection of original furniture of exceptional quality, the house, garden and estate had been in decline for half a century under the ownership of Simon Yorke, who loved the house but became a recluse, with a deep distrust of outsiders, especially officialdom. The decline accelerated in the 1940s and '50s because of the effects of coal mining. Simon totally refused to negotiate with the National Coal Board after they took out a seam of coal right under the house, the resulting subsidence being disastrous.

Philip Yorke unexpectedly inherited from his brother in 1966 and until he finally gave it to the Trust in 1973 he lived at Erddig in ever-increasing isolation. But he retained a touching optimism and faith that somehow all would be right eventually ('on the night'), maybe recalling his days as a repertory actor. Certainly he enjoyed his unexpected last role as the squire of Erddig. I first met him for tea in the Servants' Hall, where we all sat round the table as did the servants past. He delighted in taking people round the house, which was almost totally devoid of amenities, and showing them the priceless collection of furniture, while rain dripped through the roof into a variety of bizarre containers. 'This is the State Bedroom – we call it that because it is in such a state'!

He used to spend much time on the roof with Fred Cheetham, moving slates around in an effort to plug the leaks. I saw him, aged 70-plus, clinging to a chimney stack, holding flue brushes and allegedly sweeping the chimneys. To find out which were blocked his method was to light newspapers in each grate, a nightmare prospect of chimney fires. He would don a First World War despatch-rider's outfit and go off every day on a vintage motor bike to buy bread and milk. Cakes for tea came daily, courtesy of Henry Boot's wife; 'Boot' was 'employed' to open and close the shutters and patrol the garden. However, terrifyingly, Philip was mostly alone at night until he actually signed the Deed.

The garden had been entirely let go in Simon's time, with apparently nothing done, resulting predictably in overgrown thickets of evergreens; self-sown trees and elders everywhere. Philip's answer was a little flock of sheep and goats which were effective grazers but they also barked many of the remaining desirable trees and evergreens. The 'head gardener' was a ram but he got into the house and attacked himself in one of the eighteenth-century mirrors, with obvious results. Sadly the flock came to a grizzly end when a pack of marauding dogs cornered them in the garden.

The local Boy Scouts, who were permitted to use the park, were by all accounts persuaded to cut down the many young trees – hornbeams, sycamores, willows and beech – that had seeded on the lawns. In typical Boy Scout style they were all cut off at knee height, leaving someone else to deal with the stumps. There were mountains of brambles and nettles, occasionally containing some precious link with the past, for example an almost unrecognisable fallen mulberry in the Laundry Yard, one branch of which retained sufficient vitality to survive and flourish once cleared. It is now a fruiting tree.

As Merlin Waterson wisely remarked, 'the repair of Erddig was as much a matter of reviving a community of staff, as it was of physical reconstruction', and no one played a greater part in this than Mike Snowden, along with his wife June. When the post of 'head gardener' was advertised in the winter, there were only two credible applicants and only Mike turned up for interview, fresh from the supreme order-liness of Bodnant, where he was propagator under the still-Edwardian regime of Charles Puddle. By then the canal and fish pond at Erddig had been dredged and the works on house and garden were approaching their most destructive phase – all mud and rubble and no prospect yet of anything like proper gardening. That the Snowdens could see through the chaos and imagine the outcome is a tribute to their foresight. Even the head gardener's house, recently the home of the sheep and goats, was still no more than a repaired shell.

In June 1973, with an endowment of £1m from the sale of land near Wrexham, the Trust was able to begin the restoration in earnest. In the garden this was through the energetic efforts of Ted Jones, appointed estate foreman, and Barry Roberts, for whom no job was too strenuous. They organised the dredging and felled many trees, mainly those that had sprung up thirty or forty years earlier close to garden walls and buildings.

After many years of decline and half a century of total neglect, the first jobs at Erddig in the 1970s consisted of removing trees, including stumps of old beeches and many seedling trees; then dredging the lakes. We preserved as much of the original grass sward as possible. (1976)

Our principal guide in reversing half a century of decline was the remarkably precise survey by Thomas Badeslade, published in 1740. This depicts almost the whole garden in its eighteenth-century prime after John Mellor had rebuilt the house and gone on to extend and replan the garden to a much grander formal concept, more than twice the size of that of his predecessor Joshua Edisbury. Although remaining enclosed by walls, a new axial view eastwards into the park was created and given emphasis by a wide grand path leading to a formal canal, with a fish pond north of it and a bowling green to the south.

Clearly the garden was to be as much useful and productive as impressively ornamental. There were orchard blocks, presumably apples, on either side and the extensive archive confirms a diverse and sophisticated range of wall-grown fruit occupying every aspect – peaches and plums on the south (facing) wall; pears and plums on both the east and west walls – some in the main garden and some in the narrow vegetable garden on its south side. In the north-east corner was a baffling arrangement of niched hedges overlooked by a brick arbour that had survived. After extensive enquiry, the very helpful 'queen bee' of the Bee Research Organisation confirmed that the niches were most likely to have been there to provide shelter for bee skeps which stood on wooden stools. The estate was evidently largely self-sufficient: truly 'sustainable' in the modern jargon.

The parkland was equally contrived, with extensive walks and bosky woodlands and avenues. The English landscape style arrived much later in the eighteenth century when William Emes redesigned the park. Luckily the conservative-minded Yorkes retained the formal garden intact.

In formulating a philosophy and principles for the garden's re-creation it quickly became clear that, while preserving the essence of the origin, the family had, quite

By 1983 the gravel paths had been laid, the limes planted for pleaching and the Edwardian formal garden re-cut and replanted.

understandably, continued to make changes and additions over the two and a half centuries since the Badeslade print; indeed it would have been very odd if they had not. Nevertheless, John Mellor's scheme was obviously the most significant point in the garden's history so we agreed to restore its overall structure as far as practicable. However, at the same time we agreed to renew and adapt such later features added by the family that could be incorporated harmoniously and sustained within the resources, especially of labour, likely to be forthcoming.

These included the copse that had replaced the eighteenth-century bowling green, a version of the nineteenth-century flower garden in the south-west quarter and the Edwardian parterre east of the house (an area not shown in the Badeslade engraving). This partly pragmatic approach meant that evidence of each generation of the Yorkes would be represented, their taste and their values at the time. While this approach would be regarded as standard practice now, it was novel in the 1970s, when restoration to a particular date was the rule.

The avenue of overgrown Irish Yews was buried in undergrowth and their stems had been badly damaged by sheep. After removing the competition, a year later they were cut back very hard and by 1979 they were beginning to regrow.

Nowadays there would be archaeologists exhaustively and expensively crawling everywhere for months on end, which is no doubt the proper way if you can afford it. In practice I doubt it would have made much difference; we were anxious to avoid destroying anything significant and we made a conscious decision to adapt and move on. On this basis we were able to bring back the Edwardian parterre simply by finding the surviving edges of the beds in the grass. The Victorian garden needed adaptation and some creative thinking based on photographs and what we discovered on the ground. Restoration of the Irish Yew walk, c.1860, was a great success, the overgrown yews having been totally submerged in undergrowth and subsequently browsed by sheep and goats to within an inch of death. Having cleared around, mulched them and given them light for a

season to refurnish, we went for the radical option. I advised cutting back hard to stumps and Mike Snowden had the courage to try. Thanks to his subsequent care and pruning, every one grew back to its proper tulip shape, the genuine article renewed rather than the soft option of replacement.

Having agreed the conservation philosophy at the outset, we faced some huge practical challenges. At some time probably before 1900, the outer walls of the original seventeenth-century garden, incorporated by Mellor into the new garden, were removed (probably being by then derelict) and replaced with beech hedges either side of the main lawns east of the house. According to Erddig tradition these seem to have been neglected and allowed to turn into close rows of trees, predictably becoming unstable and falling from time to time. By the 1970s there were several large beech and a variety of small ones. If we were to have a garden along the lines of the Badeslade engraving, they would have to go, before anyone, staff or visitors, had time to argue for the retention of any. Getting these out, together with their massive stumps, through a narrow gateway, the only access, was Mike's first major challenge. Curiously Philip Yorke seemed to take this total transformation of the garden in his stride, being perhaps more involved in the house repair.

With a clear site and no shade we were able to reinstate the orchards; also to revive the sheep-grazed grass sward, improving it by cultivation rather than replacement. It was easy to discern where the gravel paths used to be, now covered in grass. Ingeniously, Mike lifted off the turf for use elsewhere or for sale to buy gravel to replace it. In place of the overgrown beech hedges we decided on pleached limes which were started off in the new nursery area by the head gardener's house and transplanted when large enough to be trained on strained wires supported by galvanised angle-iron because timber structures would have been too cumbersome.

Another important consideration at the outset was the garden's vulnerability to gale damage, the house occupying a ridge facing west with the garden

At the opening of the garden by the Prince of Wales, he is accompanied by Philip Yorke on the left, with white hair, and in the foreground on the right with a beard, Mike Snowden, head gardener throughout restoration.

behind. With essential fellings around the house and in the garden, this danger was becoming more acute, especially for the avenue of tall, close-planted limes which again, Erddig style, seemed to have been allowed to grow out from narrow double-rows of pleached trees, probably before the First World War. Reducing their overall height by 8–10 m (26–33 ft) was the successful prescription, subtly supervised by Mike.

The unique tradition at Erddig was to commemorate all the staff with a framed picture and a few lines of doggerel, a testament to the family's close and unusual relationship between master and servant. If ever there were to be a person through whom to continue this unbroken record it should be Mike. He not only rebuilt an enthusiastic team of gardeners in recreating the garden but also, after a property management crisis, took on the unenviable role of 'temporarily' managing the whole enterprise at a crucial moment in the restoration, and for a much longer period than he would have wished.

Erddig was a great adventure and remains a successful and highly influential landmark for the Trust. It was at the time the largest and most comprehensive restoration of house and garden in Britain, as well as being hugely satisfying for everyone involved. The garden will never be the same as before but it is an honest attempt at reflecting John Mellor's original layout and the Yorke family's gardening taste; as much as that of their gardeners.

CANONS ASHBY

NORTHAMPTONSHIRE

The inspiring story of Canons Ashby's rescue by the National Trust from the brink of disintegration is well told by Merlin Waterson in *The National Trust: The First Hundred Years* (1994). It was thanks to the extraordinary perspicacity of the Trust's architectural adviser, Gervase Jackson-Stops, whose explosive stutterings are fondly remembered, that the last-minute negotiations with the Dryden family began in 1980. After that the Trust's virtuous web of personal and corporate contacts put together a workable scheme that captured the place for the nation. Against the odds, not only the house and grounds but also most of the significant contents of the house came to the Trust with just enough funding for their repair and restoration, thanks to generous donors and well-directed grant aid. Decades of neglect by a series of tenants had left the property on the verge of dereliction and its rescue must be one of the greatest achievements, among many, of Gervase's comparatively short but eventful life.

Although the garden and parkland had suffered no less than the ancient house, there was much less to lose because it seems always to have been a modest layout, more useful than decorative. It had retained much of its early formal structure, despite having lost the avenues that stretched out to the south and west. The heyday of the garden and undeniably its most significant period was the late nineteenth century when the present arrangement was established. The garden

Canons Ashby was held up as a prime example of the 'Old English' style favoured by the architect Sir Reginald Blomfield, with its dignified formality and the relegation of plants and trees to the roles of structure and furnishing, as shown by H. Inigo Triggs in his influential book of 1902. The south front.

The west front of
the house with
its topiary pieces
cut back and
reshaped. (1992)

had escaped both the William Robinson fashion for informal plantsmanship
and the widespread influence of Gertrude Jekyll. Instead the Drydens evidently
favoured the so-called 'Old English' style advocated by Sir Reginald Blomfield –
i.e. dignified formality with a firm 'architectural' structure, within which horticulture was restrained and subservient. Canons Ashby, with its simple terraces,
controlled views and well-honed topiary, was much admired by this school of
thought and held up as a prime example by H. Inigo Triggs in his influential book
Formal Gardens of England and Scotland (1902).

As a result not only were the significant qualities of the garden made perfectly
clear, but little had been done in the twentieth century to change them irrevocably. The garden had simply been allowed to decline, leaving the terraces, walls
and buildings dilapidated but more or less intact and recoverable. This was the
first time in my experience of a convincing case for complete restoration to a particular precedent: i.e. as meticulously recorded by Inigo Triggs and subsequently
photographed for *Country Life* in 1921. However, with only one gardener to start
with, this plan would need to be modified to save labour, at least at first. The
obvious strategy was to concentrate on the paths, which had grassed over, steps,
buildings, topiary and trees, i.e. to retrieve the structure while gradually bringing
the borders back under cultivation.

None of this was in any way controversial; the one bone of contention involved
the four Lebanon cedars that flanked the steps on the main axis near the house.
Planted bizarrely about 3 m (9 ft 10 in) apart, these had formed a close group
until the famously severe winter of 1947 when three of them collapsed; the other
one followed later. Despite this precise and irrefutable precedent, there was

opposition to their replacement from two usually opposing quarters. Surprisingly some architectural opinion had reservations because the trees would screen much of the south front, although to me this seemed to have been deliberate because of this elevation being a fascinating but asymmetric assembly of different periods and styles. Arguably this is best seen obliquely and does not lend itself to being the destination of a grand formal vista. The main axial path was centred on the main door for which the trees formed an ideal frame. On the other hand, the gardeners thought that to plant forest trees on a steep slope at such close spacing was asking for trouble.

After some intense discussion I was relieved when the Gardens Panel, led by Lord Blakenham and supported by George Clive, rather reluctantly saw the point of faithful restoration, partly because no one could suggest a valid alternative. Seeing the garden thirty years later I certainly do not regret the decision as the views to and from the house reflect the scene as it was almost a century ago. Thanks largely to the pioneering work of Peter Hall, who took on the task singlehandedly, the bones of the garden were restored in the 1980s and those crucial cedars were successfully established. This was, and is, a case for no compromise and I hope that when these four cedars fail after a century or so, they will be replaced exactly according to precedent; nothing less will do.

Under Chris Smith, who has served Canons Ashby since Peter Hall moved on to Dunham Massey, the garden has been guided forward with an impressive combination of steady endeavour and appropriate restraint, especially now that more help is at hand, both professional and voluntary.

The overgrown yew topiary on the west front in 1980 before cutting back and reshaping (see p.241).

My one regret at Canons Ashby concerns the narrow lime avenues that divide the landscape south and west of the house. The precedent was clear and we were able quickly to decide on their replanting. Unfortunately the importance of their uniformity was not appreciated. Nor did I realise at the time that seed-raised, so-called Small-leafed Lime (*Tilia cordata*), an English native, would inevitably turn out to be a mixture of hybrids because they interbreed so readily. In retrospect we should have used a clone of common lime (*Tilia × europaea*). Mistakes like that last a long time.

TATTON PARK

CHESHIRE

No doubt conscious of its great historic importance and enormous scope, the National Trust accepted ownership of Tatton Park, perhaps unwisely, on the basis that the property would be leased to Cheshire County Council, i.e. managed and financed by them: an inherently problematic arrangement. Taking advice from the Trust's Gardens Advisers was specifically noted in the lease – 'No change without the National Trust's consent'. While the County Council pays the bills, not only are Trust members admitted free but its staff expect to have an influence on conservation and standards. Only goodwill and tolerance on both sides can make such an arrangement succeed in the interest of the place. This is a particular dilemma for a garden where style of management to a large degree determines the outcome, day-to-day, year-to-year and in the long term. The Trust's advisory specialists have a delicate path to tread to establish and sustain cordial and effective relationships at all levels. In the garden and park this can only be achieved by building confidence through demonstrating that advice is always well-based, realistic, and effective, as well as aimed at valid long-term conservation objectives, without claiming credit.

From the early 1980s this partnership became increasingly successful thanks to the building of trust, each side understanding and accepting what the other can offer. However, this was not the case in the 1960s and early 1970s when the Director of Tatton Park was very grand, with a local authority management structure to support his position – almost equivalent in status to the former owners, the Egertons. In those days the Council was inclined to appoint to the post ex-servicemen of mid to high rank, the result being a steeply pyramidal command structure, our visits beginning with a formal briefing at 'command HQ'. When Graham Thomas

The azaleas and rhododendrons at Tatton Park in the dazzling colours favoured by the Egertons.

The Italian Garden of the 1860s restored substantially to Joseph Paxton's original layout using the bedding Dahlia 'Princess Marie José'. (1999)

was the Trust's Gardens Adviser, Brigadier Chestnut was officer commanding (Director). Graham was inclined to demand respect and his advice was invariably prescriptive and precise; he understandably expected to see results by the time of his next visit. Almost immediately they fell out, not helped by the head gardener Colin Pritchard's understandable loyalty to the Council's command structure. Brigadier Chestnut informed the Trust that their Gardens Adviser was no longer welcome; an immovable object had been met by an irresistible force! The hiatus was eventually overcome by the Trust deploying the well-known garden designer and journalist Lanning Roper as its Garden Adviser at Tatton Park. His perceived status and high national profile as garden correspondent of *The Sunday Times* evidently appealed to the Brigadier and certainly to his successor, Wing Commander Peter Neate; Lanning's charm overcame all remaining difficulties.

Lanning's main achievements at Tatton, apart from his vital role in 'mending fences', were mainly related to flower gardening, in that he modified and somewhat improved the Italian Garden and designed a characteristically Lanning Roper mixed border above it with shrub roses, silver foliage, etc. It was pretty and effective but not at all the sort of thing Joseph Paxton, who probably designed the Italian Garden in the 1860s, would have done. Lanning also designed flower borders at the garden entrance, then arranged inappropriately through a corner of one of the great walled gardens. He also scattered some of his 'signature' trees, i.e. those species that marked his influence wherever he advised, across the main lawn – weeping silver lime, tulip tree, silver maple, etc. He also planted an attractive glade in the pleasure grounds with a variety of flowering cherries, crab apples and trees for autumn colour, like *Liquidambar* and *Parrotia*. It was not until the 1980s that the principles of historic garden conservation and restoration became a strong enough force to penetrate Tatton Park.

With this management regime still intact, it was a challenge for me to follow the much-loved Lanning as gardens adviser. I had to tread carefully at first. However, a breakthrough came when Sam Youd succeeded as head gardener in charge of this large and complex garden and its fifteen or so staff. Although employed by Cheshire, he was temperamentally loyal to the National Trust. Whereas his predecessor was always cautious and defensive, Sam was invariably ambitious and cooperative, with a droll Liverpudlian sense of humour. We got on very well and for the first time I began to engage with his staff in charge of the various elements of this huge garden – glasshouses, Italian garden, rose garden, fernery, etc.

With crucial help from the regional Historic Buildings Representative, Julian Gibbs, we gradually began to embrace some of the bigger conservation issues as well as to take on parts of the pleasure ground that had not been actively managed for many years. The overcrowded but important pinetum was surveyed and catalogued by Michael Lear ahead of thinning and replanting. The maze was closed for renovation. Rhododendrons were cut back and regenerated and new paths made. Many decrepit trees, especially conifers, were removed and new trees and shrubs planted. Slowly standards improved and the place took on a more dynamic character. However, this kind of cyclical renovation needs to be sustained indefinitely if the garden is to retain its freshness.

One success was the total restoration of the Italian Garden, attributed to perhaps the greatest gardener in the history of Britain, Joseph Paxton. It had been much simplified over the years. Although always colourful, it was bland and had lost much of its rather heavy-handed Victorian grandeur; also missing were the evergreens that had furnished it and given it a firm structure. Many photographs had survived and it was comparatively easy to identify the box hedging, Italianate topiary and overall layout of the original. More of a challenge was to clothe the steep banks (always a problem for mowing) in laurels, as shown in the photographs. We decided on a slower-growing but round-leafed form of the common laurel, *Prunus laurocerasus* 'Mischeana', to save pruning. They were established with some difficulty by creating little flat-topped planting platforms after killing off the grass and leaving it intact to prevent erosion. Incidentally, the laurels solved the problem of erosion to the banks caused by children rolling down the steep slopes.

Fortuitously, I heard through Paul Temple (a fellow judge at the Chelsea Flower Show) that Japan's Expo 1976 had made a handsome profit amounting to the equivalent of millions of pounds sterling. The Japanese government had appointed a small committee under Dr. Shintaro Sakamoto to identify projects abroad that could be part-funded to raise the profile of Japan. The Royal Botanic Gardens Kew were immediately in on the act and, after one or two false starts and prompting from Julian Gibbs, Cheshire County Council arranged to entertain Dr Sakamoto to consider the Japanese Garden at Tatton as a candidate for grant aid. Sam Youd always had his eye to the main chance and pursued the possibility with single-minded enthusiasm and eventual success. Not only did Tatton get its grant

but Sam also turned himself into something of a Japanese garden pundit. With my backing, he obtained a Churchill Scholarship to study garden conservation in Japan, a tour he managed to extend into China. Following the Japan-British Exhibition of 1910, Tatton's Japanese Garden was made for the Egertons by Japanese craftsmen, to an impeccable standard, with no expense spared. Under the Egertons it had been faithfully cared for and, thanks crucially to Lanning Roper, was fenced off when the garden changed hands and was opened regularly to visitors. But it had become overgrown and circumscribed; after eighty years the restoration came at the right time. The enabling grant was conditional on a matching response from the National Trust, a potential difficulty that was solved by a grant from the Gardens Fund. It is now probably the best preserved example of its kind in Britain. The restoration was organised by the National Trust, which brought in Japanese craftsmen to help, led by Professor Masao Fukahara who has generously continued to lend his expertise in an advisory capacity.

After the Trust acquired Tatton in 1960 and leased it to Cheshire, the County Council used some of the grander kitchen garden buildings for visitor services and access but knocked down much of the extensive range of functional buildings that made up, in its heyday, one of the greatest walled kitchen gardens in the country. At the time there was no foreseeable prospect of restoring this huge complex to its original purposes. Much survived, including the walls (once heated) and several of the greenhouses designed for particular purposes – pineapples, peaches, vines, etc. – but others were demolished. The main walled garden was leased to the (amateur) Tatton Garden Society and soon became a whimsical mixture of interesting and productive garden features, arranged to suit the needs of hobby gardeners. On the whole they managed it and cared for it well by the standards of the time, and it served a need. Similarly, when I joined the staff of the National Trust, walled kitchen gardens were looked upon as expensive luxuries. What few staff could be afforded were employed on essential upkeep in gardens strictly modified to make best use of scarce labour; garden volunteers were unheard of. Nevertheless, the Trust was able to continue growing fruit and vegetables in some walled kitchen gardens (e.g. Barrington Court, Upton House, Gunby Hall, Fenton House), usually on a comparatively small scale. Sadly, many of the larger walled gardens remained empty or were commandeered for recreational uses or for car parking; sometimes they were used to provide private gardens for tenants or donors.

Conscious that many of the skills developed in large, professionally run kitchen gardens in the nineteenth century were being lost, it was my ambition for the Trust to undertake a total restoration. This would demand not only reconstruction or repair of all the buildings, equipment and physical support systems, but also sufficient skilled staff to ensure proper upkeep and training. In the 1970s this seemed at best a distant prospect and perhaps an unrealisable objective. However, I raised the possibility with Sir Marcus Worsley, then Chairman of the Trust's Properties Committee, and he encouraged me to present it to the Gardens Panel as one of our strategic objectives. Although there was as yet no money they readily agreed and we began the process of selecting the best prospective restoration. I set down the criteria – major walled garden, substantially intact, centrally located, well recorded, easily accessible – and produced a short list. Eventually Tatton was chosen, partly because it would give the Trust greater opportunities to influence the garden generally, and partly because eventual funding (we then thought EU) may well have been conditional on partnerships between different organisations. Cheshire County Council eventually agreed.

The Trust's Gardens Fund was again raided, this time to carry out a full feasibility study and outline costing. Peter Thoday (an old friend who had come to prominence with the television series 'The Victorian Kitchen Garden') was appointed as consultant and he conducted the historical research and physical survey, setting

The Vineries under repair in Tatton's great walled garden. (2001)

The lofty Fernery is a rare survival, having been under continuous cultivation for a century and a half.

out the reality of the challenge and identifying the infrastructure that needed to be restored. After two years we had a proposal to put to Cheshire County Council who had been kept in the picture throughout. Through Julian Gibbs the Cheshire County officers and elected councillors were persuaded, and a joint bid to the Heritage Lottery Fund was prepared, assisted by £100,000 from the Trust's 'Tatton Fund'. Although Julian supervised the project for the Trust, the direction of the work had to be taken on by the County Council and their officers. It soon became their project, from that point on being subsumed almost entirely as an initiative of the County Council. Thanks to the enthusiasm and professionalism of Julian Gibbs and the Trust's regional archaeologist Jeremy Miln, James Wyatt's vinery/pinery greenhouse and orchid house were restored according to historic precedent. The whole restoration was a great achievement by all concerned but its impact was perhaps muted by the extended timescale, by which time other walled garden restorations were well under way or had even been completed. Nevertheless, it remains perhaps Britain's most comprehensive walled garden restoration.

The lesson learned at Tatton is perhaps a universal truth – that a great deal more can be achieved if one never seeks credit.

In 1884 the plight of Sayes Court, Deptford, largely because of the likely loss of its exceptionally important historic garden, was a turning point leading to the creation of the National Trust. Despite this the Trust has always been reluctant to take on gardens. The first few seem to have come to it almost by accident and it was sixty years before it acquired one (Hidcote) in its own right. Gardens are considered expensive because they need skilful and consistent upkeep, although the cost of their conservation over a given period is usually less than that of a house of comparable importance, while income from visitors to gardens is always greater. The equivalent of periodic electrical rewiring, fixing the roof, eradicating dry rot, etc. in houses, all done expensively on contract, applies in gardens only to structures like bridges, walls, garden buildings and waterworks. The principal cost of gardens comes with the employment of expert gardeners at all levels, a human cost which conserves special skills, local continuity and values characteristic of the place. Just what the National Trust should be spending its money on, perhaps?

On the other hand, the Trust has rightly given high priority to the acquisition of our dwindling unspoilt coastline and in the twentieth century was the nation's leading agent of its protection and conservation. Coleton Fishacre came to the Trust in the early 1980s with a superb stretch of South Devon coastline, along with a distinguished house built for the D'Oyly Carte family between the wars. The garden occupies an idyllic coombe, complete with a gentle stream running down to a delightful cove at sea level: spectacular views and perfect peace. However, it was almost completely unknown, never having been open to visitors and hardly even to guests for two or three decades during the ownership of the reclusive Rowland Smith.

Coleton Fishacre with its surrounding Lutyen's-like terraces designed by Oswald Milne for the D'Oyly Carte family, on a site exceptionally favourable for tender plants.

View of flower
garden. (c.1999)

Under the Chairmanship of Lord Gibson the Trust was particularly sceptical about gardens unless they were, like Biddulph Grange, of national importance. Plantsmen's gardens were a blind spot. As a result, despite Oswald Milne's handsome Arts and Crafts house and imaginatively arranged terraces, Coleton was at first overlooked as a place worth opening regularly to visitors. How values change! At the outset there was pressure to offset some of the cost of the purchase by leasing the house and garden to a private tenant, the coast being the perceived point of the exercise. Luckily the then Regional Director, Peter Broomhead, thought I should see it before any irrevocable decisions were made. In fact, the procedure should have been for the Gardens Adviser to make recommendations and for the Gardens Panel to state a view on any new acquisition.

My first visit was a revelation. For many years there had been only one gardener, Eddie Shepperd, for the 8 ha (20 acre) site (including woodland shelterbelts) and I was glad to meet him for a private tour. His deeply serious opening comment was 'you know, Mr Sales, this place is paradise', and I could instantly see what he meant. At first Eddie was defensive about his lack of knowledge and the standard of upkeep. However, there was so much to admire that he soon began to relax as he led me through an ever-more astonishing assembly of mostly uncommon trees and shrubs, some of them fine specimens and many semi-naturalised to form huge clumps – flowering dogwoods and mimosas spreading like natives in the almost frost-free conditions. Understandably, he had been spending a lot of time cutting grass on the steep slopes; otherwise gardening consisted of caring as best he could for the borders near the house and keeping paths open and views unobstructed. The garden was living on borrowed time, gradually reverting to semi-exotic woodland, much of its rich plant collection and diverse structure in danger of being lost as brambles and introduced colonisers took charge. I was in no doubt that this was a garden of special significance because of its glorious site, diverse plant collection and special relationship to the house and the D'Oyly Cartes.

It seems that Lady Dorothy D'Oyly Carte had been the gardener in terms of interest and inclination, and she must have influenced the layout of Oswald Milne's terraces, including the little Lutyens-style rill garden and shell-shaped reflecting pool, through which the stream is channelled. However, the layout and planting were otherwise entirely conventional, a competently professional job, of its time. Predictably there were flowering cherries and laburnums, hardy hybrid rhodo-dendrons and choicer trees like the ironwood (*Parrotia persica*) and tulip tree (*Liriodendron tulipifera*). Wisely, extensive shelterbelts were planted on either side of the valley but seem never to have been managed or thinned. Half a century of unrelieved forestry-style density had resulted predictably in impenetrable masses of stalky trees, now vulnerable to catastrophic storm damage.

Sadly the D'Oyly Cartes' life together did not last, as Rupert found his pleasures elsewhere. While her marriage broke up, Lady Dorothy's interest in gardening blossomed, and she began to realise the horticultural potential of this delightful place. With lime-free soil, little frost and adequate rainfall, she found she could broaden her plant palette to include less hardy plants of all kinds, especially from Mediterranean climates and the southern hemisphere, many of which flourished in the bright light and remarkably equable climate of Coleton Fishacre. In essence, she successfully applied an overlay of tender exotics to the established structure of conventional trees and shrubs. The result was indeed the plantsman's paradise I had been promised. After thirty years of minimum intervention it had become an exotic jungle where self-sown seedlings of scarce ornamentals had to be mown off to preserve the pathways and keep views open.

With a minimum requirement of two or preferably three gardeners, it is hardly surprising that the Trust would baulk at the prospect of direct management and the capital cost of opening regularly to visitors, especially with Coleton's difficul-ties of access along narrow lanes, limited space for car parking and doubt about the appeal of the house. On the other hand, it seemed highly unlikely that the Trust would find a tenant sufficiently rich and able to take the lease and restore and conserve this large and complicated garden, needing expert care and rare plant knowledge. Nor did it seem likely that anyone would want to take the garden on in its own right, with a separate tenant in the house, and open it to visitors.

I first met Jane and Dick Taylor soon after they had built a house together in the Forest of Dean on what amounted more or less to a slag heap from one of the many small shallow coal mines in the area. Surrounded by desolation, they soon caught the gardening bug in a big way, digging out all kinds of rubbish and discarded mining gear and creating topsoil by incorporating massive quantities of shredded bark and composted wood chip. They had an extraordinary hunger for information as well as for plants, maintaining an exhaustive card index system for every plant. Their garden was immaculate but not perhaps to everyone's taste, every plant accompanied by a plastic-encapsulated white label providing details of its identification, source, country of origin, taxonomy, etc. For the many little plants each label was attached to a metal spike. In the winter, the labels flapping in the wind, the effect was extraordinary.

The Taylors' ambitions soon outgrew their modest horticultural beginnings as Jane's plant knowledge became formidable. At that stage they came to me looking for a garden of significance where they could exercise their talents at their own expense, according to the Trust's policy and direction. They jumped at the chance

RIGHT Alongside the house a stream was channelled in a rill through a little formal rose garden. In the soft climate and with increasing shade the 1980s roses were failing.

BELOW In a bold move we replaced the roses with semi-tender plants giving an exotic 'sub-tropical' effect.

The lower terrace below the house has a little dripping fountain to reflect the sunlight onto the concave stonework above.

of gardening at Coleton Fishacre despite the lack of money and a tenant in the house. They would sell up and invest their entire capital in moving to take a lease of the garden and set up a plant nursery near Coleton. Dick would continue part-time to sell insurance, while Jane would run the garden and nursery, in the hope that they would be able to live increasingly off profit from plant sales. They worked extremely hard and made rapid progress in the garden, although clearly irked somewhat by the Trust's insistence (through me!) on respecting the D'Oyly Carte legacy, when they would have preferred unbridled plantsmanship.

With a separate tenant in the house and limited facilities, the Trust had no willingness to increase visitor numbers unduly, and opening remained comparatively low-key. As the Taylors' plant sales failed to meet their targets, tensions rose and they blamed the Trust for their plight. The arrangement suddenly came to a sad end when Dick died in an accident. In these tragic circumstances, Jane Taylor had to leave but she did not lose her interest in plants, soon becoming a distinguished and successful author.

No one was content with the outcome of this unfortunate episode, which cost a lot in every way to all concerned. On the positive side, the excellent tenants in the house proved that it was possible to manage the garden separately and open it to visitors, given tolerance and respect on both sides. Now that regular opening had been established and the garden had already become popular, the Trust was virtually forced to accept the new situation. At considerable expense and some perceived risk, the Trust decided to go ahead and appoint a head gardener. This was a great relief to me, even though facilities for gardeners and visitors were expanded only minimally to save cost. After one false start, David Mason was eventually appointed in the late 1980s, ultimately with one assistant. The place has never looked back.

After a life working and travelling the world, David had come to the Trust on a government-sponsored training opportunities scheme, ready to give up his peripatetic life. Being mature and bright, he learned quickly during his time at Killerton and we received glowing reports of his progress. So when the vacancy arose at Coleton, despite his comparative lack of training and horticultural knowledge, we were confident that he would rise to the challenge, which he did. It was a steep learning curve, not only to come to terms with a plant collection that would test anyone's knowledge but also with the need to act in effect as property manager, while also establishing and maintaining a good relationship with the house tenants.

Happily David was no meek steward, waiting constantly for a prescribed programme of work, and the garden prospered greatly under his leadership. We enjoyed a robust and fruitful relationship once the garden's principles of conservation had been established. This vital but often elusive ingredient in the management of any significant historic garden needs to be formulated to provide a unique discipline that guides all decision-making. As well as taking advantage of the potential of the place (all too obvious at Coleton), it needed to be true to its origin and to the people who made it. It would be easy enough to go on unselectively gathering tender rarities from all over the world but we needed to retain a link with the D'Oyly Cartes and especially with Lady Dorothy and Coleton's gradual transformation from conventional pleasure ground to a plantsman's paradise. The earlier 'layer' should not be obliterated: a principle easy enough to agree but difficult to apply consistently. A classic case arose with the Japanese flowering cherries, indispensable elements of any between-the-wars garden – and Coleton was no exception. Predictably the Taylors had not seen the point of replanting because there were so many exciting alternatives but David Mason soon began to understand the conservation philosophy although it was difficult to find appropriate new sites, cherries never succeeding well where they have been grown before. Furthermore, they are always short-lived, seldom exceeding fifty or sixty years.

On the other hand, there seemed little point in persevering with the hopelessly unsuccessful roses in the rill garden. Not only was the soil unsuitable and 'tired' of bush roses, the site had become much more enclosed over the years. Roses of the period were martyrs to black spot and there seemed to be little justification for planting modern roses. Better, we thought, to do something totally different and make a spectacular contribution reflecting these changes, much as a private owner, even perhaps Lady Dorothy, might have done in the same circumstances. Few people regretted the demise of the sickly roses and we devised a colourful planting scheme with a sub-tropical theme, a luxuriant arrangement of strong colours and bold foliage deemed by all to be a success. This transformation took place a few years before Christopher Lloyd decided to do much the same to his rose garden at Great Dixter, creating a well-publicised confection of exotic luxuriance to great acclaim. He never said where he got the idea from but he certainly visited south Devon every summer!

With historic garden conservation, innovation is always a dilemma, perfectly legitimate in gardens, which are always changing, but to be closely argued and rigorously justified in historic as well as horticultural terms. The principal question to be asked is why? Is this something that, given similar circumstances, the former owner might have done? Does the proposal reflect the continuing history and development of the garden and its style of layout and planting? Is the change likely to be irrevocable or could it be reversed in the future?

DUNSTER CASTLE

SOMERSET

With Anthony Salvin's towers rising romantically above a wooded hill, you only have to see the Dunster Castle from the coast road to Minehead to want to go there. Below is the honeypot village of Dunster with its pretty main street unspoilt except for the plethora of tea rooms and souvenir shops. For 600 years the Castle had been the home of the Luttrells, who latterly had been opening it and the grounds, without being able to tempt sufficient visitors to climb the hill from the village to make it sustainable for the future.

Although it was obviously worthy on grounds of quality and historic significance, in the absence of an adequate endowment the National Trust's acquisition in 1976 depended upon its potential for attracting visitors in large numbers. The Trust had learned that good gardens attract visitors and repeat visits. The Luttrells had been keen gardeners for generations and the higher windswept castle slopes are remarkably free of hard frosts, suffering only from thin, dry soil. They had assembled a wide range of often choice trees and shrubs on the sheltered lower slopes, especially near the riverside leading to the Castle Watermill, now a working corn mill. On the upper terraces near the house there is a little Victorian flower garden

Seen from the main road Dunster Castle is irresistible.

and a now-restored orangery and conservatory. Here the microclimate allowed the Luttrells to grow a variety of tender plants among the hardy Chusan palms which provide a distinctly south-of-France effect on stepping out of the castle. Here, too, against the south wall of the house is the famous Dunster lemon, which has grown with only the protection of an unheated glass case for 150 years at least.

However, three-quarters of the 6.9 ha (17 acre) pleasure grounds had received little attention over the years, some of the steep slopes being covered by huge cherry laurels, gloomily exterminating all competition. Elsewhere, mainly on the west slopes, there was an acquired ecosystem of trees and shrubs, including holm oaks and a lot of laurustinus, both presumably self-sown from eighteenth-century

In place of a tennis court the Castle keep became an oval lawn surrounded by mostly fragrant plants with a perimeter walk and views over the countryside. (1986)

introductions, together with periwinkles, philadelphus, spurge laurel, hypericum, buddleja, leycesteria and our native stinking hellebore and iris. This exotic mixture hinted at the possibility of taking advantage of Dunster's special climate to develop an even more distinctive woodland with an Italianate character. The opportunity to try this in part arose when a landslide, a seemingly periodic phenomenon at Dunster, forced the cutting down of the laurels. Not to be accused of half measures, we planted strawberry trees, eventually hundreds of *Arbutus unedo*, in an attempt at creating a unique effect – perhaps to naturalise?

Immediately upon acquisition the main challenge was to deal generally with the trees, most of which, especially on the north slopes above the village, were over-mature or otherwise unhealthy. This woodland, vital for shelter, had not been actively managed for many years, if ever, and there had been no attempt at regeneration or replanting. The crowns of most trees near paths had died back, making them potentially unsafe. On enquiry I discovered that sodium chlorate had been used annually for years as the preferred weedkiller – effective but soluble and deadly to tree roots as it drains through or runs off. An extensive programme of felling and replanting was called for, within sight of most of the village. Mental alarm bells rang as we contemplated the reaction from village people who were not known for their ready acceptance of change.

Luckily, or perhaps through exceptionally good judgement by the Trust's Regional Director John Cripwell, Guy Courage of the brewing family had been appointed managing land agent to cope with the huge Holnicote estate and now Dunster Castle and grounds as well. Guy was tempted into working for the Trust in middle

Big Himalayan magnolias like *M. mollicomata* thrive on the steep banks.

age after an active career in rural land agency because he lived in nearby Crow-combe and because the job was allegedly part-time. Guy was a highly effective agent of the old school – practical, direct, decisive and thick-skinned – qualities he would need in abundance. However, he was also an honourable man whose integrity and selfless determination to do the right thing always shone through.

Guy's great passion was hunting – two or three days a week – squeezing his work for the Trust into the rest of the week, in theory. We got on well and agreed to tackle the tree felling problem all at once, together with the major cutting back of several huge yews on the terraces that blocked views and had been ineffectively 'nibbled' at for decades. Guy was well aware of the character of the village opposition – mainly retired, very conservative – and he went out of his way to explain the problems and the need to take a long-term sustainable view, including replanting. Nevertheless, the row was ferocious, involving all levels in the Trust, but to his credit Guy did not give an inch. I recall the local television turning up for a controversial story and being given very short shrift as Guy pointed out a series of stumps, rotten to the core. The row soon blew over, especially as the removal of the big trees overhanging the village let in light. They were replaced by smaller species like Field Maples which now provide shelter and glorious autumn colour.

All this upheaval made a lot of extra work, both directly and by making spaces and letting in light. We needed a new head gardener who would be able to cope with the challenge. Guy, who had a great sense of humour, jokingly said that on that steep site we needed 'someone with one leg longer than the other'. After the interview he rang me and said 'you will never guess …!' Despite this minor disability Michael Marshall turned out to be a head gardener of outstanding energy and ability, always contributing constructively and getting things done. He was able to visualise the outcome of any proposal and was invariably loyal in reconciling the village and the Trust. Nothing was too much for him.

The Trust restored the conservatory and we replanted it in Victorian style. The orangery was subsequently re-roofed, allowing us to restock. In view of the lemon tradition we decided to make a collection of citrus to be grown in large terracotta pots, overwintered in the orangery and stood out on the breezily sunny south terrace for the summer. We considerably enriched the planting here with plants of borderline hardiness to reinforce the exotic character already present.

The so-called Castle Keep at the top of the hill is a level area of irregular shape with, at the time, a semi-derelict gazebo. It would have been a serious disappointment to those energetic enough to climb the winding path prior to the Trust's acquisition. Astonishingly, the family had a tennis court there, since it was the only flat area, and I guess they must have lost a few tennis balls despite the ugly high miscellaneous netting and fences! Apart from a few shrubs there was little else to see and most of the potentially spectacular views in all directions were blocked, presumably in attempts at giving shelter. We decided to start again with two principal aims – first to reopen a series of views in all directions, and second to provide a calm and sheltered open space in contrast to the enclosed winding paths en route. We regularised the shape of the lawn by creating an ellipse, working from an imaginary centre point, and then created a perimeter gravel walk with seats and openings between the trees to give views. The outer walk

The exotic theme of the orangery terrace is accentuated by Chusan palms, *Bescorneria yuccioides* and the tender rosemary *R. officinalis* 'Prostratus' cascading over the wall.

and central lawn were separated by mixed shrub and herbaceous borders, not only to give colour and interest but also shelter and fragrance where possible. So as to keep the two experiences visually separate, access from outer to inner was arranged via diagonal grass paths. Eventually it became possible to repair the pretty little gazebo above the house so as to provide a weatherproof destination.

The conspicuous scars from felling and pruning on the terraces and steep slopes revealed the castle but demanded bold treatment to furnish them according to the generally exotic character of the garden. Replanting at that stage became an exercise in large-scale ground cover, established with some difficulty on some of the steepest inclines, while at the same time adding to the already extensive range of flowering and fruiting trees and shrubs. You will go a long way to see better and more comprehensive and widespread use of large-scale ground cover plants in massive groupings – including *Hypericum*, *Mahonia*, *Rubus*, Virginia creeper, *Stephanandra*, *Symphoricarpos* and ivies, together with the woodrush *Luzula maxima*, a useful substitute for grass on shady banks.

The garden at Dunster covers a remarkable range of microclimates and soil types, allowing the continual development of contrasting effects, a clear and separate planting policy for each area. Such is the potential, the danger being haphazard planting leading to undue repetition and a meaningless miscellany.

Like the day of John Kennedy's assassination, the burning of Uppark in August 1989 was such a traumatic event that it will be vividly remembered by all who knew and loved the place. Its demise was all the more galling in that we could see a smouldering roof component gradually fanned by the wind to become a raging inferno despite intense efforts to put it out. Heroically, most of the important contents were rescued and the place was meticulously restored and reopened in 1995. However, for the garden and woodland the great storm of October 1987 was almost equally disastrous, taking much longer to restore. With another damaging gale following in January 1990, the combined effect was much as I remembered London after the Blitz. Like London it was an opportunity as well as a calamity for the garden.

Watched relentlessly by the donor family, the Fetherstonhaughs, Graham Thomas's recommendations throughout the 1960s and into the 1970s had been sensibly circumspect, mostly concentrating on gradual small-scale improvements in the pleasure ground north of the house. However, he was able to remove a seemingly pointless hedge west of the mansion and plant trees at a respectful distance further west to provide a measure of shelter. Less successful was the ha-ha dug on the south side, the purpose of which was to allow visitors to walk out to see the house properly from its best aspect. This was a questionable innovation and records, including an early nineteenth-century illustration by Humphry Repton, showed the house sitting starkly in the parkland backed by pleasure ground

Uppark house under repair after the fire. (1990)

Humphry Repton recommended a short, curving avenue up to the north front of the house, here replanted. (1995)

woodland. Evidently over a century or more, for the convenience of living there, the family had gradually taken in part of the park and blurred the distinction between it and the pleasure ground.

From the time I first saw it and realised its history, I was convinced that the house should again sit starkly in the park surrounded by sheep-grazed pasture. However, the status quo had seemed immutable, with the family using the east front privately. Almost while the embers of the fire were still warm, I began sowing the seeds of radical change with the regional staff and the Gardens Panel. House restoration understandably came first and little thought was given to the garden,

The house now sits forward of the pleasure ground in the landscape park.

except in confining salvage and reconstruction works and access to the east front away from the garden. When landscape restoration was eventually discussed I found myself happily agreeing wholeheartedly with those who wanted what had been my aspiration – to draw back the pleasure ground boundary and leave the house in the park, also to fill in the modern ha-ha. I remember very well the then Regional Director, David Sekers, putting the idea to me as his own!

The National Trust owned only the house and 21.6 ha (54 acres), but with covenants over another 359.4 ha (888 acres) of the South Downs comprising the parkland. Although not directly attributable to Lancelot Brown, the park and the disposition of house and pleasure ground are entirely in his style, and plans exist which bear a strong resemblance to his work. However, we know that Humphry Repton was employed by Sir Harry Fetherstonhaugh for work in the pleasure ground, the outlines of which already existed. Repton's Red Book for Uppark related mainly to improvements within the pleasure ground, developing it into a no doubt welcome sheltered escape from the breezy surroundings of the house. Much had been added since, part of the history of the place, but we were able to use Repton's recommendations for replanting along the short drive to the back of the house, a gentle curve of trees gradually revealing the portico and doorway. Otherwise the layout remained basically simple with trees and shrubs sheltering an enclosed lawn leading out to walks with views of the Downs. There is also a tradition for scented plants which should not be forgotten.

The garden is now well on its way to providing the cosy corners for sitting out and the sheltered walks with sweet-smelling plants that must be the ideal for anyone living at Uppark.

The garden at Dunham Massey had gone to sleep for more than a quarter of a century by the time the National Trust acquired it in the mid-1970s, along with the house and huge estate. Benign neglect and minimal maintenance had left a confusing muddle of overgrown features dating back to almost every phase of the garden's development since the sixteenth century, all slipping steadily towards natural re-afforestation. Even the Second World War was commemorated by a puzzling series of ridges on the main lawn, relics of potato growing for the War effort, presumably never lifted!

This fascinating garden occupied an important part in my life for twenty years and probably reflects more of my character than any other Trust property with which I have had the pleasure to be associated. One great advantage of Dunham was its low profile as a garden, allowing us flexibility, and the other was the availability of generous funding, something I had never encountered before.

Because it had been closed for so many years the garden was unknown, nationally and even locally. Yet it contained elements reflecting its whole history, often modified, like the Elizabethan mount and moat, but sometimes almost intact, like the eighteenth-century orangery and the nineteenth-century bark house arbour. The dominant feature was the Edwardian formal layout of paving and flower beds (long gone) which wiggled its way intrusively from the house to the orangery. There remained some fine specimen trees but many false acacias and oaks had dead crowns, apparently resulting from a breakdown at some time in the complicated estate drainage system. Perhaps the oddest legacy, but also the area of most potential, was a piece of unkempt garden woodland beyond the ha-ha, presumably enclosed from the park at the turn of the twentieth century. This contained some fine trees and many ageing birches; also a wealth of fine young English oaks, presumably self-sown during and since the last War.

Even the extensive park, a rare survival of late seventeenth-century formal taste, was not well known despite John Harris's eighteenth-century series of bird's-eye views in the house, showing the idealised 'goose foot' of avenues. However, this was already freely visited locally and, along with a deer herd, also had considerable nature conservation value.

Although the garden was managed from the local estate office, its acquisition and early restoration were piloted by Gerard Noel, the Regional Director from Attingham. He was a real countryman and land agent in the traditional sense but also a free-thinking, imaginative man of great energy and enthusiasm. He was very good with people and always established a loyal following wherever he was. He led from the front at Dunham and was not afraid to take potentially contentious decisions. Nor was he shy of attempting to put his own stamp on things. In some senses it was like having to deal with a resident donor whose many ideas were mostly sound but occasionally rash. But his drive achieved a great deal very quickly, with a minimum of bureaucratic intervention. His early masterstroke was to persuade George (Harry) Burrows to leave Hidcote to spend the last six years of his Trust career on the ground-breaking restoration at Dunham. As head gardener under Graham Thomas's direction, Harry had recovered the overgrown and run-down garden at Hidcote from the late 1950s onwards. After more than twenty years he was ready for a new challenge and was never happier than when cutting back and pruning; just the man for Dunham. He was joined by the energetic Michael Ridsdale, who went on to become head gardener at Studley Royal/Fountains Abbey. As Harry's eventual successor, Peter Hall was appointed later, having worked first at Wimpole Hall and then as a gardener-in-charge of the restoration at Canons Ashby.

We were lucky to have first Merlin Waterson and later Julian Gibbs as Historic Buildings Representatives because they both took such a special interest in gardens. As usual with garden restorations, much of the initial work entailed obvious clearance and dealing with considerations of access and circulation for the eventual opening, still years away. We closed a service path from the corner of the house and made a new entrance via the garden woodland beyond the ha-ha. This enabled us to split the visitor circulation and reduce pressure on the main lawns. The remnant of the rather pompous Edwardian layout was impractical, unsustainable and over-dominant, and we decided unilaterally to remove it from the main lawns near the orangery and to retain it only for the formal north front

The Orangery standing unconnected to its surroundings. (1980)

The Orangery now sitting comfortably sheltered among large borders of shrubs and plants. (1992)

overlooking the moat. In any historic garden, simply because something has previously existed does not in itself require its restoration. Gradually we formulated a conservation philosophy based on the garden's continuous development over almost 400 years, incorporating the ebb and flow of change and retrenchment. Separate elements had survived from each period of the garden's history and needed to be revealed and unified into a coherent concept according to their perceived value. At Dunham there was also ample scope for creativity; for moving the garden forward while respecting the past.

The Edwardian garden had had a formal rose garden surrounded bizarrely by purple beech hedges which had grown on to become uneven bands of trees. Total gloom and beech roots meant that nothing grew there, so we decided to take advantage of this and create a moss garden, a restful contrast to the flowery borders; not to everyone's taste but an acceptable innovation arising out of the garden's twentieth-century history of neglect and revival.

Perhaps the trickiest early decisions involved access and circulation, especially from the point where visitors would emerge onto the main lawn from below the ha-ha. There was a strong reluctance to lay paths across the lawns but I became convinced that anarchy would result in a muddy mess of 'sheep tracks'. We called upon the Gardens Panel, led then by the redoubtable Viscount Blakenham (once Minister of Agriculture in Macmillan's government), to validate our proposed conservation philosophy and resolve the paths dilemma. Their combined wisdom was invaluable in exploring every alternative and casting fresh light to clarify our half-formed ideas. They agreed a simple layout of informal paths, to cater unobtrusively for the expected 'desire lines' that visitors could be expected to follow, a crucial decision that allowed me to agree the precise routes. The aim was to keep the main lawn uncluttered, furnished only with some carefully placed specimen trees. New planting would be confined to the edges but especially aimed at creating large borders either side of the orangery, so that this lovely building would be framed with trees and shrubs as an important incident in the circuit.

The severe, even dull, north façade of the house needed a lift, and we decided to retain the essence of the Edwardian layout, a parterre set in paving, which I

LEFT The north front showing the bleak area of paving at its centre and insubstantial beds around.

RIGHT The north front after removing some of the Edwardian paving to create a large central bed planted mainly with permanent plants and bulbs.

redesigned to make it bolder, including an oblong bed in the centre containing permanent planting. The colour scheme was a challenge because of the extraordinarily brash hedges of golden yew, through which the scarlet *Tropaeolum speciosum* (glory vine) grew in abundance. With a setting like this subtlety is hardly appropriate but we found an old zonal pelargonium cultivar with yellow foliage; we also concluded that violet blue was a successful complementary colour (from *Verbena rigida*). As four topiary pieces I specified *Quercus phillyreoides*, a rare Chinese oak (to test the botanically-minded visitor) with glossy, evergreen leaves, which clips well and resembles the European *Phillyrea latifolia*. All this gorgeous colour needed the antidote provided by the site of the Elizabethan mount, now a flattened hump on a peninsular on the moat, covered in false acacias which had suckered overall. We planted evergreens as a visual break and made a circular path around the grassy mount, keeping all the planting low-key: a restful interlude.

Harry Burrows soon began making splendid inroads into the overgrown evergreens, especially the leggy hollies along the streamside and ha-ha wall, relieving much of the gloom. Perhaps Harry's greatest achievement, however, was with the courtyard, entirely enclosed by the house, which had been paved overall, apart from a fountain pool in the centre. The house exhibited little architectural merit from this aspect and the whole enclosure was dank and gloomy with slippery paving. Our answer was to cover the walls with climbers and to restore four big beds that had evidently been paved over with flagstones at some time. According to orientation we used mostly large-leafed climbers like the teinturier grape (*Vitis vinifera* 'Purpurea') and Chinese gooseberry (*Actinidia chinensis*). As the courtyard's only access is through the house, this was a huge horticultural and logistic challenge. The only way of removing the slabs and replacing the topsoil was by hand-barrowing over a gantry constructed through the house. As half

The Inner Courtyard with Harry Burrows, then head gardener, and Richard Dykes, laboriously removing some of the paving to create flower borders. (1977)

the courtyard is in almost constant shade and the other half at times subject to intense heat, design and planting provided another big challenge. We decided on pale colours to penetrate the gloom, but dead white can seem funereal in such circumstances. So we went for mostly creamy colours and pale yellows, with light blue for contrast, mostly bulbs and herbaceous to soften the hardness of the paving. With my colleagues in Cirencester I produced the plans and all went well with the planting until the local jackdaws decided that these little plants were ideal for nest-making, the most expensive nests ever known in Cheshire!

The Inner Courtyard showing the four herbaceous beds which replaced paving. The colour scheme is creamy white and pale yellow with some blue for contrast. (c.1989)

Harry and his wife, Vicki, occupied the head gardener's house in the walled garden across the road opposite the main garden. He brought many plants from Hidcote and made a small but fascinating plantsman's garden where he entertained groups of garden enthusiasts. After his retirement this served as a valuable stock bed for some of the large-scale plantings in the main garden.

Meconopsis
x *sheldonii* at
Dunham Massey.
(1980s)

After living in the village and working as Harry's assistant, Peter Hall succeeded as head gardener at a time when the garden needed the management ability, horticultural expertise and attention to detail that marked him out as one of the most accomplished and effective head gardeners the Trust has ever employed. Under his perceptive care the garden developed into one of the Trust's most popular gardens: a paradise for discerning plantsmen. Not that gardening is easy at Dunham with light, sandy soil, second only to Biddulph Grange for acidity (mostly pH 4.5 or even lower) and devoid of natural fertility. This had to be built up slowly, using magnesian limestone, and laboriously, by copious applications of farmyard manure, of which there was a plentiful local supply. On the other hand, the high water table enabled us to plant large areas of herbaceous perennials in the mid-1980s, well ahead of the modern trend for this style of planting. Apart from this, the predominant style became late-Victorian 'William Robinson' informal, incorporating the best of the surviving trees and features.

In the 1970s herbaceous perennial plants were steadily making a comeback after years of neglect during and after the War, when new plantings had become dominated by 'labour-saving' bush roses, shrubs and ground covers, while local authority parks departments clung to their colourful displays of bedding plants. Thus far we had not seen herbaceous planting on any really generous scale. At Dunham in the early 1980s we were able to pioneer lush and flowery planting in extensive, sometimes mixed, drifts mainly along the streamsides. These plantings were much admired and were followed in the 1990s by the use of herbaceous plants, on the truly landscape scale associated with Piet Oudolf and much copied, to great effect.

Special efforts were made to make the new planting interesting and colourful throughout the year, especially in the summer. The garden already contained many hardy hybrid rhododendrons and other ericaceous plants for spring colour and we extended the range to include many cultivars of *Rhododendron yakushimanum*. We also made a speciality of hydrangea in all its many species and

cultivars, planted with big grasses and bamboos for contrast of form. At one of the RHS Vincent Square shows I saw some late azaleas exhibited by Cheshire-born Denny Pratt, followed by an article in *The Garden* about his attempts to produce June- and July-flowering cultivars by using late-flowering American species crossed with Knap Hill azaleas. I invited Denny to Dunham and he was thrilled by the prospect of finding a permanent home for some of his horticultural off-spring. Then in his late eighties (having begun hybridising in Fittleworth, Sussex, only after retirement), he was extremely generous, and I recall a wonderful day with Peter Hall setting out groups of his cultivars in the garden wood, a highlight of Denny's later life I guess. Peter and Sally Hall became his great friends and he subsequently bequeathed half his stock of seedlings to Dunham (the other half went to the Ness Botanic Garden).

In the house John Harris the Younger's amazing early eighteenth-century series of bird's-eye views are an unsurpassed record of the park at that time, then a recently completed complex of avenues radiating from the house, still substantially intact after 250 years. Near the house the six lines of trees, three either side, had disappeared, probably due to their close planting. They are shown as small mop-headed trees and their replacement implied a sustainable programme of intensive management. Perhaps wrongly we chose seed-raised limes, the native *Tilia cordata*, but their inevitable variability did not matter because they would have to be regularly pruned. Each needed secure protection from deer and I specified training their crowns initially into a pyramidal shape to take account of apical dominance, pollarding back to this shape at regular intervals.

As soon as possible Julian Gibbs commissioned John Phibbs to survey the whole park to reveal its full history and development and to devise a long-term plan

Some hybrid rhododendrons and Japanese maples had survived until the 1970s well enough to be restored to good health.

Azalea 'Anneke' is one of Denny Pratt's spring-flowering hybrid azaleas but he subsequently bred for flowers in late June and July.

for its conservation. This involved several stimulating discussions to tease out a workable replanting policy that took account of practical considerations. Replanting would be phased over several generations so as to lend long-term resilience to the outcome, eventually with trees of all ages. In the 1980s the need to accommodate historic significance, landscape and garden aesthetics, access and function alongside nature conservation were not well understood. With my nature conservation colleagues in the Trust's advisory office in Cirencester, I resolved to tackle this problem by convening a meeting between the Nature Conservation Panel of invited experts and the Gardens Panel, then led by Lady Emma Tennant, whose broad perception and wise counsel served the Trust well for many years. Dunham Massey was the ideal case for consideration, exhibiting all the conflicts that are likely to arise. The discussions were exploratory, largely inconclusive and a steep learning curve for most people present, revealing some extraordinarily narrow thinking, mostly among highly-specialised experts in any particular field. However, they aired the problems and enabled us to begin formulating policy principles that were later refined, leading to a much better understanding of the issues. However, the equitable application of the guidelines would inevitably remain dependent on the fair-minded judgement of those in charge.

Thanks to the work of Professor Donald Pigott at the University of Lancaster and the University of Cambridge, by the 1980s we were beginning to recognise the different clones of lime (*Tilia*) in the Trust's parks and gardens. These were mainly clones of the hybrid so-called common lime (*Tilia* × *europaea*), raised almost entirely in the Netherlands in the seventeenth century and imported in their thousands as young trees for planting formal avenues. Many ancient avenues have been degraded by interplanting with the 'wrong' clone, often with forms of *Tilia platyphyllos* (large-leafed lime). It seemed vital that somewhere there should be a nursery where the nucleus of a stock of these clones could be raised and compared, commercial sources being very limited. Peter Hall went to a lot of trouble to create a lime nursery at Dunham in the redundant walled garden, raising several batches of young trees of known provenance by layering and stooling.

BIDDULPH GRANGE

STAFFORDSHIRE

My first visit to Biddulph Grange was with a garden history group in the mid-1970s, having little idea of what to expect. I was totally overwhelmed – in turns amazed, intrigued, excited, baffled and lost in the mixture of styles, moods and plants; that was the intention perhaps? Here was something entirely different in the world of gardens and gardening. I cannot admit to finding all of it beautiful in terms of our time but the varied buildings, muscular rock work and towering trees were deeply impressive among the lugubrious groves of overgrown yews. Clearly it was something of originality and historic interest but at that time the National Trust's involvement was mere hope in the minds of a few, particularly Peter Hayden and Keith Goodway of the Garden History Society.

The garden was being run by the Regional Health Authority along with the house and a large modernist 1924 award-winning hospital extension. Thanks to the sympathetic attitude of some of the health service officers, the three dedicated gardeners – Bill Shufflebottom, Fred Hancock and Eric Bowers – had been retained since the 1930s. By sheer diligence and loyalty they had kept it in good order, preserving the structure as well as they could, maintaining if not cultivating the garden and protecting many of its plants through a period of every-increasing austerity and of disdain for this style of gardening. Anyone would find it difficult to get the hang of the place at first and to grasp why and how it was made. The full story of the garden's rise and decline is well related In Peter Hayden's book *Biddulph Grange, A Victorian Garden Rediscovered*, published in 1989 at the time of the Trust's eventual reopening. However, you do not need the full story to recognise special significance, personal preference being irrelevant to any one seriously interested in historic garden conservation. The more you find out, the more rewarding it becomes.

Already known and revered in the comparatively small world of the Garden History Society, Biddulph Grange came to prominence through its inclusion among a series of postage stamps illustrating historic gardens in 1983. Each period of garden design was represented, Biddulph being considered an outstanding example of mid-Victorian garden-making.

By the time the protracted negotiations had been completed for the Trust to acquire the garden and part of the house, I had visited several times and learned something of its history and content. Luckily the Trust was able to take over de facto management in 1986 some two years before its eventual acquisition, while Eric Bowers remained in charge of the gardeners. Sadly they had been giving way to the incursions of local youths whose drinking parties and minor misdemeanours had been taking their toll, especially with the buildings. With no perimeter fence the gardeners had been losing the battle, gradually retreating from confrontation. That the garden had survived is testament to their dedication but also to its robust construction. The Trust was fortunate in having Julian Gibbs, Regional Historic Buildings Representative, available to take on the huge task of project manager, one of the principal proponents of the acquisition who had campaigned long and hard within the Trust. Thereafter he was the lynchpin in guiding and managing this thrilling restoration, unsurpassed anywhere in it complication and significance.

The two-year interregnum before legal acquisition allowed us, without the spotlight of publicity, to take some of the obvious first steps in any restoration. First priority was protection, and despite an expensive security contract vandalism was not overcome until a complete 'unclimbable' perimeter fence could be built. Equally urgent was to commission a thorough historical and botanical research project based on a full study of the records linked to a precise survey of the whole garden. Particularly important was a detailed record of all the surviving plants, including their critical identification, together with analysis of contemporary photographs, descriptions and written record. Similar research was needed to cover all the garden buildings and structures whether existing or gone, although much had to be learned about these artefacts from archaeology revealed during reconstruction.

It is important as soon as possible to establish the motives and aspirations of those who made the garden so that the welter of detail can be read as part of the bigger picture. The garden at Biddulph Grange was created by James Bateman, and to a lesser degree his wife, Maria, from the 1840s for the principal purpose of growing the world's plants in appropriate surroundings, both environmentally and stylistically. The artist Edward Cooke was employed to create, in effect, 'stage sets' on a 6 ha (15 acre) site, within which ideal growing conditions would be provided for the many exotic plants that were then arriving from distant lands. Edward Cooke used this opportunity to create an imaginative series of linked architectural excitements based loosely on foreign precedent, such as 'China' and 'Egypt'. One suspects that the now wide appeal of the garden derives largely from this series of contrasting experiences, excitingly discovered through exploring the garden, never knowing what next to expect. Except among plantsmen this

The Dahlia Walk at Biddulph had to be excavated, revealing some of the original walls and even the roots of the yew hedging.

undeniable impact tends perhaps to take precedence over the principal purpose of the garden: to grow and display the plants of the world.

To a large degree the garden's restoration was based on a series of articles by Edward Kemp which appeared in the *Gardeners' Chronicle* in 1856 and 1862. In considerable detail these articles not only described the extraordinary range of novel features in the garden but also listed many of the plants, their sources and their arrangement, together with several precisely drawn plans. With the many contemporary photographs it was possible to gain an accurate impression of most of the garden.

LEFT The Chinese Terrace in 1987 after vandalism and before repair. The shrub growing out of the wall at water level was identified as *Spirea japonica fortunei*, the name assigned to a plant collected in the wild by Robert Fortune and the only one in the garden.

BELOW The Chinese Terrace after restoration. (1991)

The vital importance of the comprehensive plant survey and analysis, carried out so brilliantly by Michael Lear, was justified time and time again. It revealed, for example, the only survivor of an original introduction by the nineteenth-century plant collector Robert Fortune, *Spirea japonica* var. *fortunei*, which was growing out of a mortar joint at water level in 'China' and would not have survived the first week of the reconstruction of the Chinese Terrace. Similarly, the scientific and historic significance of the golden larch, *Pseudolarix amabilis*, in 'China' was emphasised by establishing it as the sole survivor of the first-ever introduction of this species into Europe.

These seedlings and many other plants were imported on board ship in Wardian cases, closed and glazed packing cases shaped like small greenhouses, which had been designed by Nathaniel Bagshaw Ward and first used successfully in 1833 by Loddiges' Hackney nursery to convey plants to and from Australia. That Nathaniel Ward's son, Stephen, married Edward Cooke's sister, Georgiana, and that Cooke himself married a Loddiges, indicates the close personal as well as professional ties that existed among those involved at Biddulph.

The plant survey distinguished the plants, mostly ubiquitous hardy hybrid rhododendrons, that had been introduced with the best intentions by the hospital management some time since the war to fill gaps. We decided to remove this overlay entirely in favour of original species and cultivars as far as possible. On the other hand, we agreed to retain plants introduced by Robert Heath, who bought Biddulph Grange in 1872, unless they destroyed the Batemans' intentions. This led us to formulate a planting policy, novel at the time, which categorised the choice of plants for the restored garden on historic grounds, bearing in mind that the eventual selection would also need to take account of horticultural and aesthetic considerations. First preference would be plants known to have been in the garden in the Batemans' time. Second preference would be plants deemed to have been identified from contemporary photographs but not documented. Failing these, the third choice would be plants widely available at the time the garden was made.

The Dahlia Walk in the 1990s.

In every case the exact form or the current cultivar would be sought and in the case of true species plants of wild or known source origin would be preferred. The procurement of rare and unusual plants is a slow and painful process with a plant collection of this magnitude and had to be started as soon as possible. Furthermore, a nursery was essential for propagating the existing stock, evaluating and caring for new plants, and for raising from seeds and cuttings plants which were not otherwise available.

Because the Trust did not own the property, it was not able legally to spend money and carry out irreversible work during the period from 1986–88, but much preparatory work was accomplished. For a century or so the garden had been maintained – in the sense of being raked, weeded, swept and trimmed – but not cultivated as gardens must be – pruned, mulched, lifted and divided, replenished, thinned and renewed. As a result much of the topsoil had been gradually weeded away and taken with the weeds to an ever-increasing rubbish dump, situated for convenience on the former bowling green in the centre of the garden. Up to 1.5 m (4 ft 11 in) deep, it had to be taken back but unfortunately the dump had been contaminated with Japanese knotweed, no doubt originally introduced as an ornamental. Over three years this was successfully exterminated and the topsoil relocated along with the large quantities of farmyard manure brought in to raise fertility. Being on the edge of heathland, the soil at Biddulph is naturally poor, free-draining fine sand, mostly devoid of nutrients and fertility until improved. This poverty was soon made clear in our soil testing, which also revealed the most acid soils ever encountered in National Trust gardens (pH 4.3–4.5 – almost acid enough to scorch your socks!). This was no doubt in part due to acid rain fallout

The formal gardens and Rhododendron Ground in 2005, seen from the house terrace.

from the local heavy industry around Stoke-on-Trent (whence Bateman's wealth was derived!). Correcting such a serious nutrient imbalance cannot be achieved quickly because of the likelihood of counter-reaction to sudden remedial applications. The two years' grace before starting any major structural works were fortunate in giving time for repeated small applications of magnesian limestone to raise the pH, together with heavy mulching to raise fertility, while also destroying any persistent weeds.

As soon as possible the Trust appointed its own head gardener, while Eric Bowers generously stayed on for a while to pass on his knowledge and help out. The admirable Nigel Davis was eventually moved in to a restored gatehouse and pioneered the garden restoration. With a reputation for vandalism and at least partial neglect, Biddulph was not an easy assignment but Nigel rose to the occasion, steadily clawing back control over the whole garden and dealing with the contractors involved in the early stages of restoration and repair. He and Julian Gibbs were invariably positive and resilient even in the midst of seeming chaos, with heavy machinery bogged down and mud everywhere.

The other key early appointment was Anthony Blackley, an outstandingly able conservation architect, as consultant, responsible for drawing up plans and procedures for repairing or reconstructing all the garden's buildings and other artefacts. Working mostly from contemporary sketches, paintings and photographs, together with archaeological evidence, he put together designs and working drawings of extraordinary precision. His observation of detail and ability to visualise the final product were shown to be right in almost every case, although Julian Gibbs had an important part to play in every decision. Anthony even drew out the precise dimensions of the yew hedges in the Dahlia Walk as they had been a century earlier.

After a couple of years of ground-breaking endeavour, Nigel moved on to become head gardener at Sheffield Park and was succeeded by Bill Malecki. I first met Bill as a student at Askham Bryan, in my part-time role as National Moderator for National Diploma 'sandwich' courses in amenity horticulture in the 1970s. I used to interview a sample of students at either end and the middle of the range of academic achievement. Bill was top and said, when asked of his ambitions, that he wanted a job like mine with historic gardens. He asked for my suggestions both for his sandwich year and for his subsequent employment, and I suggested experience in a garden of outstanding historic importance and horticultural merit. He could hardly have done better than going to Bodnant for his sandwich year, and did so well that they offered him a job when he finished the course. Within a few years at Bodnant the head gardener Martin Puddle appointed him, aged twenty-seven years, his general foreman in charge of the day-to-day work of a large staff caring for this hugely complex garden, which annually attracted at the time the most visitors of any garden owned by the National Trust. I asked Bill at his interview

Clematis 'Miss Bateman'.

why he should wish to leave such a great garden on a glorious site containing an unmatched plant collection in favour of Biddulph? Obviously anticipating my question, he replied that it was the equivalent of moving from being leader of a great orchestra to becoming musical director and conductor of a chamber orchestra of great potential; not a bad answer, I thought.

As well as having the best possible background and experience for his role as head gardener and property manager, Bill was calm, methodical and extremely good with people, including staff at all levels, architects, contractors, archaeologists, academics, committee members and even Gardens Advisers. Looking back, my advisory visits to Biddulph in the 1980s and early 1990s were some of the most challenging, effective, productive and enjoyable of my entire career with the National Trust. In spite of a whole series of difficulties, Julian Gibbs drove the restoration forward with remarkable energy and resilience. Being so diverse, it represents perhaps the Trust's greatest achievement in garden restoration and renewal: historic plant conservation and replacement, avenue renewal, archaeological excavation, historic buildings repair, reconstruction of lost features, flower garden restoration, repair and conservation of sculptures and ornaments, visitor services and car parking, all on a site of 6 ha (15 acres).

After long discussions with the local planners and owners of neighbouring properties, Julian eventually obtained consent for the car park, obviously vital to any open garden, on condition that we produced a layout and planting plan which satisfied the local planning officer, whom we were due to meet. Although he had brought the outline survey plan with him and we had discussed it earlier, we had done nothing about the planting plan. Julian had forgotten the appointment until 1 pm, the appointment being for 2 pm. He did not want to put it off so we settled down over lunch and produced an outline sketch scheme for access and car parking with detailed tree positions and screen planting for the whole site, 'completing' it with ten minutes to spare. To our relief it was accepted without query, saving the professional fees of a landscape architect for a 'posh' plan.

After an entirely successful spell managing the spectacular rebirth of the garden at Biddulph Grange, Bill Malecki was eventually appointed to my staff at Cirencester in the early 1990s as a Gardens Adviser, having earlier successfully completed a six-month 'sabbatical' from Biddulph as an Assistant Adviser. He soon became a highly effective and a much-loved adviser in a wide range of gardens, especially in Devon and Cornwall, the Home Counties, Yorkshire and the East Midlands, continuing after my retirement to play an ever-more important role in the conservation of the Trust's gardens generally, especially with historic plant propagation and conservation. His tragic death from a brain tumour in 2006 was a sad blow to all who knew him, a man of outstanding qualities, personal and professional – deep insight, good humour, exceptional judgement, wide interests, acute observation, real humanity, genuine humility, logical persuasiveness and sharp intelligence. As he had been a mentor and friend for nearly thirty years, his death was a deep personal loss to my wife, Lyn, and me, but he will be remembered for his works, especially at Biddulph, for his wise counsel to head gardeners and others, and for his support of the plant conservation nursery at Knightshayes.

One of Bill's great achievements at Biddulph was the replanting of the great wellingtonia avenue, in fact originally a complicated triple avenue with hedges, contouring and background planting for shelter. The original central avenue of alternating wellingtonias (*Sequiadendron giganteum*) and deodars (*Cedrus deodara*) had been thinned after the Batemans' time by removing the wellingtonias, originally the intended survivors. By the 1980s some of the cedars had fallen and the general effect was picturesquely decrepit but not sustainable. We agreed that half-measures would be inappropriate because the feature was originally intended as a complicated, typically Victorian, set-piece of three ranks of trees planted at different levels. Tree felling is always emotive and this would involve the removal of a local skyline, quite a challenge for local public relations! From the start, total felling and replanting was presented as a decision, never a matter for negotiation, and a crucial move by Bill was to persuade every one of the many voluntary guides that the whole procedure would be not only necessary

The wellingtonia avenue in the 1980s. Bateman intended the deodars as interplanting between the wellingtonias but the 'wrong' trees were removed after Bateman's time.

but also a thrilling prospect. Two years before the act, display boards were put up to explain the original intention, and our proposals and volunteer guides briefed to explain these to every interested visitor. The local press was also informed on several occasions. Meanwhile, as much publicity as possible was given to the acquisition of wellingtonia seeds from California for propagating the trees. By the time of the actual felling, although massive and traumatic, most local people were already aware. Carried out in the closed season as quickly as possible, the actual felling and extraction passed off astonishingly well with little local or national reaction. From that point the avenue resumed its role as an important feature of the garden, restarting a process begun almost 150 years earlier by James Bateman.

'Egypt' consists of a pyramid of clipped yew growing on top of a subterranean corridor and chamber containing a stone figure of the Ape of Thoth whom the Egyptians credited with the invention of botany. Renewal of the pyramid of yews, still clinging to life but starved and eroded, was a special challenge which we solved by 'prefabricating' the yew topiary in deep boxes grown together in the nursery and clipped to shape. Eventually, with some considerable difficulty, we were able to replace the original yews over the repaired roof structure and quickly reform the pyramid.

Where the intricate formal gardens near the house and the extraordinary Dahlia Walk had been totally obliterated, complete reconstruction was necessary. This was a difficult but immediately rewarding experience, exciting and good for the ego. Elsewhere it was a case of careful conservation, repair and renewal, a far more difficult procedure, needing careful analysis and frequent tricky judgements involving horticultural considerations – timing, priority, public access, fellings, major prunings, etc. Whatever the public's perception, restoration as a part of conservation can never cease if the garden is to be cared for with a view to its ultimate survival as a great work of art, artifice and gardening, continuing to reflect its special qualities and values.

The Wellingtonia Avenue in 1995 after felling the pines and Deodars and restoring the avenue of *Sequiadendron giganteum* raised from Californian seeds in the nursery at Biddulph. They were planted on mounds for drainage, a common Victorian practice.

Egypt in the 1980s before restoration of the structure and replacement of the pyramid yews.

Eventually a long-term conservation management plan was written, one of the first of its kind for an historic garden of such horticultural and historic complexity, which had to address some of the dilemmas of comprehensive restoration like changed surroundings and the impact of many visitors. An important philosophical dilemma arises out of the fact that the garden was owned by the Batemans for less than thirty years and was in their time entirely new with many young plants, especially trees at an early stage of development planted presumably at unsustainable spacing. A garden like Biddulph needs to be in a constant state of renewal and reworking, deliberately felling and replanting to avoid any sense of uniform maturity; not a place for the faint-hearted.

Chapter 7

ICONS AND SHRINES

The Tower at
Sissinghurst seen
from the Cottage
Garden.

I first went to Hidcote in 1960, soon after I began lecturing in horticulture at Writtle College, and long before I worked for the National Trust. The whole property, including the house, farm and most of the village of Hidcote Bartrim, had been acquired by the Trust through the will of Lawrence Johnston, who famously made the garden after 1907. In an historic change of emphasis Hidcote was the first place to be accepted by the National Trust primarily on account of its garden, thereby setting a precedent, soon to be followed by Bodnant, Nymans, Mount Stewart, Sissinghurst, Sheffield Park and others. As it was arguably Britain's most important and influential garden of the twentieth century, this was a wise and far-reaching decision. It was also the very beginning of serious historic garden conservation as we know it.

Much has been written about Lawrence Johnston and Hidcote but detailed evidence is scarce and much of it based on hearsay. As far as the garden is concerned, his gardening style began from the Arts and Crafts tradition of Broadway and the Cotswolds, and he seems to have been much influenced by Edith Wharton's *Italian Villas and their Gardens* and Thomas Mawson's *The Art and Craft of Garden Making* in laying out the garden's structure. However, his garden-making was entirely original and no one has successfully copied his style, although many have tried. As well as being an imaginative designer of spaces and contriver of views, Johnston became an accomplished plantsman and there is no doubt that Frank Adams, his head gardener, had a large part to play in developing Hidcote's catholic plant collection, as well as in its arrangement, cultivation and management. Great gardens are rarely made entirely through the genius of a single individual but they always come about from the pursuit of a unique ideal, persistently sought and perfected, as at Hidcote in the mind of Lawrence Johnston.

The much underrated Norah Lindsay was a huge influence at Hidcote in the 1930s, significantly after Johnston's mother died, and there seems little doubt that much of the garden's colour scheming can be attributed to her dominant impact. She reigned as the country's most effective and influential flower garden designer between the wars, but the memory of her work quickly faded because she rarely drew plans on paper and never wrote a book, unlike Gertrude Jekyll and Vita Sackville-West. Norah Lindsay, however, was part of Johnston's restricted circle of friends and frequently stayed at Hidcote. It is said that Johnston intended leaving Hidcote to Norah Lindsay but in the event she died first, to the benefit of the nation.

Deliberate development of the garden at Hidcote virtually ceased after the outbreak of the Second World War, coinciding significantly with the death of Frank Adams in 1939. He was succeeded by Albert Hawkins, formerly in charge of the vegetable garden, who kept things going remarkably well with what help he could get until the onset of Johnston's dementia; then came the Trust's acquisition in 1948. However, there was no money and a lack of direction; the Trust had to learn how to manage its gardens, and it was not until 1955 that Graham Thomas was appointed as Gardens Adviser. In the interregnum the garden seems to have drifted. A complex garden demanding strict control and constant detailed decision-making, it had clearly become over-mature and overgrown. Despite this it seems that many, if not most, of the key plants survived, bearing in mind that plantsmen's gardens of this kind invariably contain a shifting population, coming and going, many lost or rejected as unsuitable.

After Johnston's death Norah Lindsay's daughter, Nancy, assumed the right to run the place based on her assertion that it would have been her mother's wish. Although knowledgeable about plants, she had neither the aptitude nor the consistency of purpose to succeed. To confuse the situation further, the Trust appointed a high-powered committee to run the garden, chaired by Lord Aberconway. Committees have a role but they have managed neither to make a significant garden successfully nor to care for one in a way that retains its special qualities and individuality.

Someone had to take a grip and it effectively fell to Graham Thomas to manage the process of restoration and renewal, in the face of many conflicting views and interests, with minimal resources and little real authority. There was no endowment. Several of the garden's buildings were ruinous or too dangerous to use, let alone allow visitors to enter. Difficult decisions, including demolition and radical adaptation, had to be made, giving priority to what at the time seemed most important. With visitor numbers as low as 3,500, the utmost economy was necessary, and at the time few people foresaw the boom in garden visiting and National Trust membership of the 1960s and '70s. With his steady, consistent approach and never-failing drive, Graham achieved a huge transformation with the head gardener George (Harry) Burrows, who was a great worker and an enthusiastic pruner. In fact, they saved the garden from dereliction.

Penstemon 'Hidcote Pink'.

At that time there was no accumulated experience of historic garden conservation to draw upon: no established principles and certainly no guidance. Graham's approach was effectively a common sense one, respecting the qualities for which the garden was acquired while renovating, re-working and renewing in the light of a complete change of use from private to public, including all the paraphernalia of public visiting. He quickly assumed control and, by any standard, achieved a remarkable amount. Having visited Hidcote in the 1930s, and with a very remarkable memory for plants and plant associations, his touch was sure but in the last resort his own taste was the touchstone. Luckily his preferred gardening style was close to the Hidcote idiom, a combination of Johnston's plantsmanship and Lindsay's colour sense.

Renovation and renewal included a great deal of tree work to reopen views and lift some of the gloom created by the many holm oaks; also the reduction of overgrown hedges, formal and informal, to restore their scale in relation to the series of room-like spaces and vistas imagined by Lawrence Johnston. Harry Burrows was in his element pruning back

ABOVE The main axis from the Old Garden through the Circle, the Red Borders and up to the Stilt Garden in the 1980s.

A 1963 view of one of our first visits to Hidcote from the southern gazebo with Lyn Sales and our oldest son, Nick.

overgrown hollies and rediscovering plants long hidden by luxuriant shrubs and ground cover. Replanting was closely directed by Graham according to his appraisal and governed by his perception of the appropriate colour scheme or theme for each border or area. While he mostly used plants known to have been in the garden, there was no compunction at the time about introducing compatible new plants as Johnston would have done, particularly ephemeral plants for the red borders and elsewhere.

As an ordinary, occasional visitor during the 1960s, I was fascinated by Hidcote and intrigued by the pollarding of overgrown holm oaks, the radical reduction of overgrown hedges and the generous sophistication of the renewed plantings. However, latterly, like many visitors, I became irritated by inadequate facilities, especially car parks and tea room, together with overcrowding and poor circulation in the garden. These problems intensified during the 1970s and '80s, made worse by the Trust using parts of the garden for raising and selling plants and merchandise.

Conservation aims for important gardens should include as far as possible preventing the erosion of character and values arising from overcrowding, over-regulation, over-interpretation and over-commercialisation. As visitor numbers spiralled, it became increasingly clear that the infrastructure for car parking, visitor reception, catering and shopping was hopelessly inadequate and that it was unrealistic to expect to let the house to a private tenant, thereby forcing visitors to enter via the garden yard.

Unfortunately the response of the National Trust, regionally and nationally, was at no stage adequate, bearing in mind Hidcote's supreme importance as the most significant and influential garden of the twentieth century, in Britain if not in the world. The property was consistently under-funded, despite being financially in credit, and unlike other great gardens like Sissinghurst and Stourhead, it had

A detail of one of the Red Borders seen from the steps. (1983)

no far-seeing master plan to provide visitors with facilities for a welcome in line with the Trust's usual standards. The Trust's national priorities lay elsewhere and the regional management response was, perhaps unavoidably, too piecemeal and narrow.

This lack of vision and foresight was revealed at the time Harry Burrows moved to Dunham Massey, thus creating the key vacancy for a head gardener. No post in the Trust's gardens could possibly be more important but the Burrows had always lived in a flat overlooking the garden, above the tea room, suitable perhaps for

LEFT One of the Red Borders showing too much purple foliage. (1983)

BELOW Mrs Winthrop's Garden in 1986 (Mrs Winthrop was Lawrence Johnston's mother). The colour scheme should be primrose and greenish-yellow with bronze foliage and strong blue for contrast.

a childless couple but hardly adequate for a family. In the event the region was unable or unwilling to offer an acceptable alternative, despite owning the village. As a result the post was turned down by at least one promising candidate and the eventual appointment was severely hampered.

In the final analysis the unique quality of Hidcote rests largely on the choice, arrangement and cultivation of its plants – creating a series of effects by associating plants in ways that should seem casual and unforced, but nevertheless relying upon the discipline of a different ideal for each part of the garden. As well as distinct colour schemes, there are contrasts of clipped and loose, open and closed, light and dark, intricate and plain, all to be manipulated as a going concern, never static and always developing. To be true to Lawrence Johnston each border and each area needs to be rigorously analysed so that a subtle ideal can be established, always to be an aspiration, probably never to be fully realised.

Nevertheless, throughout the 1980s and '90s the flower gardens were well cared for and were at times outstandingly good. The important hedges and topiary were kept meticulously clipped and trim. However, the garden was always run on a shoestring with minimal, if dedicated, staffing. There was a curious reluctance to employ specialist contractors for jobs like lawn renovation and peripheral hedge-cutting, and an aversion to the recruitment and deployment of volunteers to undertake some repetitive work.

The hedges and topiary at Hidcote need to be crisp and smart in contrast to the profuse planting. This shape became a favourite motif of Norah Lindsay, who had a profound influence on the garden during the 1930s (see Blickling Hall parterre).

Around the time I retired Hidcote received a generous anonymous windfall, consisting of a promise of match-funding for any monies raised by an appeal for resources for restoration and renewal up to £1m. This offer was initially attracted through two of the gardeners and subsequently taken over by the incoming head gardener and property manager. They pursued it vigorously and it has been the means of a long-overdue series of structural restorations, including

reconstruction of the shelter house and a re-routing of visitors so that they enter the garden appropriately from the house rather than through the garden yard. These funds have also enabled a thorough restoration of Johnston's tennis courts, reflecting his third great passion, along with his garden and his dogs. The rock garden has been renovated and at last catering and trading have been granted sufficient space and funding, although what is being offered for lunch can still be smelled immediately on entry!

While buildings and other structures can be repaired or replaced exactly according to precedent, plants are more difficult. Hidcote represents a life's work – the realisation of a unique concept arising from a continually developing ideal, always being re-worked and perfected. How can it be possible to re-create these processes and recapture the dynamism of the original? Hidcote is the creation of an artist–plantsman and its conservation demands similar talents backed by constant reassessment and critical endeavour. To what extent are these precepts understood by the National Trust's management and the necessary skills being valued and conserved?

The White Garden is an example of the huge amount of restoration and renewal carried out by Graham Stuart Thomas between 1955 and 1980 while Harry Burrows was head gardener. White flowers with silver foliage is the principal theme.

No garden had greater influence than Sissinghurst in the second half of the twentieth century. Vita Sackville-West and Harold Nicholson first realised their concept in the 1930s, inspired by the ancient and romantic setting, and Vita continued to embellish the garden's ever-developing structure until the 1960s. While Hidcote, with its loosely room-like layout, must have been an influence, Sissinghurst is an original work of art, a unique concept with a series of inspired set-pieces that nevertheless were constantly reworked towards Vita's evolving ideals. Partly through her writings but also because of the garden's imaginative layout and planting, Sissinghurst led the fashion for garden visiting that became a principal summer sport of the middle classes from the 1960s and '70s.

Vita was a passionate gardener, outstanding in the English tradition of artist–plantsmanship which has been our foremost creative expression for generations, especially, it seems, among women. Although she was never able to afford such upper-class extravagance, it was Norah Lindsay's work that Vita most admired, with its contrived casualness and gloriously colour-schemed abundance. However, Vita was no copyist, instead taking Sissinghurst ever forward to inspire a new generation of gardeners and designers across the western world as well as in Britain, including Christopher Lloyd (at Great Dixter) and Graham Thomas. Easier to recognise than to analyse, any distinctive style of gardening has to be learned, not only by study and observation but also by emulation and practice; it is the cumulative impact of a series of gardening decisions, judgements and actions, large and small, that constitutes a particular gardening style.

The White Garden at Sissinghurst in 1978 seen from the tower. White flowers and silver foliage predominate in patterns of sharply clipped box but dark green foliage and dark shadows are important elements too.

Pam Schwerdt and Sibylle Kreutzberger were taken on in 1959 as joint head gardeners by Vita, three years before she died, long enough to absorb the values that inspired the garden and to learn the special techniques that lay behind its appeal. By the time that the National Trust's acquisition had been completed in 1967 the garden had already responded to their high standards of care and cultivation. Its growing reputation led to a rapid increase in visiting, many members coming

BELOW The Rose Garden seen from the tower showing the narrow perimeter band of paving that was laid to reduce wear and tear on the grass.

OPPOSITE TOP The iconic White Garden in 1989. When the rose-covered central Prunus collapsed after Vita Sackville-West died, Graham Stuart Thomas suggested a light steel arbour as the central feature over which the rose was trained thereafter.

BELOW The Nuttery as it was in the time of Vita Sackville-West before disease confirmed the biological impossibility of repeating the same scheme year after year indefinitely. With Pam Schwerdt and Sibylle Kreutzberger the Nuttery was subsequently transformed by Graham Stuart Thomas into an exercise in ground cover planting.

repeatedly to experience the change and development that is inherent in flower gardens. Trained under the eagle eye of the redoubtable Miss Beatrix Havergal at Waterperry College, Pam and Sibylle were perfectionists, intelligently critical of every aspect of structure, planting and management. They honed their skill and judgement jointly through constant enquiry, inspiring their slender team of gardeners with their ever-improving standards and leading from the front. Under their control and the Trust's management, Sissinghurst set a new standard for gardens open to the public which has never been surpassed.

The resulting exponential increase in visitors, to a garden made originally for personal enjoyment and entertaining friends, had inevitable impacts which, to the Trust's credit at that time, it strove to minimise as far as possible. Despite some narrow paths having to be paved with brick and some paved areas sensitively extended, it seems incredible that so many thousands of visitors have been accommodated without significant wear and tear, thanks mainly to careful grass cultivation and attention to detail. Crowding limits enjoyment and can only be controlled by a timed-ticket system, which was used for a period. However, there was another more subtle impact of consistent visiting on this scale, which involved the pressure to keep every part of this constantly scrutinised garden not only trim but also horticulturally interesting and attractive. Whereas Vita enjoyed the luxury of being able virtually to ignore parts of the garden before or after their main display, under the National Trust people were inclined to want their money's worth from spring opening to autumn closure. Hence Sissinghurst rightly became famous for its consistent successional display as well as for the richness and subtlety of its planting.

Although always within Vita's concepts of colour, texture and character, this became in effect a new style, highly demanding of planning, organisation and judgement. It was taken up and developed by others as the predominant flower garden style of the last quarter of the twentieth century. While inevitably losing something of its elements of surprise and innovation, under Pam and Sibylle the garden matured into something much richer and more complex, with every part of it performing to a well-rehearsed schedule, choreographed with remarkable foresight and imagination. As in Vita's time new plants were freely acquired and rigorously discarded if they were deemed not to accord with the Sissinghurst style. The alternative would have been arbitrarily to have frozen the plant collection, thereby weakening the garden's vitality and continuing creativity.

Rosa 'Sissinghurst Castle'.

Although the historic setting and structure of buildings, walls, hedges and water are of course vital to the character of Sissinghurst, its *raison d'être* is the quality of its gardening, which places it as one of the world's greatest gardens. However, even among garden historians and intellectuals its qualities remain misunderstood, even to the extent of someone, who should know better, criticising Sissinghurst in an article for allegedly remaining unchanged, obviously failing to appreciate the constant renewal and reworking needed to sustain the complex subtleties of this always-developing ecosystem. The critic's suggestion was to retain the structure and to replace the planting with a modern scheme: a failure to realise the true significance of the place.

Although for various reasons I spent a good deal of time at Sissinghurst, I never advised there. Until the 1980s Graham Thomas visited regularly and he was succeeded by Jim Marshall. In the Trust the job of a gardens adviser, as well as providing continuity, should be to respond to the needs of the place according to its

The full garden staff at Sissinghurst in 1996 with Pam Schwerdt in the pale jacket and Sibylle Kreutzberger behind her; their successor, Sarah Cook is third from the left.

The Rose Garden in spring.

condition and to its staff according to their qualities and experience. Sissinghurst has consistently enjoyed staff of the highest quality. Pam and Sibylle were succeeded as head gardeners by Sarah Cook and Alexis Datta, who overlapped with their predecessors so that the skills and traditions of the place would be handed on. The adviser's role therefore at this level should be to stretch the abilities and perceptions of the gardeners, at which Graham was an expert, and to act as a sounding-board for fresh approaches, at which Jim Marshall was adept: also to provide continuity and act as a buffer to over-commercialisation and obtrusive 'interpretation'.

Vita's ideals, as far as they can be understood, should always remain dominant, but Sissinghurst has had to respond to its role as an iconic garden of the late twentieth century, giving untold pleasure and inspiration throughout its half-century non-stop performance. The garden has evolved without being vulgarised: a triumph of conservation.

CHARTWELL

Soon after I retired from the National Trust I was invited, through the Trust, to give a lecture in Santa Barbara, California, on Sir Winston Churchill as a gardener. All expenses paid plus a fee: who would turn it down? The lecture was one of a series on great statesmen as gardeners. They had begun with George Washington and Thomas Jefferson, and were looking abroad for well-known names, all to raise funds for their botanic garden. I said 'yes' of course but rather sheepishly, knowing well that Churchill's specifically gardening exploits could hardly be characterised as anything special. Everyone knows of Sir Winston Churchill's outstanding qualities as world statesman, visionary, orator and leader; also as author and artist. However, in a different life he would never have made a great gardener – charismatic, quixotic and altogether too impatient. I would never have taken him on! On the other hand, as a man of astonishing energy, enthusiasm and drive, he obviously enjoyed projects and was closely involved in all the landscaping and construction works which in the 1920s transformed Chartwell from a run-down and overgrown Victorian mansion and garden into the Churchills' family home. Through his architect Philip Tilden, Churchill imposed his personality on the park and garden as well as the house. Tilden designed the elegant Marlborough Pavilion and together they created the terraces and the chain of ponds and rockery between the Chart Well and the swimming pool. Churchill spurned any kind of professional landscape layout, preferring to develop the garden and parkland in his own way. He was in his element with the waterworks, supervising construction of the lakes from a series of ponds through the valley, perhaps to echo Blenheim on a different scale. The famous kitchen garden wall building was evidently part of this passion for making a mark with his own hands.

Winston Churchill was attracted to Chartwell by the glorious views it affords over the Weald of Kent. Here is the terrace in 1995.

The Butterfly Terrace planting at Chartwell is unmistakenly a product of Lanning Roper's influence. During the 1980s we cut back the overgrown yew hedges, left, and extended the silver theme across the paved path.

Churchill said he chose Chartwell for the view over the Weald of Kent and his principal gardening motive seems to have been to embellish the foreground and create a congenial place to live and work. As well as trees, birds and animals, he enjoyed flowers and plants but left gardening to his wife Clementine. She loved roses, irises and lilies, and especially wanted cut flowers for the house, a tradition that has been well preserved by the Trust. Her gardening style reflected the conventional country house good taste of the time – generally soft colours, good foliage and informal planting within a formal framework of terraces and lawns.

Chartwell was bought for the Churchills by a group of friends in 1946 and given to the National Trust with an endowment. Apart from fruit and vegetables, the garden could hardly have been a wartime priority but after Victor Vincent took over as head gardener the place was in comparatively good shape, apart from the abandoned kitchen garden. With reduced staff and different priorities, the garden needed to be adapted to a new, less labour-intensive regime while also preserving and renovating features loved by the Churchills. Lanning Roper was appointed adviser in 1965, after Sir Winston's death, by agreement with the family. He continued in this role until he died in 1983, after which I took over. Lanning was much loved at Chartwell, deftly guiding the garden's renewal to the satisfaction both of the family and of the Trust; not an easy trick to pull off. He charmed most people but not my predecessor Graham Thomas. Although he would rarely criticize, Graham seemed reluctant to give credit to people among his peer group he had perceived as his competitors. On the other hand, he was invariably generous of his time and knowledge with junior colleagues, students and acolytes generally.

Lanning was advising at Chartwell before the term 'historic garden conservation' had any real meaning, and he was undoubtedly part of the garden's post-war reincarnation for the Churchills. He was also a leader of the predominant garden style of his time both through his writings and his works, being for perhaps two decades the favourite garden designer of the country house set. To this extent he occupies a special place as part of the significant history of Chartwell. He certainly left his mark, mainly positive, in the flower garden where soft colours and silvery foliage betray his influence, especially along the Butterfly House Walk. He also did his best to incorporate the Golden Rose Garden that was rather plonked down through the middle of the former kitchen garden for the Churchills' Golden Wedding in 1958, the kitchen garden having been cleared and grassed over by Lady Churchill and Victor Vincent after the War.

Lanning Roper's principal achievement was to adapt the garden to the unprecedented onrush of visitors to the house and garden in 1966 after Sir Winston's death the previous year. With the house treated as a 'shrine' and managed carefully as a museum, pressure on the garden and park was sudden and intense. I did not witness the occasion but by all accounts the initial damage from car parking in the parkland and from crowds of people in the garden was serious: mud everywhere. This was perhaps the Trust's first experience of having to deal with a property's total transformation from quiet retreat to famous honeypot in one leap. It

The Golden Rose garden was a gift to Sir Winston and Lady Churchill from their friends to mark their Golden Wedding anniversary in 1958. It was accommodated here in the former kitchen garden.

Margaret Thatcher planting an oak tree typically without assistance from either the head gardener Mick Boakes or the Chairman of the National Trust Lord Chorley! The ceremony was to mark recovery after the 1987 storm, which severely affected Chartwell. (March 1998)

was forced to learn quickly through Lanning Roper. He had to help rapidly to design the car park and entrance facilities, and also to arrange a new access route and wider paths for circulation.

Although with hindsight Chartwell finished up with rather too much paving in the garden, Lanning's impact was highly effective and generally unobtrusive, a difficult compromise. The large new car and coach parks were functionally efficient but Lanning was adamant about his choice of trees and shrubs, essentially exotics like his favourite silver maple that stand out in contrast to the traditional park trees instead of blending with them. With the car park situated sensibly alongside the boundary tree belt, the best approach would have been to extend the belt to encompass it, eventually bringing the canopy of traditional park trees eastwards over the cars. Similarly, if the strips between the cars had been planted with native and traditional small trees and evergreens, like hollies, yews and thorns, this understorey would have screened the cars more effectively. However, Lanning was intent on gardening the new visitor facilities, which added unduly to the cost of upkeep and reduced the impact of the garden on entry. It was a valuable lesson for me anyway.

Similarly Lanning, while highly effective in gardens, was undeniably unimaginative when it came to tree planting in semi-parkland, i.e. large pleasure-ground lawns. He was inclined to use, as at Tatton Park, a range of favourite trees dotted about apparently indiscriminately and too frequently. In time these would have overwhelmed vital views and diluted the essential contrast of simple open space and intricate gardening which is the stuff of garden design. Tree planting, felling and removal are invariably and understandably emotive challenges. Every action at Chartwell was critically watched and Lanning's reputation was for ever sacred. With the trees getting bigger and more difficult to tackle, I could see little prospect of radical change until the great storm of 1987 came unexpectedly to our aid. As well as seriously damaging some young specimens, the storm felled a huge number of trees at Chartwell, and that gave us the opportunity to make

Victor Vincent was head gardener at Chartwell throughout the post-war period and continued to live there into the 1990s. Mary Digby was the assistant head gardener throughout her time at Chartwell, responsible for growing and arranging the many cut flowers which are a tradition there. (1993)

fundamental changes. As part of the consequent replanting, we were able to move some of Lanning's trees to more suitable sites and to remove a few completely. In this we were governed by the principal panoramic view and the need to furnish the fringes of the parkland and screen some unsightly incidents. Sir Winston had not planted sufficiently to screen the change of levels between the two lakes, as Lancelot Brown would certainly have done at Blenheim. We remedied this omission and placed a commemorative oak, ceremonially planted by Margaret Thatcher, to help achieve this purpose.

The 1987 storm struck this part of Kent with a ferocity not known for centuries and Chartwell was hopelessly exposed. Apart from the areas nearest the house, none of the old woodland in the property's 32 ha (79 acres) had been dealt with in any way since the Churchills acquired it, more than half a century earlier. They and the National Trust were content to enjoy these glorious old hanging beech woods. However, they were ready to fall and they did so more or less together on 16 October 1987, along with many nineteenth-century conifers either side of the road from Westerham. The initial outcome was that Chartwell was entirely isolated from the rest of the world, the roads being blocked by hundreds of fallen trees.

Mr Vincent retired just before I began to advise at Chartwell and Mick Boakes was appointed head gardener, with Mary Digby as assistant head gardener. Mick brought energy and good practical management skills to the job but never claimed to be an expert plantsman or a knowledgeable horticulturist. This role was ably assumed by Mary, who was a student when I was lecturing at Writtle College. She was in charge of the greenhouses and managed the provision and arrangement of cut flowers, always an important feature at Chartwell. Mick Boakes was a man of action, who enjoyed his pint of beer, and was proficient with the chainsaw. There was no one to help after the storm and the task was daunting. The Chartwell community had to extricate themselves and Jean Broome, one of the best property managers I encountered in the Trust, devised a cunning plan of incentive and

reward for Mick Boakes and his team. At strategic intervals along the road she placed crates of beer so that when they reached each goal they could have a long break for liquid refreshment. While it was never less than a Herculean task, team spirit plus a pint of beer now and again made it bearable. Within a few days they had the road open again; hundreds of tons of timber had been shifted.

Perhaps my trickiest moment at Chartwell involved the unsolicited gift of a statue of Sir Winston and Lady Churchill seated together. In shiny glass fibre its realism is undeniable despite its monumental scale. The gift had been well canvassed and was not to be refused. There was even a strongly supported suggestion that it should be sited between car park and house, where it would undoubtedly not be missed, being hopelessly out of scale with the site and overwhelming in its impact. Some swift thinking was required to head off a potential aesthetic disaster. Bearing in mind the huge scale of object I felt sure it needed a site in the parkland and suggested the present site at the end of the lake; not without argument, this was eventually found acceptable.

POWIS

After Kew I began as a very junior Assistant Lecturer at Writtle College, Essex, where my most important role other than teaching was in managing the garden. I did this for twelve years, a wonderful opportunity to develop the grounds, make mistakes and learn something of the realities of running a garden. Before I arrived a rather grand head gardener (of the late-middle-aged, panama hat variety) had been appointed. Acknowledged as a sad mistake by all concerned, he was already applying for other jobs and soon announced that he had been appointed for Powis Castle, about which I had heard but not seen. His description intrigued me and I could only imagine that the National Trust was looking for a traditional figurehead who would be happy with the status quo. When I joined the Trust eleven years later I soon learned that the Powis garden had indeed marked time under his tenure. However, I was horrified that one of his few decisive actions seemed to have been a negative – he had cut down one side of the yew walk, the whole point of which is to provide an enclosed, evergreen corridor with only occasional glimpses out over the great lawn. Predictably he had done this to save work, and I resolved, if nothing else, to restore the original intention. This is a perfect example of how pragmatic management can erode distinctiveness if carried out without regard to any kind of plan, setting out the special significance of the garden as a whole and of each part of it, together with ideals and aspirations for future development.

The vacancy for head gardener at Powis arose in my second winter with the Trust, during the period of Graham Thomas's 'hibernation'. Partly to keep me busy, I suppose, I was despatched to help the Regional Agent to interview the candidates. I am not sure whether Graham would have been so keen but the outstanding candidate for us was Jimmy Hancock, who had spent much of his career with hospital gardens in Yorkshire. Above all, it was his obvious drive and enthusiasm that impressed. He was also entirely well motivated, although perhaps a touch opinionated and voluble (which would not have gone down well with Graham!). We appointed him in 1972 and he never looked back. He gradually became one of the Trust's most effective and creative head gardeners, raising the status of the Powis garden from being an 'also ran' alongside a great house to realising its full significance as one of the world's greatest gardens. He was always totally committed and fiercely loyal to the place and to his staff. He was sometimes prickly, but he knew how to fight his corner. He needed this quality at a time when resources were very short and raising the status of gardens tended, as now, to figure low in the Trust's priorities. However, he did not come to the Trust fully formed. Of course he learned by experience, but above all he was shaped by the standards demanded by Graham and the challenges that he devised while the garden was being almost totally renovated. Not that Jimmy would ever allow that Graham was his mentor, the relationship always being mutually critical, with Jimmy bridling at Graham's over-prescriptive approach and Graham forever complaining about Jimmy being argumentative and having too much to say! However, this was an entirely creative tension and, whatever Jimmy may have said, their interaction through the garden was the making of the man as head gardener. Ultimately it was the means by which the garden became a national source of ideas and reservoir of horticultural excellence. This indeed is how great head gardeners and great gardens are made and sustained; head gardeners (and Gardens Advisers) are to a large degree made, not simply born, learning their profession initially by formal training but thereafter from experience accompanied by criticism, discussion and encouragement, opening their eyes gradually to excellence that they had never before appreciated.

The structure of the flower garden at Powis speaks for itself as one of the most impressive and beautiful survivals of late seventeenth-century formal design, given a unique sense of continuity by the massive yew hedges and topiary pieces, clipped by successive generations of gardeners for 300 years. The terraces seem to have been made largely for production as well as gentle exercise, and some wall-trained fruit trees remain to this day. The dominant influence of the twentieth century was Violet, the 4th Earl's wife, who was a keen gardener and an admirer of Gertrude Jekyll. It seems that she made the flower garden, setting out the borders in their present form, backed by the ancient brick terrace walls, which show signs of having been repaired and partially rebuilt from time to time. In addition there were rectangular, sloping beds on the aviary terrace, probably originally for growing early salad crops, which Lady Violet planted with blocks and groups of herbaceous flowers and dwarf shrubs for summer colour, like the hardy plumbago (*Ceratostigma plumbaginoides*), but these became infested with weeds and were eliminated by the Trust in the late 1960s in favour of simple aprons of lawn sloping away from the borders.

By the early 1970s the flower borders were infested with familiar country house perennial weeds – ground elder, bindweed, etc. – which commonly gain a foothold slowly among herbaceous rootstocks over a generation or more. The only solution is total and meticulous eradication; a miss is as good as a mile, any tiny scrap, even in the box hedges, being a potential source of reinfestation. Although Graham remained as adviser at Powis for some years, I frequently visited him in the 1970s as the extensive orangery terrace double borders were cleared, saving clean stock of anything of value. A phased 'scorched earth' eradication programme was carried out, leaving the borders empty for a year. On this scale, with walls and hedges harbouring weeds, nothing short of this consistent and determined blitz is good enough, using effective (but not persistent) herbicides, like glyphosate. There is no evidence that this approach, sensibly applied, has any significant damaging effect on wildlife or on the environment, especially compared with the methods used on a vastly larger scale in agriculture, forestry and the public utilities. The organic movement has much to commend it but it should not become a fundamental quasi-religious belief, rejecting courses of action on purely emotional and subjective grounds, against objective evidence. The borders at Powis are now a conservation success, more diverse than any comparable area of rainforest.

Deep cultivation and the incorporation of large quantities of organic material from a new composting system, devised by Jimmy Hancock, raised the fertility of the starved borders. Thereafter heavy annual mulching has been the key to

The Orangery west border at Powis in the 1970s while it was being given the scorched earth treatment to clear it of perennial weeds accumulated over many years.

continuing success, and Jimmy always put down the absence of slugs and snails to blackbirds and other birds being encouraged by the mulch. At that time it happened that Graham was in the process of writing *Perennial Garden Plants*, published in 1976 – in my opinion, his best book. I realised later that his highly sophisticated planting plans for the orangery terrace borders were based on his researches for that book, recommending uncommon and even obscure species and cultivars that he had encountered at Sunningdale and seen at Wisley, Kew, Edinburgh Botanic Garden and nurseries like Bressingham, Kelways and Slieve Donard. His design style was rooted strongly in Gertrude Jekyll's principles, and the planting plans he drew up for the orangery borders were based on her ideas

One of the Orangery Terrace borders in 1988 long after its replanting to a scheme designed by Graham Stuart Thomas; subsequently 'tweaked' by Jimmy Hancock while I was advising there.

After a partial collapse of the Aviary terrace wall in the 1980s we decided to move the hybrid musk roses from this dry site to the valley. They were replanted with a scheme of drought-resistant plants in strong colours, with silver foliage.

of colour association, with stronger colours to the east and softer colours towards the west. In other respects these borders set a new standard in deploying herbaceous plants (with some shrubs) remarkable for their richness and diversity. From the start Jimmy was keen to make adjustments in the light of his experience of the relative vigour and stature of the species and cultivars assembled at Powis but Graham would have none of it, insisting, perhaps a little too dogmatically, on adherence to the plan. By the time I took over as Adviser in the early 1980s, I was confident in Jimmy's judgement, but he would always discuss major changes. Borders like these consist of artificially contrived ecosystems which cannot by nature remain fixed from year to year. They need to change and develop, ebb and flow, according to a clear understanding of the ideal in terms of plant content, colour association, textural contrasts, periods of display and aesthetic effect; not in any way a free-for-all dependent on the whims of the person in charge.

Lady Violet was evidently fond of the repeat-flowering hybrid musk roses, so popular between the wars, like 'Buff Beauty', 'Cornelia', 'Felicia' and 'Penelope'. She planted them on the aviary terrace on the eastern side. Unfortunately this is a very dry site, made worse by being in rain shadow from the high terrace wall behind. Being susceptible to mildew, they suffered badly enough to be crippled annually. When part of the wall collapsed and had to be rebuilt, probably something that must have happened several times in its long history, the roses had by necessity to be removed, and we decided to re-site them permanently in the formal (former kitchen) garden, where the soil was deeper and heavier: a great success. By then I had taken over as Adviser and proposed agreeing a general philosophy, covering all the terraces in an effort to sharpen the distinctiveness of each and create a logical progression based upon suitability of site as well as aesthetic considerations.

With the orangery terrace borders already established in their lush, Jekyll-style splendour, I proposed Jimmy's favourite sub-tropical style exotics for the top terrace and in contrast mainly small-leafed, dry-soil species for the aviary terrace,

strong colours east and soft colours west, reflecting the orangery terrace colour schemes. The apple slope terrace borders had been sumptuously replanted at the western end according to a plan by Graham for an early autumn, mainly September, scheme. This further adds to the diversity and provides something in its prime when the other borders are going over. Similarly, I encouraged Jimmy to develop the delphinium border in the formal garden, which gives an early burst of colour, followed by summer-flowering mallows and hollyhocks, regularly sprayed with fungicide to combat rust. He responded well to being given this freedom to develop his ideas within an agreed policy.

Pots on the Orangery Terrace balustrade in 1983. One of Jimmy Hancock's great skills and abiding traditions was to adorn the terraces with a glorious arrangement of pots, set out already in full bloom.

Under Jimmy every aspect of this very diverse garden was renovated and improved beyond compare – propagation for sale, apple slope shrubs, wilderness planting, formal garden hedges, etc. – but his forte was with plants in pots and vases. From the start he was creative and experimental, actually encouraged by Graham. Every year they were different, gradually becoming bolder as he created sufficient propagation space to grow the large tender exotics for which Powis became famous. The containers were eventually planted and established under glass and stood out in full flower, a huge annual endeavour.

One area where we agreed to disagree was with the castle forecourt where the central equestrian sculpture of 'Fame' was meant to proclaim the glory of the place. However, over the years it had sagged almost out of recognition and at vast expense was to be sent away for conservation. Unsurprisingly, the forecourt had been adjusted piecemeal and changed gradually over the years in response to pressure, mostly from vehicles. A review of its history by the Historic Buildings Representative, Christopher Rowell, showed graphically how it had been urbanised, formalised and fragmented in a variety of ways, with bits of ornamental planting adding to the incoherent effect. We liked it best in its earliest, quietly informal, guise with simple unobtrusive eighteenth-century-style planting and a large area of grass. Predictably, Jimmy Hancock wanted lots of horticultural riches but he

In front of the Aviary arches, the balustrade carries precious lead sculptures.

lost the argument and we agreed on my plan for a much larger elliptical area of lawn around 'Fame' and borders around the sides reflecting this shape, containing mostly eighteenth-century-style shrubs and small trees, mostly evergreen with a preference for silvery foliage and white flowers, if any. This low-key scheme was meant primarily to furnish and soften the forecourt without being assertive, framing the castle's west entrance. Jimmy never agreed but loyally carried out the scheme, despite being supported in his view by the adjacent restaurant and shop staff, who would probably have had seats with umbrellas, hanging baskets and tubs of busy-lizzies, given a free hand! The point in cases of this kind is to seek a workable solution that is right for the place and to avoid being distracted by current single-issue arguments connected with commercial pressures, visitor preference, vehicular access, etc. More in the way of flower display would have merely added to work and detracted from the impact of the terraces.

It takes a rare talent to follow someone like Jimmy Hancock, who totally identified himself, and was identified, with the garden at Powis. He never properly anticipated his retirement and it took him months to move out, both mentally and physically, from the wonderfully cluttered head gardener's house in the garden. Changes of this magnitude should not be left to chance and need, if possible, to be planned in advance. Although he was always anxious to share decisions and involve his staff, he was totally committed to every detail and inevitably dominant in every aspect of the garden. His successor needed to be an experienced and expert horticulturist, able to pick up and develop the garden's tradition for unsurpassed excellence while redefining the head gardener's relationship with the staff and their respective roles. Peter Hall had worked his way up in the Trust from Wimpole and Canons Ashby to carrying out a major renovation of the garden at

The Croquet Lawn border has a spectacular early-summer display of delphiniums followed by hollyhocks, with roses and climbers on the wall behind.

Dunham Massey. I had long realised that he had the right qualities of character and all the skills for Powis. Luckily he decided to accept the challenge and, after a predictably difficult start, made a huge success of the task of consolidating the improvement and carrying the garden forward.

The amphitheatre of the great lawn at Powis invites big events, and a string of property managers, land agents, public relations consultants, etc., have thought it their personal brainwave to hold them there. Having been a late seventeenth-century water garden, with a culverted stream running underneath, the lawn is usually wet, its heavy clay soil being prone to waterlogging. The gardeners and Gardens Advisers have long been well aware of this, but there is a tendency to regard this kind of advice as mere negativity: spurious reasons to reject a wonderful opportunity. Consistent objective argument has mostly avoided any disasters, and a comprehensive and expensive drainage system, with sand-slitting on the football pitch model, was installed in the 1980s. However, in our considered view, well recorded, the lawn remains suitable only for light use, bearing in mind the strong likelihood of wet weather in this part of Wales. Against this, two unwise events were pushed through without sufficient consultation, leading to extensive damage and severe financial losses as stages, expensive machinery and heavy equipment became almost inextricably bogged down. Unsurprisingly, this resulted in deep distress and loss of morale among the gardeners, who are rightly proud of the garden's high standards. They are invariably expected to clear up the mess, costing huge sums of money and loss of time at the expense of the conservation of this internationally important garden. These were not honest mistakes; they were wilful misjudgements made without proper consultation or objective consideration. On a different scale, these conflicts are inclined to recur elsewhere where managers with full authority fail to consult either their staff or their advisers in any serious way and fail to learn from, or even about, past mistakes. Every property needs to abide by its own carefully considered events policy with realistic objectives based on the special character and history of the place and on an assessment of actual physical and staffing constraints likely to be met.

Together with Fountains Abbey, the largest monastic ruin in the country, Studley Royal is a 'blue chip' property of unsurpassed historic importance in the National Trust and now a World Heritage site. It has everything except a flower garden and everything is of outstanding quality and significance – deer park, water garden, historic buildings, archaeology, fine trees and wildlife. Everyone who knows it loves it, each for their own set of reasons. However, from a visitor's point of view it has suffered from a split personality, always having been visited separately from either end. Whilst never owning it, English Heritage and its predecessors have maintained the Abbey precincts, admitting people from an inadequate car park at the western end, most of their visitors being hardly aware that a garden of great beauty and significance lay beyond the Abbey. Nor is it possible properly to appreciate John Aislabie's incomparable water garden or the glorious historic parkland by approaching it from what was the traditional monastic western entrance.

Of course a monumental ruin as complex and as richly significant as Fountains Abbey is perfectly able to absorb any visitor for a full-day visit if interested in sufficient depth. However, the many years of separate ownership and management have inevitably altered its character. Under English Heritage and its predecessor, upkeep has been understandably governed by precepts formulated for the preservation of archaeology and historic buildings – what I would call the graveyard approach: no trees or shrubs, close-clipped grass, and crisp edges around every artefact. The rule was to separate anything living from everything dead and even the Fountains Abbey pink (*Dianthus* 'Fountains Abbey') was barely tolerated on the ruins until a local naturalist, Beatrix Molesworth, identified the importance of the flora growing on and around the precincts. Thankfully, as the years have passed this early approach has changed somewhat. Sealing the ruin in cement mortar was found not to be the best way of preserving it, after it stood for half a millennium unprotected. Fashions change in the world of historic buildings conservation as they do in historic gardens conservation. No precept is too sacred to be challenged in its detailed application, if not in general principle.

Looked at from an historic garden perspective, the abbey ruin constitutes the great picturesque culmination of a tour of Studley Royal's garden, a superb example of the early use of the gothic ruin in the borrowed landscape incorporated in the late eighteenth century, after the fashion for formal gardening had waned and a more romantic mood prevailed. The right way to see Studley Royal is to drive through the grand gates at Studley Roger, where Ripon Cathedral can be seen to the east, then follow the main avenue towards William Burges's St. Mary's Church. Along the drive down to your left are Aislabie's great lake and water garden. Before you drop down, catch a glimpse of the handsome stable block near the site of the former great house and see some magnificent trees, including wonderful old sweet chestnuts, oaks, limes and wild gean cherries which grow better here than anywhere else I know. A walk through the park and along the picturesque Mackershaw Valley would alone make a more than satisfactory outing.

There are some remarkable examples of very early planting of some species. One sweet chestnut in the valley is probably the tallest in Europe, with others reaching almost incredible proportions. The unchallenged expert on lime trees, Dr Pigott, identified four specific eighteenth-century lime clones, including one clone not known anywhere else.

John Aislabie made his dramatic formal, but asymmetric, water garden piece-meal (in common with most great English gardens), starting after the South Sea Bubble scandal wrecked his Parliamentary career in 1716. It is arranged to be seen principally on foot, as a series of views and experiences governed by romantic allusion and furnished with classical buildings, designed for the enjoyment of each consecutive dimension of the place. The garden was subsequently developed and extended by his son William to embrace the picturesque taste of the late eighteenth century, with the acquisition and incorporation of Fountains Abbey as a final westerly flourish. The park and water garden were privately owned until acquired by West Riding County Council in 1967 and transferred to North Yorkshire in 1974. In 1983 the National Trust purchased the estate. Despite its consistent popularity since the eighteenth century, the perceived significance of the Studley Royal garden seems to have been gradually diminished as the importance of Fountains Abbey has been realised. Even now, by calling the property Fountains Abbey and Studley Royal, the National Trust appears to continue to undervalue the garden in relation to the monastic ruin.

On my first visit I met John Walker, who had undertaken a great deal of diligent research on the history of the buildings and landscape while employed as architect-in-charge for the West Riding. He had assembled a fascinating pictorial

The landscape park at Studley Royal was formed around this main axis from Ripon Minster (now Cathedral) as an avenue through the park, later broken up to accord with late-18th century taste.

chronology of the development of the park and garden which aided him in some of his pioneering work of conservation. If nothing else, this convinced me of the physical and historical complexities and contradictions of the place right up to the present day. Clearly much more research needed to be done and, through his work as archaeologist for the National Trust, Mark Newman has revealed more and more over the years.

Our approach needed therefore to be cautious but not timid, looking for imperatives and for the manifestly obvious while avoiding the irreversible in case we had got it entirely wrong. Jumping to conclusions is always dangerous and it soon became clear to me that while mostly right about other things, John had got it wrong about the main lime avenue through the park, which had been gappy when he started. It is easy, particularly for an architect, to assume that avenues should always be continuous, until you look at the history and realise that this avenue was almost certainly deliberately broken up in places, probably by William Aislabie, while the park and garden were being converted to the picturesque taste. After twenty years or so, West Riding Council's regiment of lime replacements were already substantial trees; as a result it became 'politically' difficult to remove them and even more difficult to explain the desirability of their removal to the layman.

Perhaps one of the greatest mistakes ever made was to sell off the shooting rights of Studley Royal in perpetuity as a separate entity. No doubt Henry Vyner, who was responsible for the break-up of this great Yorkshire estate, saw this sale as a source of funds at a time when he was in desperate straits, but the result has compromised restoration in important parts of the historic landscape and hampered it almost everywhere. It seems that owners of the shoot are entitled, according to their judgement, to veto anything that may adversely affect the game and the convenience of the guns. The strict application of these rights has wide ramifications. It seems ludicrous that in a World Heritage site such considerations should have precedence.

In the late 1980s the Trust was committed to closing the overcrowded, and at times dangerous and squalid, west (Fountains) car park, and sought a new site with sufficient capacity to take virtually all visitors. Entry through the park was ruled out because the residents of Studley Roger were understandably against more vehicles passing through the village. After much deliberation Swanley Grange, a piece of farmland directly north of the abbey with strong historical connections, was acquired for a new visitor centre and the inevitable car parks. The splendid new building became in effect a monument not only to cater for the property's needs but also to satisfy the ambitions of those who conceived it as a project and as a design. Little expense was spared to make this fine building fit into its surroundings and comply with the strict planning conditions applied to screen it from the surrounding landscape. As ever the costs exceeded expectations both for construction and maintenance, making it obligatory for the building to pay its way in its own right. The substantial amount of tree planting and its subsequent upkeep absorbed the equivalent of as much as one gardener full-time. While it was obviously necessary, the scale of endeavour absorbed by the new building and its landscape had the effect of depleting the gardening staff upon whom progress in restoration and renewal depended. Luckily the Trust had recruited an outstanding head gardener in Michael Ridsdale, who had more than enough of the necessary management, landscaping and arboricultural skills, combined with never-flagging drive and sound common sense. Together with the land agent Andrew McVety, who seemed to be able quietly to overcome every challenge of construction and repair, he has given the whole landscape a new lease of life, a huge continuing task which must never be allowed to slip; mere 'maintenance' will never do.

Although situated inside the 'elbow' of the valley and therefore more or less adjacent both to the abbey and to the water garden, access from the visitor centre was concentrated on a route directly to the ruin. This was understandable because for a majority of visitors this was their principal goal. However, it had the effect of further emphasising the division between garden and monument. For the important minority of visitors wanting to see the landscape in the sequence designed by John Aislabie and his son, a route from the visitor centre to the northern garden gates is needed. This could be arranged via a pleasant walk down the picturesque valley of Kendall's Walk or perhaps by electric buggy.

There was plenty to do. Bearing in mind that felling and clearance inevitably leave gaps and planting needs time to take effect, we gave priority to the water garden. The geometric precision of the ponds and the contrasting patterns of still water and fine turf were judged to be indispensable. This necessitated a contract to provide crisp new revetments around every one of the ponds, a demanding task organised and supervised by Andrew McVety. The effect was a revelation, especially after the fine lawns between the ponds had been resown. Studley Royal garden was back on the map. Precision was essential and anything less would amount to failure. But not everyone shared our values; there is always loss as well as gain in landscape restoration. The old broken-down edges provided habitat for

The Water Garden shows no sign of the frequent flooding that occurs when the river brings down huge quantities of silt from upstream. (1989)

a variety of small waterside plants but it was the frogs and tadpoles that caused the most grief. The problem was to explain how the little frogs would escape the ponds with a foot or more of vertical freeboard to climb. This potentially bitter controversy was resolved and the nature conservation lobby pacified by erecting little wooden ramps in each pool. This was picked up by the local and national press who wanted a picture of the little frogs wending their way. Embarrassingly, no one had seen a single frog on any of the ramps at any time (and yet they did get out somehow). My suggestion was that we should nail a toy rubber frog onto one of the ramps for a photograph to please the journalists!

There was a lot of overdue renovation crying out to be dealt with on the steep slopes: scrub had to be reduced and an impoverished woodland community restored according to historic precedent as far as possible. Priority was given to repairing the ugly gashes where young people had been increasingly taking short cuts to slide down the steep banks. Thank goodness we tackled this before the Trust's preoccupation for 'engagement' with visitors and for providing entertainment at almost any cost (perhaps preserving the eroded earth-slide as a diversion for young people?). Reducing yews to reopen views and make space for a new generation of trees is inevitably a long-term project for which clear historic precedents and aesthetic judgements are required, set out in terms of a conservation plan. A great deal of planting has rightly been done by the Trust both within the water gardens and in the park, always to good effect, but it is important with historic landscape always to take the long view. It is easy, almost selfish, to plant too much during a given period, thereby reducing the long-term resilience of the tree population as a whole, which ideally should consist of the widest possible diversity of age and species as is consistent with historic precedent. Once an equilibrium has been achieved, new tree planting should not need exceed 10 per cent of the population in any decade. Within historic parks and gardens tree removal often turns out to be at least as important as planting for the achievement of conservation objectives.

One dilemma encountered at Studley Royal, in common with most historic gardens that have been consistently cared for at some level, is that it contains an overlay of trees and shrubs of later introduction. At Studley Royal these are mercifully infrequent but nevertheless part of the history of the place. Careful mature judgement is required to decide whether, and to what extent, these trees and shrubs disturb the historic and aesthetic imperatives set out in the property's statement of significance, the key to the conservation of any historic property. Generally trees of highly-distinctive shape or strong foliage colour are difficult to integrate within pre-nineteenth-century landscapes, but every group and specimen should be considered on its merits before contemplating removal.

In 1983 the Trust assumed management of the immediate landscape around Fountains Abbey, formerly maintained by the Department of the Environment, as well as the park, garden and estate. Until then the style of management matched that employed at almost every ancient property in DoE guardianship. Instead of the weedy romantic ruin among trees incorporated by William Aislabie in the eighteenth century, we had a sanitised monument sitting starkly by the river Skell with all vegetation held back at a respectful distance: grass closely mown and

The Temple of Piety with the November mist slowly lifting.

edges trimmed. Principal views from the garden were marred by the valley having been turned into a regularly mown oblong field with a tarmac drive down one side. Our attempts to bring back elements of the picturesque included reopening views of spectacular rock faces, planting to screen the drive and frame the view, and treating the valley as a meadow with wildflowers, left to be cut annually in late summer. Change was more difficult around the abbey ruin, mainly because of archaeological sensitivities, with an assumption of no tree planting anywhere. However, never taking no for an answer without query, we arranged a meeting with the DoE archaeologists, who turned out to be entirely reasonable. When asked direct questions as to why we should not put a tree here or there, with some understandable difficulty they gave a straight yes or no, and we found sites for several trees, which will in time have a significant effect. Never take for granted a blanket bureaucratic negative.

Flash floods are a recurrent cause of crisis at Studley Royal, as the Skell seems more frequently and more quickly to rise to a torrent. This brings down enormous quantities of silt from the moors to give the water gardens a morbid combination of thrombosis and dropsy on a giant scale. The cost of dredging and repair for each flood is huge; nothing new perhaps, but apparently getting worse and frustratingly impossible to alleviate, leading managers now to think on a grander scale. World heritage designations can seem obscure but surely Studley should not have to endure the ravages of constant flooding when other designated sites, such as Venice, enjoying positive notoriety and funding for flood mitigation.

In the late 18th-century William Aislabie incorporated the ruins of Fountains Abbey as the final revelation of the garden tour. (1986)

Studley Royal incorporates the whole range of conservation challenges encountered in historic gardens, made more difficult by the long-standing neglect of any consistent measures of repair and renewal over 300 years. The establishment and pursuit of long-term programmes of pruning and replenishment, especially of the enormous bosquets on steep slopes, requires courage, persistence and regular funding in the face of ill-informed criticism. Effective conservation involves facing and resolving inevitable conflicts in the interest of retaining and enhancing the qualities, values, processes and characteristics of the place. At Studley this demands constant reworking according to pro-active cycles of renewal and replanting on a vast scale on a schedule measure in centuries.

POSTSCRIPT
SHADE UPON SHADE

Covering less than a third of the total number of gardens owned by the National Trust, this book does not purport to be a guide. Although I was responsible with my colleagues for advice relating to cultivation, management and conservation of all gardens, including their contents, and I had direct experience of most, my memoir is a selection. I enjoyed the privilege of working with historic significance, great art, unrivalled plant collections and fascinating associations (including people). I was party to the way the National Trust learned about caring for gardens visited by ever-increasing numbers of visitors, along with an ever more intense examination of its methods and procedures.

That my memoir does not imply any kind of judgement is obvious from the omission of some of the National Trust's greatest acquisitions, e.g. Stowe, Bodnant, Waddesdon Manor, Cliveden, Wakehurst Place. Nor does it underrate significant places rightly appreciated by many people, e.g. Attingham, Hanbury Hall, Kingston Lacy, Lanhydrock, Lyme Park, Mottisfont Abbey, Polesden Lacey, Saltram, Sheffield Park. All gardens are the products of enlightened and creative individuals or dynasties, and it is reasonable to leave them under the control of resident families, provided they have sufficient interest, resources and expertise. This is the case even with huge estates like Bodnant and Waddesdon; also successfully at Antony, Ascott, Buscot Park and Coughton Court. Gunby and West Green are cared for by tenants, and Wakehurst is permanently leased to the Royal Botanic Gardens, Kew.

But between them the smaller gardens also hold a wealth of historical evidence, great beauty, wonderful plants and for me unforgettable moments. When briefing me before my first visit to The Weir in 1971, Graham Thomas enigmatically suggested that I decline any invitation into the house. Sure enough I was greeted at 10.30 am by the tenant with an invitation to join him for a glass of champagne (and perhaps more?). At Lindisfarne I had to try to make sense of Gertrude Jekyll's scribbled plan, perhaps drawn after a good lunch, for the tiny,

The walled garden at Lindisfarne Castle, Northumberland.

One source of the Keating family's fortune was Keating's Powder, much used in the first world war for controlling lice on soldiers in the trenches.

isolated walled garden on which she used only cultivar names of several species and left huge gaps, presumably for salad crops? My first visit to Plas yn Rhiw with Ian Kennaway the Regional Director, included, as well as a delightful tour of the quirky garden, tea and Battenburg cake with two of the three legendary Misses Keating, Eileen, Lorna and Honora, who gave the property and a great deal more of the west Lleyn Peninsula. My only successful experience of (re)designing as well as restoring a garden by committee was at Fenton House in Hampstead, guided by what existed and the combined ideas and efforts of an historian, three gardens advisers

Fenton House, Hampstead, London.

The Argory, Co. Armagh.

in succession and the gardener. I shall never forget my first visit to The Argory at Moy, County Armagh, N.I., with John Lewis-Crosby, Regional Director, and Peter Marlow, Historic Buildings Representative, in November 1979 on what they call a "soft day" in Ireland when it seemed to be dark by 3.30 pm. The garden, overlooking the River Blackwater, was far from its all-time best, and in the gathering gloom we were shown the acetylene gas plant, solely by which the house was lit. Mr MacGeough Bond (of Brook Bond tea) demonstrated the 1824 cabinet barrel organ and then gave us tea in his cluttered study, perhaps the only warm room, surrounded by his modern sculptures and lit only by the distinctive, piercing light of the gas lamps; unforgettable.

Yes, there is a lot more to tell.

ADDRESSES OF GARDENS

ACORN BANK   (page 75)
Temple Sowerby, near Penrith, Cumbria, CA10 1SP

ANGLESEY ABBEY   (page 113)
Quy Road, Lode, Cambridge, Cambridgeshire, CB25 9EJ

BENINGBROUGH HALL   (page 71)
Beningbrough, York, North Yorkshire, YO30 1DD

BIDDULPH GRANGE   (page 272)
Grange Road, Biddulph, Staffordshire, ST8 7SD

BLICKLING HALL   (page 228)
Blickling, Aylsham, Norfolk, NR11 6NF

CALKE ABBEY   (page 192)
Ticknall, Derby, Derbyshire, DE73 7LE

CANONS ASHBY   (page 240)
Near Daventry, Northamptonshire, NN11 3SD

CHARTWELL   (page 296)
Mapleton Road, Westerham, Kent, TN16 1PS

CHASTLETON HOUSE   (page 202)
Near Moreton-in-Marsh, Oxfordshire, GL56 0SU

CLUMBER PARK   (page 163)
Worksop, Nottinghamshire, S80 3BE

COLETON FISHACRE   (page 250)
Brownstone Road, Kingswear, Devon, TQ6 0EQ

CRAGSIDE   (page 188)
Rothbury, Morpeth, Northumberland, NE65 7PX

DUNHAM MASSEY   (page 264)
Altrincham, Greater Manchester, WA14 4SJ

DUNSTER CASTLE   (page 256)
Dunster, near Minehead, Somerset, TA24 6SL

ERDIGG   (page 234)
Wrexham, LL13 0YT

FELBRIGG   (page 46)
Felbrigg, Norwich, Norfolk, NR11 8PR

FLORENCE COURT   (page 102)
Enniskillen, County Fermanagh, BT92 1DB

GLENDURGAN   (page 123)
Mawnan Smith, near Falmouth, Cornwall, TR11 5JZ

HAM HOUSE   (page 54)
Ham Street, Ham, Richmond, London, TW10 7RS

HARDWICK HALL   (page 174)
Doe Lea, Chesterfield, Derbyshire, S44 5QJ

HIDCOTE   (page 284)
Hidcote Bartrim, near Chipping Campden, Gloucestershire, GL55 6LR

HINTON AMPNER (page 120)
Hinton Ampner, near Alresford, Hampshire, SO24 0LA

ICKWORTH (page 65)
The Rotunda, Horringer, Bury St Edmunds, Suffolk, IP29 5QE

KILLERTON (page 222)
Broadclyst, Exeter, Devon, EX5 3LE

KNIGHTSHAYES (page 150)
Bolham, Tiverton, Devon, EX16 7RQ

LITTLE MORETON HALL (page 62)
Congleton, Cheshire, CW12 4SD

MOUNT STEWART (page 143)
Portaferry Road, Newtownards, County Down, BT22 2AD

NYMANS (page 208)
Handcross, near Haywards Heath, West Sussex, RH17 6EB

OSTERLEY PARK (page 85)
Jersey Road, Isleworth, London, TW7 4RB

PACKWOOD (page 158)
Packwood Lane, Lapworth, Warwickshire, B94 6AT

PECKOVER HOUSE (page 59)
North Brink, Wisbech, Cambridgeshire, PE13 1JR

PETWORTH (page 217)
Petworth, West Sussex, GU28 0AE

PLAS NEWYDD (page 133)
Llanfairpwllgwyngyll, Anglesey, LL61 6DQ

POWIS (page 302)
Welshpool, Powys, SY21 8RF

PRIOR PARK (page 95)
Ralph Allen Drive, Bath, Somerset, BA2 5AH

ROWALLANE (page 196)
Saintfield, County Down, BT24 7LH

SCOTNEY CASTLE (page 138)
Lamberhurst, Tunbridge Wells, Kent, TN3 8JN

SISSINGHURST (page 291)
Biddenden Road, near Cranbrook, Kent, TN17 2AB

SIZERGH CASTLE (page 129)
Sizergh, near Kendal, Cumbria, LA8 8DZ

SNOWSHILL MANOR (page 50)
Snowshill, near Broadway, Gloucestershire, WR12 7JU

STANDEN (page 178)
West Hoathly Road, East Grinstead, West Sussex, RH19 4NE

STOURHEAD (page 80)
Near Mere, Wiltshire, BA12 6QF

STUDLEY ROYAL (page 309)
Near Ripon, North Yorkshire, HG4 3DY

TATTON PARK (page 244)
Knutsford, Cheshire, WA16 6QN

TRELISSICK (page 169)
Feock, near Truro, Cornwall, TR3 6QL

UPPARK (page 261)
South Harting, Petersfield, West Sussex, GU31 5QR

WALLINGTON (page 182)
Cambo, near Morpeth, Northumberland, NE61 4AR

WEST WYCOMBE PARK (page 108)
West Wycombe, Buckinghamshire, HP14 3AJ

WESTBURY COURT (page 38)
Westbury-on-Severn, Gloucestershire, GL14 1PD

WIMPOLE HALL (page 90)
Arrington, Royston, Cambridgeshire, SG8 0BW

SELECT BIBLIOGRAPHY

Brown, Jane, *Lanning Roper and His Gardens* (Rizzoli International 1987)

Dutton, Ralph, *The English Garden* (B.T. Batsford 1937 rev. 1950)

Elliott, Brent, *Victorian Gardens* (B.T. Batsford 1986)

Hadfield, Miles, *Gardening in Britain* (Hutchinson 1960)

Harney, Marion (ed.). *Gardens and Landscapes in Historic Buildings Conservation* (Wiley Blackwell 2014)

Harvey, John, *Mediaeval Gardens* (B.T. Batsford 1981)

Hayward, Allyson, *Norah Lindsay* (Frances Lincoln 2007)

Jacques, David, *Georgian Gardens* (B.T. Batsford 1983)

Laird, Mark, *The Flowering of the Landscape Garden* (University of Pennsylvania Press 1999)

Lees-Milne, James, *Ancestral Voices* (Chatto and Windus 1975)

Newby, Howard, (ed.), *The National Trust: its next hundred years* (The National Trust, 1995)

Sales, John, *West Country Gardens* (Alan Sutton 1980)

Strong, Roy, *The Renaissance Garden in England* (Thames and Hudson 1979)

Stroud, Dorothy, *Capability Brown* (Faber and Faber 1975)

Taylor, Patrick (ed.), *The Oxford Companion to Gardens* (Oxford University Press 2006)

Thomas, Graham Stuart, *Gardens of the National Trust* (Weidenfield and Nicholson 1974)

——, *Perennial Garden Plants* (Dent 1976 rev. 1980)

——, *Plants for Ground Cover* (Dent 1970)

Waterson, Merlin, *The Servants' Hall* (Routledge and Kegan Paul 1980)

——, *The National Trust: The First Hundred Years* (BBC 1994)

——, *A Noble Thing* (Scala 2011)

Watkins, John and Wright, Tom (ed.), *The Management and Maintenance of Historic Parks, Gardens and Landscapes* (Frances Lincoln 2007)

Weideger, Paula, *Gilding the Acorn* (Simon and Schuster 1994)

Woodbridge, Kenneth, *The Stourhead Landscape* (The National Trust 1982)

ACKNOWLEDGEMENTS

Above all, the publishing of this book owes a great deal to the persistence and patience of Brent Elliott, who persuaded me to write it and edited the text with his customary precision; he also introduced me to Unicorn, who gave me the full run of their resources and fought tenaciously to ensure the book was published with the backing of our sponsors. I would also like to thank and praise Lyn Sales who turned my ever-changing handwritten scribble into intelligible text.

Without hesitation Anna Pavord wrote the Foreword with great generosity and I shall be eternally grateful for her giving her time and expertise.

I am also indebted to several friends and former colleagues who have kindly read and, where necessary, amended some of the garden accounts – Robin Allan, Richard Ayres, the late Steve Biggins, Peter Broomhead, John Cripwell, Laurence Harwood, Julian Gibbs, Paul Kendrick, The Lady Mary Keen, the late Bill Malecki, the late Peter Mansfield, David Masters, the late Anthony Mitchell, Michael Ridsdale, Mike Snowden, Matthew Ward, Merlin Waterson; and also the special help and encouragement of The Lady Emma Tennant.

PICTURE CREDITS

Photographs by courtesy of the author except as listed below.

Brent Elliott: pp.52, 113, 116, 128, 153(b), 162, 167, 186, 187, 213, 251, 279, 281, 289.

GAP Photos Ltd: pp.149, 173, 195, 294.

National Trust Images: front cover, pp.10, 50, 53(t), 53(b), 61(b), 71, 74(t), 74(b), 75, 89, 93, 100, 106, 107, 122, 156, 168, 204, 205, 231, 232, 262(b), 263, 270, 282, 292, 295, 310.

RHS Library Collections: 64 (photo Paul Miles), 240.

University of Cambridge aerial survey: 93(t).

Every effort has been made to trace copyright holders and to obtain their permission for the use of copyright material. The publisher apologises for any errors or omissions in the above list and would be grateful if notified of any corrections that should be incorporated in future reprints or editions of this book.

INDEX

Locators in *italics* refer to photographs and drawings. Those in **bold** indicate the page numbers with the most significant information. Plant names are indexed under their common name (where different from the botanical name). Lords and Ladies are indexed under their titles. NT refers to National Trust.

Florence Court

ARMAGH   DOWN

ISLE OF
MAN

IRISH SEA

ISLE OF
ANGLESEY
Plas Newydd   CONWY   DENBIGH-
                                    SHIRE

                                FLINTS

                GWYNEDD

                                    Powi

CARDIGAN BAY   W A L E S

                        POWYS

                CEREDIGION

ST GEORGE'S CHANNEL

                PEMBROKESHIRE   CARMARTHENSHIRE

                                WEST
                                GLAMORGAN   MID GLAMORGAN

                                    SOUTH
                                    GLAMORGAN

                        BRISTOL CHANNEL

                                Dunster Castle

                                    Knightshayes

                        DEVON
                                    Killerton

ATLANTIC OCEAN

                CORNWALL

                                        Coleton Fishacre

                Trelissick

ISLES OF SCILLY   Glendurgan